Sports and the Racial Divide

Sports and the Racial Divide

*African American and Latino
Experience in an Era of Change*

Edited by Michael E. Lomax

University Press of Mississippi / Jackson

www.upress.state.ms.us

The University Press of Mississippi is a member of
the Association of American University Presses.

Copyright © 2008 by University Press of Mississippi
All rights reserved
Manufactured in the United States of America

First printing 2008

∞

Library of Congress Cataloging-in-Publication Data

Sports and the racial divide : African American and Latino experience in an era of change
/ edited by Michael E. Lomax.
p. cm.
Includes bibliographical references and index.
ISBN 978-1-60473-014-2 (cloth : alk. paper) 1. Discrimination in sports—United
States—History. 2. African American athletes—History. 3. Mexican American athletes—
History. I. Lomax, Michael E.
GV706.32.S745 2008
306.4'830973—dc22
2007051865

British Library Cataloging-in-Publication Data available

In Loving Memory of
Donald and Ollie Scott

Contents

Contents

Foreword

—Kenneth L. Shropshire

There has been a long trail of scholars attempting to sift through issues related to race and sports. Virtually all scholars who study race and sport agree that this millennium begins with marked progress. We have witnessed the first African American athletic director hired at the University of Georgia and the first African American head football coach hired at Mississippi State and the Southeastern Conference, a moment with an African American as head of the United States Olympic Committee, a Latino with majority ownership of a Major League Baseball franchise and an African American with majority ownership of a National Basketball Association franchise. This was all, without question, so difficult to imagine when Jackie Robinson integrated Major League Baseball over fifty years ago, but the news is not all good.

Some were quietly celebrating the death of the myth of the inappropriateness of the African American quarterback. In the midst of that silent celebration, Rush Limbaugh raised his baritone voice and revealed the still existing racist attitudes of a lingering few. He cautioned us that the All-Pro quarterback Donovan McNabb was not as good as our eyes told us he was, that it was all media hype, designed to prop up a successful black quarterback for the masses. Regardless of high profile hirings at the University of Georgia and Mississippi State, we can also look closely at the head coach position in college football. There, the number of African Americans in those positions of power remains woefully low. The same is true about people of color as well as females in athletic director positions at NCAA Division 1A schools. The mountaintop is still seemingly a ways off.[1]

The truth is, however, even with these setbacks, that blatant, unrestrained, public, conscious racism is now the exception. Yes, every year we get our share of racist outbursts, but most of that can now be squarely pinned on the ignorance of the individual uttering the words from Marge Schott and Hootie Johnson to John Rocker and Reggie White. Real racism and other forms of discrimination that occur in sports are now largely clandestine, sophisticated, and not allowed to see the direct light of day.

Formerly, no matter what the game, you knew the closer you got to the ball, the more likely the player in that position would be white. These were, after all, the thinking positions. Quarterbacks, point guards, centers, pitchers, and catchers were almost exclusively white. This racially preferred positioning was based on skin color, not talent. In addition to what one hopes is changing societal hearts and minds there is also a new incentive—money. In most sports money comes with winning. Winning comes with fielding the best players and fielding the best players comes with ignoring their race, and seeing simply who can get the job done. As this has become the guiding principle of owners, general managers, and coaches, racism has trickled out of decisions of who sets foot on the field of play. With less deliberate speed this is trickling to the head coach position and other top-level jobs as well.[2]

With this progress comes the enlightened thinking too that the issues of race and sport go beyond black and white. That if progress is to continue to be made in bringing about equality in sports the issues of other races and ethnic groups must be brought into the discussion. But, at the same time, we must constantly be aware that the issues related to blacks and sports are foundationally different, will remain different, and should not be diluted by a new world diversity thrust.

This book accepts this new millennium's new age challenge. The selections appropriately deal with the historic black and white past as well as focus on the interests of ethnic groups that people sports today. The book covers the important themes of racial identification, the foundational civil rights protests of the 1960s as well as the prime participants, related cultural and gender issues from cheerleading to Title IX. These pages also contain valuable information and commentary on the broader cultural issues that have brought us to our current point in sports today.

Our efforts at purifying sports from the stain of race have a way to go. These pages take us that much closer to an understanding of how to accomplish that ultimate goal and the elements that, at the same time, make reform so difficult.

Notes

1. Although his primary focus is on the construction of whiteness, Douglas Hartmann analyzes the Limbaugh controversy in "Rush Limbaugh, Donovan McNabb, and 'A Little Social Concern': Reflections on the Problems of Whiteness in Contemporary American Sport," *Journal of Sport & Social Issues* 31 (February 2007): 45–60.

2. For studies that deal with stacking, see, for example, John W. Loy and Joseph McElvogue, "Racial Segregation in American Sport," *International Review of Sport Sociology* 5 (1970): 5–24; John D. Massengale and Steven R. Farrington, "The Influence of Playing Position Centrality on the Careers of College Football Coaches, "*Review of Sport and Leisure* 2 (June 1977): 107–15; Jomills Henry Braddock II, "Race and Leadership in Professional Sports: A Study Of Institutional Discrimination in the National Football League," *Arena Review* 5 (September 1981): 16–25; D. Stanley Eitzen and David C. Sanborn, "The Segregation of Black by Playing Position in Football: Accident or Design," *Social Science Quarterly* 55 (March 1975): 948–59; Joseph Dougherty, "Race and Sport: A Follow Up Study," *Sport Sociology Bulletin* 5 (1976): 1–12; Donna R. Madison and Daniel M. Landers, "Racial Discrimination in Football: A Test of the 'Stacking' of Playing Positions Hypothesis," in Daniel M. Landers, ed., *Social Problems in Athletic Essays in the Sociology of Sport* (Urbana: University of Illinois Press, 1976), 151–56; Clarence Eugene Burns, "Position Occupancy Patterns as a Function of Race: The National Football League Draft 1968 to 1983," (PhD diss.: University of California–Santa Barbara, 1988); Barry D. McPherson, "The Segregation by Playing Position Hypothesis in Sport: An Alternative Explanation," in Andrew Yiannakis, Thomas D. McIntyre, Merrill J. Melnick, and Dale P. Hart, eds., *Sport Sociology: Contemporary Themes* (Iowa City: University of Iowa Press, 1976), 177–86; Marshall H. Medoff, "Positional Segregation and the Economic Hypothesis," *Sociology of Sport Journal* 3 (1986): 297–304.

Introduction

The African American and Latino Athlete in Post–World War II America: A Historical Review

—Michael E. Lomax

In 1960, the Houston Oilers of the newly formed American Football League (AFL) instituted a "block seating" policy for the team's home games at Jeppenson Stadium. African American patrons could sit only in folding chairs in an area from the goal line to the east stands. In response to these restrictions, *Houston Informer* sports editor Lloyd Wells encouraged black Houstonians to boycott Oilers' home games and worked with local and national civil rights organizations to establish picket lines at the stadium. The boycott failed.[1]

A proposed August 1961 boycott of a National Football League (NFL) exhibition game in Norfolk, Virginia, proved somewhat more effective, however. Three Norfolk lawyers asked black players on the Baltimore Colts to sit out the game against the Washington Redskins, who had no African American players. Colts officials worked out an agreement with the boycott's organizers, but in accordance with Virginia law, seating in the stadium would remain segregated. The incident led Colts' management to pledge that the team would never again deal with the "unsavory task of playing in an atmosphere of discrimination."[2]

By the end of the 1950s, the United States was on the cusp of great social changes, with the civil rights movement about to fundamentally reshape how Americans perceived race and racial issues. The struggle for equal rights for African Americans had roots going back more than a hundred years, but in the wake of World War II, the movement gathered steam and became increasingly tied to the integration of professional sports. The

1960s marked the start of what historians August Meier and John Bracey call a "revolution in expectations" among American blacks, who developed a new sense of urgency about dismantling barriers to racial equality.[3]

Jackie Robinson initiated African Americans into the postwar sporting arena when he made his debut with the Brooklyn Dodgers in 1947. His quiet dignity—and, not incidentally, his stellar play—in the face of opponents', teammates', and fans' racism provided the initial model for minority activism in sports. Like all athletes, blacks and Latinos have had only limited avenues for activism both inside and outside the sports arena. Team owners have considerable autonomy about which players to employ. National Collegiate Athletic Association eligibility regulations, the autocratic rule of coaches, pressure from alumni and boosters to field winning teams, and classroom pressures restrain individual and collective action at the college level. But ten years after Robinson's debut, with some teams, including the Redskins, Major League Baseball's Boston Red Sox, and squads representing numerous southern colleges and universities, still dragging their heels on integration, African Americans, as Cleveland Browns All-Pro fullback Jim Brown has suggested, found their own ways to protest.[4]

Brown and other black football stars voiced their opposition to being segregated from their teammates on road trips and to block seating. In 1961, Brown and another African American Cleveland player, Bobby Mitchell, indicated that they would refuse to play in a game in Dallas, Texas, if for any reason they were "restricted from living with" the rest of the players, and Philadelphia Eagles fullback Clarence Peaks announced that he would refuse to accept any Jim Crow living quarters as long as he was a professional athlete. Two years later, four black Oakland Raiders—Clem Daniels, Art Powell, Bo Roberson, and Fred Williamson—forced the relocation of a game against the New York Jets when they refused to play in a stadium that had segregated seating. In May 1969, outfielder Willie Horton of the defending World Series champion Detroit Tigers walked off the field to protest not only the fact that he had to stay separately from the rest of the team during spring training but also the team's failure to give young black players a chance to play in the Majors.[5]

Some evidence suggests that by the early 1960s, African American players created what can best be described as "black enclaves" within the various professional sports leagues. In Major League Baseball, blacks created, in the words of *Sports Illustrated* journalist Robert Boyle, a "private world that [blacks'] white teammates do not enter." Milwaukee Braves outfielder Bill Bruton, Cincinnati Reds pitcher Brooks Lawrence, and other veteran leaders helped young blacks make the transition to the big leagues. African American athletes established an informal code of behavior to create a sense of identity and professionalism. Black players, for example, shared with one another, did not fight with each other on the field, and did not criticize one another in front of whites. In this way, black ballplayers mobilized, closed ranks, and moved toward a position of group strength.[6] Brown stressed a cardinal rule for black football players: "Assert your dignity." Black players should neither engage in buffoonery to win friendship nor establish false friendships to win whites' favor. Rather, blacks should send a message that they shared with whites the desire to succeed and to be professional. This approach represented a radical change from the message Brown had received during his rookie season: Keep his mouth shut and don't make waves.[7]

The existence of these "black enclaves" did not mean that African American athletes segregated themselves from the rest of their teammates. St. Louis Cardinals teammates Curt Flood and Bob Gibson worked to bring together the separate social worlds inhabited by black and white players. Although Flood and Gibson's efforts at first were rejected, they persevered, and white teammates eventually began to accept postgame invitations to go out for drinks—but not until after the African American players had demonstrated that they could help the team win ball games and that their presence on the field did not repel white fans. Racial harmony among the Cardinals represented the ideal of pluralism, an amicable coexistence in which blacks could keep intact their own subculture. White and black Cardinals players worked toward a common goal—winning—that would advance the economic interests of all players.[8] However, black athletes also had reservations about Latino players, who thus faced not only racial but ethnic challenges.

Since World War II, sports have played a pivotal role in American society, not only supporting dominant ideas about race and racial supremacy but also serving as a platform from which to address racial and social injustices within the larger society. The presence of African Americans and Latinos in the sports arena went from nearly nonexistent to overwhelming in a span of less than forty years. This anthology analyzes the forces that shaped the African American and Latino sporting experience in mid-twentieth-century America, exploring the intersections among race, ethnicity, and sport.

Reassessing sociocultural issues raised by scholars from a political, economic, and social perspective is essential to the study of history. However, since the 1980s, no part of the American experience has won such a broadly accepted academic point of view as the African American and Latino experience in post–World War II sports: the trials and triumphs of black and Latino athletes as they confront racist America; the integration of sports as a universally desired objective and an unqualified good; the promotion of an ethnic consciousness and building of community solidarity; and the United States as a society in transition, with equality in professional and collegiate sports serving as a metaphor for equality in American society. While these efforts have dramatically expanded our knowledge, gaps remain in the research literature. This volume will begin to fill in some of those gaps.

Scholarly studies of the African American sporting experience in post–World War II America naturally began with Jackie Robinson and the integration of modern organized baseball in 1947. In "The Paul Robeson—Jackie Robinson Saga and a Political Collision" (1979), historian Ronald A. Smith examines Robinson's July 1949 appearance before the House Un-American Activities Committee in response to anti-American statements made by entertainer and former All-American football star Paul Robeson. Smith argues that for symbolic reasons, the federal government asked Robinson to aid in removing Robeson from his role as a black leader. Utilizing a comparative analysis of the two men's early lives, Smith asserts that they approached change from different directions, with Robinson willing to compromise with white society for positive racial goals and Robeson wanting reform on his own terms, not necessarily those of white society. Yet, Smith concludes, both men fought for equal rights.[9]

Scholars have also examined black and white press coverage of the Robinson saga. In "The Black Press and the Assault on Professional Baseball's 'Color Line,' October, 1945–April, 1947," (1979), Bill L. Weaver challenges sociologist E. Franklin Frazier's assertion that the black press created and perpetuated a world of make-believe for the black bourgeoisie. Instead, according to Weaver, the black press, including periodicals such as *The Crisis* and *Ebony*, provided a valuable service by contributing to the integration of sports.[10]

One of the most insightful investigations of the link between the press and the Robinson epic is historian William Simons's "Jackie Robinson and the American Mind: Journalistic Perceptions of the Reintegration of

Baseball" (1985). Simons argues that the maxims of the American creed significantly shaped contemporary press coverage of Robinson. Newspapers typically described an American public endowed with the belief that Robinson ought to succeed or fail based on his merits, not his skin color. Whereas the media acknowledged criticism of the Dodgers' signing of Robinson, particularly from residents of the South, few articles denied that a liberal consensus supported his entry into organized baseball. Robinson, characterized as the "right type" of black athlete, could redeem organized baseball from its sins of racial exclusion and allow the sport to embody American values. But as Simons points out, such assertions of liberal support were inaccurate, and Americans could deal effectively with racism only when they recognized that it was more than a regional affliction.[11]

The most definitive monograph about the integration of organized baseball is historian Jules Tygiel's *Baseball's Great Experiment: Jackie Robinson and His Legacy* (originally published 1983; expanded edition 1997). Tygiel focuses primarily on Robinson and Brooklyn Dodgers general manager Branch Rickey but also analyzes the forces that denied blacks access to organized baseball and the plethora of individuals and societal pressures that attacked the conspiracy of silence. Tygiel provides an in-depth and critical look at Rickey's strategy for integration, demonstrating that his motives included a combination of a desire for economic gain, a desire to exploit a new source of baseball talent, a commitment to humanitarian principles, and an interest in moving beyond the limited world of baseball to influence broader societal developments—as well as an uneasy caution. Furthermore, Tygiel provides an extensive examination of Robinson's ordeal and explores his impact on attendance at games, on Americans' racial views, and in the black community. For Tygiel, Robinson, more than any other individual of his generation, brought attention to the inequalities in American society and simultaneously confirmed that the dream encompassed all, regardless of race.[12]

In *Pride against Prejudice: The Biography of Larry Doby* (1988), Joseph Thomas Moore chronicles the much less well known story of Cleveland Indians outfielder Larry Doby, the first African American to play in the American League. Although, as Moore acknowledges, Doby benefited from the fact that Robinson bore the burdens of being Major League Baseball's first black, Doby's experiences epitomized the trials of other African American players who followed.[13]

Two important studies analyze the impact of integration on the Negro Leagues. Donn Rogosin's *Invisible Men: Life in Baseball's Negro*

Leagues (1983) argues that the integration of Major League Baseball has usually been told as if the Negro Leagues never existed. Popular portrayals have focused on how Rickey's benevolence and Robinson's courage combined to shatter the color line and do not relate the integration of the Major Leagues as an inevitable consequence of the history of black baseball and changing race relations in the United States. Incorporating this perspective, notes Rogosin, would have stressed the social rather than individual dimension of baseball's integration. Rogosin criticizes Robinson's marginalization of the Negro Leagues and their role in helping integrate the Major Leagues. Rogosin also analyzes the Negro League players' reaction to the Robinson signing. Negro Leaguers took part in the general euphoria that swept through black America, but their joy was tempered by their critical assessment of Robinson's baseball abilities and the belief, held by some, that other players—for example, Josh Gibson or Satchel Paige—should have been chosen to break the color line. In addition, although the Negro Leaguers admired Robinson's courage, they also had an ulterior motive for praising him—that is, the hope that other African American players would soon have the opportunity to join Robinson in the Major Leagues. Although he focuses primarily on sports in Pittsburgh's black community, Rob Ruck's *Sandlot Seasons: Sport in Black Pittsburgh* (1987) argues that the general absorption of black athletes into the mainstream of American sport destroyed the Negro Leagues. Major League Baseball took first the Negro Leagues' best players, then their fans, and eventually the attention of the black press.[14]

In *Winning Is the Only Thing: Sports in America since 1945* (1989), Randy Roberts and James Olson assert that the integration of the Major Leagues led whites to confront their most entrenched racial attitudes. African American athletes' exceptional performances in professional baseball, football, and basketball ran counter to the stereotypes that portrayed blacks as instinctive rather than thoughtful, physical rather than intellectual, and compliant rather than ambitious. The result was a new stereotype, with whites believing blacks to be naturally talented; gifted in quickness, reflex, and strength; but intellectually lacking.[15]

Arnold Rampersad contributes to the growing literature on Robinson with the definitive *Jackie Robinson: A Biography* (1997), written with the cooperation of Robinson's widow, Rachel, who granted Rampersad access to most of her personal letters and to the archives at the Jackie Robinson Foundation.[16]

In *Blackout: The Untold Story of Jackie Robinson's First Spring Training* (2004), journalism scholar Chris Lamb uses Robinson's first spring training in organized baseball to provide insight into the paradox that the United States claimed to advocate equality for all yet simultaneously discriminated against a million of its own citizens. Lamb also examines how the nation's black press and mainstream white publications covered the events of that spring.[17]

Other scholars have looked at how Major League teams dealt with the problem of segregated southern facilities after the advent of African American players. In *The Baseball Business: Pursuing Pennants and Profits in Baltimore* (1990), historian James Edward Miller traces Baltimore Orioles general manager Lee MacPhail's efforts to house black players in the same hotel as whites during spring training. In February 1961, the Orioles' Miami hotel agreed to lodge the team's black players. The action was largely symbolic, since the Orioles' lone black player chose to stay in segregated housing, but MacPhail won himself and his club a measure of respect from Baltimore's black elite by taking a stand. Patrick J. Harrigan's *The Detroit Tigers: Club and Community, 1945–1995* (1997) touches on the Tigers' 1963 switch of hotels as a result of the refusal of their former Lakeland, Florida, accommodations to house black players. At the same time, the team removed the signs designating "white" and "colored" entrances to the spring training field. In *September Swoon: Richie Allen, the '64 Phillies, and Racial Integration* (2004), William C. Kashatus tells the story of how Philadelphia Phillies players and management fought segregation in Clearwater, Florida, with mixed results. Although the Phillies found a hotel that would allow Mexican-born infielder Ruben Amaro to room with his teammates, the establishment refused to serve him in the cafeteria. And according to "Baseball's Reluctant Challenge: Desegregating Major League Spring Training Sites, 1961–64" (1992), by Jack E. Davis, when St. Louis Cardinals officials, acting at the request of the team's African American players, pressured the squad's St. Petersburg hotels to end segregation, they refused. In response, the Cardinals simply bought their own hotel.[18]

One of the most insightful studies of the late 1990s analyzes Jews' roles in the struggle to break the color barrier in Major League Baseball. Stephen Norwood and Harold Brackman's "Going to Bat for Jackie Robinson" (1999) makes clear that the Jewish contribution to breaking baseball's color line has been essentially forgotten. The authors highlight the important influences of Jewish journalists such as Walter Winchell and Shirley Povich and assert that Jews could empathize with Robinson because the few Jews who had played in the Major Leagues were subjected to anti-Semitic taunts from opposing players and fans. Norwood and Brackman also examine a notable 1947 conversation between Robinson and Hank Greenberg in which the prominent Jewish veteran player encouraged the rookie to endure the taunts and racial slurs and offered advice on how to cope. Although Robinson and Greenberg devoted significant attention to this conversation in their autobiographies, demonstrating the importance that both men attributed to the meeting, scholars had virtually ignored the incident.[19]

Around the turn of the twenty-first century, three studies examined the American Communist Party's role in breaking Major League Baseball's color line. The first of these works, Kelly E. Rusinack's "Baseball on the Radical Agenda" (1998), analyzes the U.S. Communist Party's use of its newspaper, the *Daily Worker*, to champion the cause of ending segregation in baseball as part of a campaign to abolish discrimination against African Americans in all phases of American life. The *Worker*'s sportswriters were among the first voices to urge an end to discrimination in baseball, seeing it as a way to make revolutionary changes in American society. Similarly, Irwin Silber's *Press Box Red: The Story of Lester Rodney, the Communist Who Helped Break the Color Line in American Sports* (2003) traces the efforts of the *Daily Worker*'s sports editor to end segregation in Major League Baseball. According to Silber, Rodney made integration the signature issue of the publication's sports page, commissioning his correspondents to pressure baseball officials, including Commissioner Kenesaw Mountain Landis and National League president Ford Frick, and printing headlines that blared players' and managers' support for integration. Rodney also provided generous coverage of the Negro Leagues, marginalized by most white newspapers, and thereby brought to his readers' attention the injustice of excluding Paige, Gibson, and other black stars. The *Worker* also spearheaded a petition drive in which more than one million people protested blacks' exclusion from the Majors.[20]

In contrast, Henry Fetter's "The Party Line and the Color Line: The American Communist Party, the *Daily Worker*, and Jackie Robinson" (2001), finds that the Communist Party and the *Daily Worker* played no significant part in integrating baseball. Fetter argues that although the *Worker* ran numerous articles challenging baseball's exclusion of African Americans, scant evidence supports the idea that these or other party efforts played an important role in the sequence of events that brought Robinson to Brooklyn. Moreover, according to Fetter, the Communist paper's sports staff approached the breaking of baseball's color line with the belief that class, not race, constituted the determinate fault line in

American social life. Furthermore, the *Worker* consistently downplayed the racism Robinson confronted and the loneliness and difficulty of his struggle for acceptance and respect. Fetter concludes that integrating organized baseball was a marginal issue for the Communist Party.[21]

Two recent studies have reexamined the intersection between black baseball and integration. In his seminal work on the Negro League's Homestead Grays, *Beyond the Shadow of the Senators: The Untold Story of the Homestead Grays and the Integration of Baseball* (2003), Brad Snyder contends that the *Baltimore Afro-American*'s Sam Lacy and other black journalists initially believed that Washington Senators owner Clark Griffith represented the most likely person to integrate the Major Leagues. As the manager of the Cincinnati Reds in 1911, Griffith had pioneered the practice of passing off light-skinned Cubans as white Major Leaguers, and led by primary scout Joe Cambria, Griffith's Senators continued to sign Cuban players. Griffith also developed a good relationship with Washington's black community and encouraged the development of the Negro Leagues. However, the conservative Griffith made so much money by renting his ballpark to the Grays that he refused to sign their top stars, Josh Gibson and Buck Leonard. Griffith also had a secret ally in Grays' owner Cumberland Posey and eventually became one of the most outspoken supporters of segregation.[22]

In his excellent *Negro League Baseball: The Rise and Ruin of a Black Institution* (2004), Neil Lanctot asserts that the gradual postwar trend toward integration led to the decline of black business. As African Americans, most black baseball owners as well as other business leaders disapproved of racial segregation; however, they also had a vested interest in the maintenance of separate facilities because it created a convenient market for their goods and services. The modest and flawed nature of most black enterprises, Lanctot argues, became less acceptable when compared to the new opportunities in the integrated (that is, white) business community. Postwar blacks came to value the success of individuals within an integrated setting far more than the preservation of black institutions. Black baseball and other separate institutions lost their relevance after integration. Thus, as first Robinson and then other blacks entered the Major Leagues, many fans permanently turned away from black baseball, ultimately leading to its demise.[23]

There is of course, much more to understanding the post–World War II African American sporting experience than just Jackie Robinson and the integration of Major League Baseball. In *Outside the Lines: African*

Americans and the Integration of the National Football League (1999), Charles
K. Ross provides an important scholarly investigation of the integration
of professional football, which occurred a year before Robinson's Major
League debut when Kenny Washington and Woody Strode entered the
NFL and Marion Motley and Bill Willis entered the All-America Football
Conference. According to Ross, the black press considered the matter a
leading news story, and he highlights Lacy's crusade against Washington
Redskins owner George Preston Marshall, who refused to draft or sign
such exceptional black players as Jim Brown, Lenny Moore, Jim Parker,
and Roosevelt Grier. Despite Lacy's attacks, Marshall was the last NFL
owner to relent, and his Redskins did not have a black player until pressure
from civil rights groups and low-level Kennedy administration officials
became irresistible in the early 1960s.[24]

Scholars have also begun to examine the African American experience
in college athletics. In "The Integration of Intercollegiate Athletics in
Texas: North Texas State College as a Test Case, 1956" (1987), Ronald E.
Marcello examines a trailblazing integration case. Other southern colleges
did not desegregate their athletic programs for another decade, but North
Texas State president James Matthews sought to follow the letter of the law
and minimize potential conflicts, the school's coaching staff developed a
practical policy to promote team harmony, and a small cadre of white
players sought to create a comfortable environment for the black athletes.
This combination resulted in a general acceptance for Abner Haynes and
Leon King on the football squad, at least on the field: Haynes and King
were prohibited from staying in the athletic dormitory and had to walk
two miles to the black side of town. Three years passed before Haynes and
King were permitted to stay on campus and eat in the school's cafeterias.
Moreover, as Marcello notes, the desegregation was not voluntary but
occurred only because of a federal court order, and the black athletes were
an equal part of the team but not an equal part of the college.[25]

Charles H. Martin has contributed a great deal to the investigation of
the desegregation process in college athletics, publishing a series of works
on football, baseball, and basketball in the South and Midwest. In Martin's
view, during the 1950s and 1960s, white and black liberals urged an end to
Jim Crow in southern college sports in the hopes that doing so would
not only open opportunities for individual blacks but also create a highly
visible model of interracial cooperation that would hasten integration
in other areas of American life. This approach eventually succeeded and
represented an important turning point in southern race relations, leading

whites to adopt the attitude that integration was not merely inevitable but potentially beneficial.[26]

Andrew Doyle's assessment of University of Alabama head football coach Paul "Bear" Bryant, "An Atheist in Alabama Is Someone Who Doesn't Believe in Bear Bryant: A Symbol for an Embattled South" (1996), links the civil rights struggle to the gridiron squads of the South's traditionally white colleges and universities. Bryant, a racial moderate, maintained a cautious silence on the volatile race issue, but many of his fans regarded the success of his all-white teams as symbolic of the viability of white supremacy. Like other aspects of southern life, football was viewed through the lens of racial politics. Doyle ponders what might have happened if Bryant had used his prestige to advance desegregation.[27]

Two studies provide insights into the African American female sporting experience, another topic in need of additional scholarly attention. In her excellent *Coming on Strong: Gender and Sexuality in Twentieth-Century Women's Sport* (1994), Susan Cahn states that in the late 1930s, black women moved into track and field, a sport largely abandoned by middle-class white women, who considered it unsuitable. African American women excelled both nationally and internationally, achieving a preeminent position by 1950. However, in keeping with customary racial prejudices, the success of Olympians Alice Coachman, Mae Faggs, and Wilma Rudolph reinforced disparaging stereotypes of black women as less womanly or feminine than white women.[28]

Pamela Grundy's *Learning to Win: Sports, Education, and Social Change in Twentieth-Century North Carolina* (2001) assesses the desegregation of cheerleading squads in North Carolina high schools. Although athletic teams often integrated with apparent ease, the selection of cheerleading squads became one of the most volatile school desegregation issues in the South and was complicated by the diverse cheering styles that had developed at black and white schools. African American girls were expected to abandon their fluid improvisational style in favor of the dominant white cheerleading approach, which relied primarily on straight-armed, almost military precision as well as elaborate gymnastic routines. In many cases, cheerleading squads remained all-white, and they came to symbolize the broader frustrations black students felt about being expected to adjust to the dominant white culture.[29]

Other recent works examining African American high school sports include "'Ba-ad, Ba-a-ad Tigers': Crispus Attucks Basketball and Black Indianapolis in the 1950s" (2000), in which Aram Goudsouzian contends

that the team mobilized the black community, provided role models for black youths, and accorded an arena where African Americans could witness their representatives legitimately facing and conquering teams composed primarily of whites. These successes provided middle- and lower-class Indianapolis blacks with an enormous source of cultural pride. Although his book is geared more toward a popular audience, Randy Roberts examines Oscar Robertson's career at Crispus Attucks in *"But They Can't Beat Us":*
Oscar Robertson and the Crispus Attucks Tigers (1999).[30]

Beginning with Thomas Hauser's authorized biography, *Muhammad Ali: His Life and Times* (1991), scholars have initiated explorations of the life of a man who both reflected and shaped the social and political events of the 1960s and 1970s. In the 1960s, the heavyweight champion of the world stood for the proposition that principles mattered, that equality among people was just and proper, that the Vietnam War was wrong. Ali subsequently evolved from a feared warrior to a benevolent monarch and ultimately to a benign venerated figure.[31]

Although he does not focus primarily on Ali, historian Jeffrey Sammons's *Beyond the Ring: The Role of Boxing in American Society* (1988) links the champion to the civil rights and Black Power movements. Sammons contends that Ali's early relationship with Malcolm X was related to the Muslim leader's efforts to stage-manage the heavyweight division to ensure that his perspective and deeply felt convictions would find a mouthpiece in one of America's most visible symbols. The heavyweight champion's throne would be the public power base of the Nation of Islam, and Ali served as its standard-bearer. This approach ran counter to societal norms that required athletes to remain humble and avoid politics. In addition, mainstream liberals, supporters of the integrationist ideal, did not want this dissenter to threaten their vision of American order and athletics' role in it.[32]

Another Ali biography, Mike Marqusee's *Redemption Song: Muhammad Ali and the Spirit of the Sixties* (1999), portrays a young man who made daunting choices and stuck to them in the face of hideous threats and glittering inducements. Ali resisted political involvement and at first rejected the burden of symbolic representation imposed on black celebrities by black and white commentators. Nevertheless, he found himself becoming more and more of a symbol. Some observers saw his conversion to Islam as an embrace of blackness, and he willingly subjected himself to the demonization that the Nation of Islam had endured for years, thereby earning himself legions of black admirers.[33]

Any assessment of the changing perceptions of black athletes in the late 1960s must include Harry Edwards's pioneering *The Revolt of the Black Athlete* (1969). According to Edwards, black athletes spoke out not only on their own behalf but also in support of their downtrodden race. Edwards also offers an insider's view of African Americans athletes' lives on predominantly white college campuses. In the late 1960s, black college athletes were steered away from challenging courses for fear of jeopardizing their eligibility to play. Vast areas of college life, such as fraternities and sororities, remained off-limits, and interracial dating was strictly taboo. Nevertheless, as Edwards chronicles, his white teammates had "the unmitigated nerve to talk to [him] about 'team spirit' on Saturday."[34]

Scholars have picked up where Edwards left off, looking at the black athlete revolt from a historical perspective. Inspirational leaders such as Ali, Edwards, and Bill Russell provided models of courage and in the late 1960s brought to light discrimination in housing, problems in player-coach relationships, inadequate academic tutoring programs, and other matters. By the early 1970s, racial tensions at predominantly white colleges and universities had begun to decline, and the problems of inflation and unemployment had diverted much attention away from the black protest movement, distracting people from anxieties about America's social structure.[35]

From the perspective of the late 1980s and early 1990s, David K. Wiggins looks back and determines that black athlete revolts on college campuses did not result in sweeping changes in the country's racial policies. Nevertheless, Wiggins believes, these protests made the problems of racial discrimination in sport and the larger society more visible to the American public and international community.[36]

In "Black Consciousness and the Olympic Protest Movement, 1964–1980" (1985), Donald Spivey provides insights into the political divisions that emerged during the movement for a black boycott of the 1968 Olympics. According to Spivey, the proposed boycott represented the awakened social consciousness of black collegiate athletes but also showed differences in points of view within black America, with Tommie Smith and John Carlos representing an activist wing; Bob Beamon, Ralph Boston, Wyomia Tyus, and others adopting a moderate position; and George Foreman taking an anti-activist stance.[37]

Two recent studies have provided a more extensive investigation of the proposed boycott of the 1968 Olympic Games. Amy Bass's *Not the Triumph but the Struggle: The 1968 Olympics and the Making of the Black Athlete*

(2002) explores the role of cultural constructions and stereotypes in what she terms "popular representations" of the black athlete. By the spring of 1968, the focus moved from individuals marginalized as militant—like Muhammad Ali—to a collective political force. But at the time of the Olympic trials, athletes remained divided about whether a boycott was the best way to present a united political posture. A fundamental obstacle to unity, Bass argues, was the lack of any input from prominent black female athletes, whose concerns were either marginalized or ignored.[38]

In *Race, Culture, and the Revolt of the Black Athlete: The 1968 Olympic Protests and Their Aftermath* (2003), Douglas Hartmann argues that the enduring image of Smith and Carlos on the victory stand can be traced to the ways in which these athletes interjected "blackness" into a ceremonial system that essentially had no place for nonnational identities such as race, class, religion, and gender. He further contends that the 1968 Olympic protest was a story not merely about racism in sport but also about how sport is implicated in the history and structure of race and racism as well as nationalism and liberalism in contemporary American culture. Broadening its focus, this athletic activism ultimately took on issues such as athletes' rights and gender equity, involving white athletes as well as black and women as well as men.[39]

Between 1969 and 1974, athletes began to launch legal challenges that revolutionized labor-management relations in professional sports. The most notable of these court cases involved African American St. Louis Cardinals outfielder Curt Flood, who took on baseball's reserve clause, which bound a player to his club until it traded, sold, or released, giving him no say in where he played and very little leverage in negotiating salary. In *The Business of Major League Baseball* (1989), Gerald W. Scully discusses the strategy pursued by Flood's lawyers, while Michael E. Lomax's "'Curt Flood Stood Up for Us: The Quest to Break Down Racial Barriers and Structural Inequality in Major League Baseball'" (2003) addresses the factors that led to Flood's legal challenge. Sarah K. Fields's "Odd Bedfellows: Spencer Haywood and Justice William O. Douglas" (forthcoming) is the first work to examine the 1971 court case that forced the National Basketball Association to drop some restrictions on who could play in the league, opening the door for players who had not yet been out of high school for four years.[40]

Scholars have also begun to examine more contemporary African American athletes—in particular, Mike Tyson and Michael Jordan. Neil A. Wynn's "Deconstructing Tyson: The Black Boxer as American Icon"

(2003) examines the interplay between race and masculinity, offering a broader insight into the reading of the boxer as a cultural text. Wynn claims that Tyson recapitulates the old racist stereotypes about black men. Simultaneously, however, Tyson serves as a different symbol for African Americans, female and male. Comparing Tyson's experiences with those of Jack Johnson, Joe Louis, Sonny Liston, and Muhammad Ali, Wynn states that these boxers' iconic status among black and white audiences varied according to the particular context of the moment as well as to their skills in the ring.[41]

Gerald Early's "Mike's Brilliant Career: Mike Tyson and the Riddle of Black Cool" (2001) discusses Tyson's relationship with boxing promoter Don King at a time when the boxer's life was in utter chaos. Because his early mentors were white, Tyson had to confront the fact that he was a creation of white men. Tyson's relationship with King served to redefine his "coolness" and masculinity by linking his persona with black fighters from the past such as Liston and with the street life from which Tyson arose. In addition, the mythology King devised complemented Tyson's embodiment of black cool because it fit nicely into the roles scripted for young and physically powerful black men in the American mind.[42]

David Andrews's collection of essays, *Michael Jordan, Inc.: Corporate Sport, Media Culture, and Late Modern America* (2001), explores the intersection between corporate and media interests, addressing broad social, economic, political, and technological questions and considering Jordan's role in and influence on the celebrity economy, corporate culture, identity politics, and the global marketplace. Jordan's business relationship with Nike brought to the forefront the extent to which the media have transformed and continue to transform sports into a spectacle that sells values, products, celebrities, and institutions of the media and consumer society.[43]

As the twentieth century closed and the twenty-first dawned, David K. Wiggins and Patrick B. Miller compiled *The Unlevel Playing Field: A Documentary History of the African American Experience in Sport* (2003). In these essays, African American journalists, sports industry professionals, and scholars both recapitulate the aspirations and concerns of their predecessors and raise important questions for the future. The authors highlight a myriad of contrasting images that form the context for much of the debate about sports and society in the contemporary period. As Wiggins and Miller point out, it is far too early to celebrate the millennium of black athletic achievement. Moreover, Anita DeFrantz's essay highlights the particular problems faced by African American women in sports. In their pursuit of equality and opportunity on the playing fields, on the sidelines, and in the front office, African American women have too often been left behind.[44]

As has been the case with African Americans, the post–World War II Latino sporting experience has been shaped by its intersections with the larger forces that shaped the United States. Sociologist Alan M. Klein's *Sugarball: The American Game, the Dominican Dream* (1991) is a groundbreaking work examining the relationship between the United States and the Dominican Republic, which adopted the sport and re-fashioned it to suit Dominican purposes. Klein argues that Major League clubs and their Dominican partners operated much in the same way as other powerful U.S. economic and cultural interests in the Third World—that is, by promoting local inferiority and subordination to powerful foreigners. The main difference however, is that while most great conglomerates provoke resentment, locals generally support the Major League teams. As a consequence, popular culture as a whole and baseball in particular wield great power in the Dominican Republic, resulting in an appreciation and greater acceptance of the U.S. presence in other areas of Dominican life. Klein also explores the factors that have resulted in the growing numbers of Dominican ballplayers in the Major Leagues—the decline of baseball in North American inner cities, increased scouting of Latin American and Caribbean countries, and, most importantly, the low prices at which players from those countries can be signed. Several Major League clubs consequently have made substantial investments in Dominican baseball academies to develop talent.[45]

In *The Tropic of Baseball: Baseball in the Dominican Republic* (1991), Rob Ruck uses oral histories to argue that Dominican baseball teams serve as social institutions that link families, athletes, and fans in a lifelong sporting fraternity. Team rivalries allow Dominicans to transcend class and color barriers and join together in a larger sense of community.[46]

Klein has also looked at baseball's impact on Mexican culture. In "Baseball Wars: The Mexican Baseball League and Nationalism in 1946" (1994), he uses the concept of invented tradition to examine how the sports page and baseball have helped to mold a Mexican nationalist consciousness. In *Baseball on the Border: A Tale of Two Laredos* (1997), Klein examines baseball in the border cities of Laredo, Texas, and Nuevo Laredo, Tamaulipas.[47]

Like Klein and Ruck, historian Samuel O. Regalado has contributed immensely in bringing Hispanic sport to an academic audience. His seminal work, *Viva Baseball!: Latin Major Leaguers and Their Special Hunger* (1998), probes Latino Major Leaguers' "physical and cultural transitions from their homeland to a new country." According to Regalado, baseball is more than a game to these men: it is a competition with far-reaching social and economic implications. Baseball provides an escape from poverty and brings distinction to their homelands, thereby providing hope to many young Latinos who might otherwise have envisioned bleak futures. Regalado goes on to provide a comprehensive look at the various cultural and racial barriers faced by early Latino Major Leaguers. For example, some U.S. sportswriters belittled Latinos' efforts to speak English and labeled them temperamental and overly sensitive. Other public relations officials attempted to Americanize Latin players' names, turning Mateo Alou into Matty Alou and Dagoberto Campaneris into Bert Campaneris, a practice that irritated some of these players.[48]

In *Clemente: The Passion and Grace of Baseball's Last Hero* (2006), *Washington Post* associate editor David Maraniss has written an excellent biography of Pittsburgh Pirates Hall of Fame outfielder Roberto Clemente. From the outset, Maraniss asserts, the Clemente saga was entwined in "memory and myth." Although Clemente played his entire career in relative obscurity, away from the media centers of New York and Los Angeles, he, unlike so many modern athletes, insisted that his responsibilities extended beyond the playing field. His willingness to assume this greater role led directly to his death in a December 1972 plane crash as he attempted to bring relief supplies to Nicaragua after a devastating earthquake, and his untimely demise further contributed to the mythologizing of his life.[49]

Jorge Iber has looked at the Mexican American experience in football, especially at the high school and college levels. In "On-Field Foes and Racial Misconceptions: The 1961 Donna Redskins and Their Drive to the Texas State Football Championship" (2004), he examines the cultural significance of this victory by a team whose star players included Mexican Americans Abel Benevides, Richard Avila, and Raul "Chief" de la Garza. Football offered these players a setting where they could compete alongside and against whites and be judged on individual merit, not their ethnicity. Football not only helped these students remain in school, graduate, and pursue college degrees but also provided other young Mexican Americans with an example of what could be accomplished in the classroom and on the gridiron.[50]

Iber and Regalado have collaborated to produce *Mexican Americans and Sport: A Reader on Athletics and Barrio Life* (2007), a broader examination of Mexican American involvement not only in baseball and football but also in soccer, boxing, track, and softball. The chapters spotlight a myriad of issues—recreation, community bonding and empowerment, and identity creation and maintenance. The authors build from the fundamental premise that people of Mexican descent in the United States have used sports to build community and challenge the majority population's notion of Mexican American intellectual, athletic, and cultural weakness. In particular, Katherine M. Jamieson's contribution to the collection, "Advance at Your Own Risk: Latinas, Families, and Collegiate Softball," provides a much-needed examination of the female sporting experience among women of color. Jamieson builds on some of the issues Iber raises in his investigation of the Donna Redskins, asking whether sports constitute a viable alternative for social advancement and assessing the cultural impact of playing softball in mostly white institutions.[51]

Although scholars have immensely enhanced our knowledge of the African American and Latino sporting experience since World War II, numerous areas still warrant further study. While a few works have examined blacks in sport from an African American cultural worldview, the overwhelming scholarly focus examines the black experience in relation to white society. This perspective has embraced an integrationist model to explore the black sporting experience and portrays African Americans as a monolithic group. But integration alone has not defined the African American experience. Scholars have yet to examine thoroughly the links between sports and the broader forces that have defined the overall African American experience—most notably, black nationalism (the rejection of racial integration, the development of black socioeconomic communities, and opposition to white racism). The ideas of Marcus Garvey and other black nationalist leaders have at times won the support of thousands and even millions of people. With the emergence of the Nation of Islam after World War II, black nationalist sentiment escalated within the rural South and urban North. Malcolm X and the plethora of boxers and basketball players who converted to Islam in the 1960s and 1970s did not emerge in a vacuum. A strong case can be made for the intersection between the postwar African American sporting experience and economic black nationalism—that is, the idea that in contrast to integration, an amiable coexistence of diverse groups will allow subcultures to remain relatively intact. Calls for black economic development appear to have resonated among athletes. Basketball great Bill Russell, for one, has stressed the need for economic development as a means of racial uplift for the black masses. These black athletes clearly recognize that to conduct business in the United States, they must negotiate with the white power structure, and they have sought solutions that integration alone cannot address. Moreover, activism has frequently come into conflict with self-help economic initiatives, although both approaches share the goal of improving the lives of African Americans. To what degree have activism and self-help complemented each other, and to what degree have they conflicted?[52]

In addition, the overwhelming focus on baseball, particularly for Latinos, limits our understanding. While football has received some scholarly attention, the works on basketball lack historical context, and hockey has been virtually ignored.[53] The height of the civil rights movement coincided with the massive expansion of professional team sports, as teams relocated and leagues added new franchises in response to declining markets, the development of new markets, and challenges from rival leagues. Expansion not only created new opportunities for black and Latino players but also meant that southern cities seeking to lure sports franchises had to come to grips with Jim Crow segregation. The NFL and AFL were the first major leagues to expand in the South, but by the late 1960s, the American Basketball Association had franchises in Miami; Louisville, Kentucky; and New Orleans, among other southern cities. To what degree did the presence of players of color on these teams affect the southern way of life? Moreover, how did these players deal with the situation, and how did club owners and league officials handle racial discrimination and segregation?

Although scholars have looked at the forces that led to the revolt of the black athlete, particularly at the college level, they have overlooked an internal black revolt in professional sports. Black athletes began to focus on issues that opportunities to play professional sports could not address— discrimination in housing, players' relationships with coaches/managers, labor relations, and upward career mobility after their playing days ended. One notable example is Frank Robinson, who as early as 1968 expressed his desire to become a Major League manager. With the support of the Baltimore Orioles, Robinson found managerial positions in the Puerto Rican winter league, and he ultimately became the first African American manager in the big leagues when he took the Cleveland Indians' helm in 1975.[54]

Although scholars have devoted some attention to the legal challenges that dramatically altered labor relations in professional sports, no in-depth examination has yet been conducted of why some players risked their careers to challenge the professional sports establishment. Furthermore, what do these challenges to the status quo reveal about the black sporting experience in the 1960s and 1970s?

Scholarly work on the pioneering efforts of African Americans in such individual sports as golf, track and field, tennis, and boxing remains incomplete. Even though hockey, tennis, and golf have attracted few players of color, understanding their pioneering efforts is necessary to advance our knowledge of the postwar sporting experience. Although boxing has received significant scholarly attention, academics have focused primarily on the heavyweight division. Such lighter-weight fighters as Roberto Duran, Sugar Ray Leonard, Carlos Palomino, Thomas Hearns, and Hector "Macho" Camacho are worthy of study.[55]

Finally, the topic of African American and Latino involvement in sports at the high school level remains underexplored. In particular, studies of McClymonds High School in Oakland, California, and Power Memorial in New York City would be valuable.

Since the end of World War II, African Americans and Latinos have left their imprint on professional, college, and high school sports in the United States. Their accomplishments on the field of play afforded them the opportunity to strive for social justice and equality off the field. Nevertheless, these men and women still endured many of the racial indignities to which their parents' generation had been subjected. Success in the athletic arena did not necessarily result in rewards off the court. But this generation of African American and Latino athletes refused to accept the status quo. They expected to live in a different America and in a different sports world. Continued athletic excellence and collective action to break down racial barriers to political, economic, and social equality have helped U.S. society work toward the ideals on which this country was founded.

Notes

The author thanks Joseph Dorinson, Billy Hawkins, Sam Regalado, and David Wiggins for providing invaluable critiques of this review essay.

1. Michael E. Lomax and Melvin Adelman, "Goal Line Stand: The Impact of Both Expansion and the Civil Rights Movement on Professional Football's Race Relations, 1957–1965," unpublished manuscript, in possession of author.

2. Ibid.; Charles K. Ross, *Outside the Lines: African Americans and the Integration of the National Football League* (New York: New York University Press, 1999), 152.

3. August Meier and John Bracey Jr., "The NAACP as a Reform Movement, 1909–1965: 'To Reach the Conscience of America,'" *Journal of Southern History* 59 (February 1993): 26–27.

4. Jim Brown and Myron Cope, *Off My Chest* (Garden City, N.Y.: Doubleday, 1964).

5. Lomax and Adelman, "Goal Line Stand."

6. Robert Boyle, "The Private World of the Negro Ballplayer," *Sports Illustrated*, March 21, 1960, 16–19, 74.

7. Brown and Cope, *Off My Chest*.

8. Michael E. Lomax, "'Curt Flood Stood Up for Us': The Quest to Break Down Racial Barriers and Structural Inequality in Major League Baseball," *Culture, Sport, Society* 6 (Summer–Autumn 2003): 44–70.

9. Ronald A. Smith, "The Paul Robeson–Jackie Robinson Saga and a Political Collision," *Journal of Sport History* 6 (Summer 1979): 5–27. For an account that examines the Robeson-Robinson saga from Robeson's perspective, see Martin B. Duberman, *Paul Robeson* (New York: Knopf, 1988).

10. Bill L. Weaver, "The Black Press and the Assault on Professional Baseball's 'Color Line,' October, 1945–April, 1947," *Phylon* 40 (Winter 1979): 303–17; E. Franklin Frazier, *Black Bourgeoisie* (Glencoe, Ill: Free Press, 1957). Journalism scholars who have examined the press coverage Robinson received include William G. Kelley, "Jackie Robinson and the Press," *Journalism Quarterly* 53 (Spring 1976): 137–39; Pat Washburn, "New York Newspapers and Robinson's First Season," *Journalism Quarterly* 58 (Winter 1981): 640–44; Pat Washburn, "New York Newspaper Coverage of Jackie Robinson in His First Major League Season," *Western Journal of Black Studies* 4 (Fall 1980): 183–92. These works, though scholarly, are essentially ahistorical.

11. William Simons, "Jackie Robinson and the American Mind: Journalistic Perceptions of the Reintegration of Baseball," *Journal of Sport History* 12 (Spring 1985): 39–64.

12. Jules Tygiel, *Baseball's Great Experiment: Jackie Robinson and His Legacy*, expanded ed. (1983; New York: Oxford University Press, 1997).

13. Joseph Thomas Moore, *Pride against Prejudice: The Biography of Larry Doby* (New York: Praeger, 1988).

14. Donn Rogosin, *Invisible Men: Life in Baseball's Negro Leagues* (New York: Atheneum, 1983); Rob Ruck, *Sandlot Seasons: Sport in Black Pittsburgh* (Urbana: University of Illinois Press, 1987).

15. Randy Roberts and James S. Olson, *Winning Is the Only Thing: Sports in America since 1945* (Baltimore: Johns Hopkins University Press, 1989).

16. Arnold Rampersad, *Jackie Robinson: A Biography* (New York: Knopf, 1997). Additional scholarly accounts in the 1990s and beyond include Steven K. Wisensale, "The Political Wars of Jackie Robinson," *Nine: Journal of Baseball History and Social Perspectives* 2 (Fall 1993): 18–28; Anthony R. Pratkanis and Marlene Turner, "The Year Cool Papa Bell Lost the Batting Title: Mr. Branch Rickey and Mr. Jackie Robinson's Plea for Affirmative Action," *Nine: Journal of Baseball History and Social Perspectives* 2 (Spring 1994): 260–76; Anthony R. Pratkanis and Marlene Turner, "Nine Principles of Successful Affirmative Action: Mr. Branch Rickey, Mr. Jackie Robinson, and the Integration of Baseball," *Nine: Journal of Baseball History and Social Perspectives* 2 (Fall 1994): 36–65; John Vernon, "Beyond the Box Score: Jackie Robinson, Civil Rights Crusader," *Negro History Bulletin* 58 (October–December 1995): 15–22; Michael E. Lomax, "'I Never Had It Made' Revisited: The Political, Economic, and Social Ideology of Jackie Robinson," *Afro-Americans in New York Life and History* 23 (January 1999): 39–60; Jules Tygiel, *Jackie Robinson Reader: Perspective on an American Hero* (New York: Plume, 1997); Jules Tygiel, *Extra Bases: Reflections on Jackie Robinson, Race, and Baseball History* (Lincoln: University of Nebraska Press, 2002); Jules Tygiel, "Jackie Robinson: 'A Lone Negro' in Major League Baseball," in *Sport and the Color Line: Black Athletes and Race Relations in Twentieth-Century America*, ed. Patrick B. Miller and David K. Wiggins (New York: Routledge, 2004), 167–90; Joseph Dorinson, "Paul Robeson and Jackie Robinson: Athletes and Activists at Armageddon," *Pennsylvania History* 66 (Winter 1999): 17–26; Michael Berenbaum, "Jackie and

Campy: Ethnicity in the 1950s," *Jewish Journal*, April 18–24, 1997, 29, 31, 47; Arthur Diamond, *The Importance of Jackie Robinson* (San Diego: Lucent, 1992); Joseph Dorinson and Joram Warmund, eds., *Jackie Robinson: Race, Sports and the American Dream* (Armonk, N.Y.: Sharpe, 1998); John Kelly, "Integrating America: Jackie Robinson, Critical Events, and Baseball Black and White," *International Journal of the History of Sport* 22 (November 2005): 1011–35; John Kelly, "Exclusionary America: Jackie Robinson, Decolonization, and Baseball Not Black and White," *International Journal of the History of Sport* 22 (November 2005): 1036–59; Richard Ian Kimball, "Beyond the 'Great Experiment': Integrated Baseball Comes to Indianapolis," *Journal of Sport History* 26 (Spring 1999): 142–62.

17. Chris Lamb, *Blackout: The Untold Story of Jackie Robinson's First Spring Training* (Lincoln: University of Nebraska Press, 2004); Chris Lamb, " 'I Never Want to Take Another Trip Like This One': Jackie Robinson's Journey to Integrate Baseball," *Journal of Sport History* 24 (Summer 1997): 177–91; Chris Lamb and Glen Bleske, "Democracy on the Field: The Black Press Takes on White Baseball," *Journalism History* 24 (Summer 1998): 51–59.

18. James Edward Miller, *The Baseball Business: Pursuing Pennants and Profits in Baltimore* (Chapel Hill: University of North Carolina Press, 1990); Patrick J. Harrigan, *The Detroit Tigers: Club and Community, 1945–1995* (Toronto: University of Toronto Press, 1997); William C. Kashatus, *September Swoon: Richie Allen, the '64 Phillies, and Racial Integration* (University Park: Pennsylvania State University Press, 2004); Jack E. Davis, "Baseball's Reluctant Challenge: Desegregating Major League Spring Training Sites, 1961–64," *Journal of Sport History* 19 (Summer 1992): 144–62, reprinted in Patrick B. Miller, ed., *The Sporting World of the Modern South* (Urbana: University of Illinois Press, 2002), 200–218. See also Lomax, " 'Curt Flood Stood Up for Us' "; Michael E. Lomax, "Separate and Unequal: The African American and Latino Experience in Spring Training, 1946–1961," in *Race and Sport: The Struggle for Equality on and off the Field*, ed. Charles K. Ross (Jackson: University Press of Mississippi, 2004), 59–94.

19. Stephen H. Norwood and Harold Brackman, "Going to Bat for Jackie Robinson: The Jewish Role in Breaking Baseball's Color Line," *Journal of Sport History* 26 (Spring 1999): 115–41. Joseph Dorinson also highlights this conversation in "Hank Greenberg, Joe DiMaggio, and Jackie Robinson: Race, Identity, and Ethnic Power," in *Jackie Robinson*, ed. Dorinson and Warmund, 116.

20. Kelly E. Rusinack, "Baseball on the Radical Agenda: The *Daily Worker* and *Sunday Worker* Journalistic Campaign to Desegregate Major League Baseball, 1933–1947," in *Jackie Robinson*, ed. Dorinson and Warmund, 75–85; Irwin Silber, *Press Box Red: The Story of Lester Rodney, the Communist Who Helped Break the Color Line in American Sports* (Philadelphia: Temple University Press, 2003).

21. Henry D. Fetter, "The Party Line and the Color Line: The American Communist Party, the *Daily Worker*, and Jackie Robinson," *Journal of Sport History* 28 (Fall 2001): 375–402.

22. Brad Snyder, *Beyond the Shadow of the Senators: The Untold Story of the Homestead Grays and the Integration of Baseball* (Chicago: Contemporary Books, 2003).

23. Neil Lanctot, *Negro League Baseball: The Rise and Ruin of a Black Institution* (Philadelphia: University of Pennsylvania Press, 2004).

24. Ross, *Outside the Lines.*

25. Ronald E. Marcello, "The Integration of Intercollegiate Athletics in Texas: North Texas State College as a Test Case, 1956," *Journal of Sport History* 14 (Winter 1987): 286–316. Additional scholarly accounts on the black experience in college athletics include Adolph H. Grundman, "The Image of Intercollegiate Sports and the Civil Rights Movement: An Historian's View," *Arena Review* 3 (October 1979): 17–24. John Watterson provides a chapter on the postwar black experience in college football in *College Football: History, Spectacle, Controversy* (Baltimore: Johns Hopkins University Press, 2000), 308–31. See also Russell J. Henderson, " 'Something More Than the Game Will Be Lost': The 1963 Mississippi State

University Basketball Controversy and the Repeal of the Unwritten Law," *Journal of Southern History* 63 (November 1997): 827–54, reprinted in Patrick B. Miller, ed., *Sporting World of the Modern South*, 219–43; Robert W. Dubay, "Politics, Pigmentation, and Pigskin: The Georgia Tech Sugar Bowl Controversy of 1955," *Atlanta History* 39 (Spring 1995): 23–33.

26. Charles H. Martin, "Jim Crow in the Gymnasium: The Integration of College Basketball in the American South," *International Journal of the History of Sport* 10 (April 1993): 68–86, reprinted in Patrick B. Miller and Wiggins, eds., *Sport and the Color Line*, 233–50; Charles H. Martin, "The Color Line in Midwestern College Sports, 1890–1960," *Indiana Magazine of History* 98 (June 2002): 84–112; Charles H. Martin, "Integrating New Year's Day: The Racial Politics of College Bowl Games in the American South," *Journal of Sport History* 24 (Fall 1997): 358–77; Charles H. Martin, "The Rise and Fall of Jim Crow in Southern College Sports: The Case of the Atlantic Coast Conference," *North Carolina Historical Review* 76 (July 1999): 253–84; Charles H. Martin, "Racial Change and 'Big-Time' College Football in Georgia: The Age of Segregation, 1892–1957," *Georgia Historical Quarterly* 80 (Fall 1996): 532–62; Charles H. Martin, *More Than a Game (Was at Stake): Intercollegiate Sports, Race Relations, and the American South, 1890–1980* (forthcoming).

27. Andrew Doyle, "An Atheist in Alabama Is Someone Who Doesn't Believe in Bear Bryant: A Symbol for an Embattled South," *Colby Quarterly* 32 (March 1996): 72–86, reprinted in Patrick B. Miller, ed., *Sporting World of the Modern South*, 247–75.

28. Susan K. Cahn, *Coming on Strong: Gender and Sexuality in Twentieth-Century Women's Sport* (New York: Free Press, 1994). Scholarly sources that examine the postwar African American female experience include Jaime Schultz, "Reading the Catsuit: Serena Williams and the Production of Blackness at the 2002 U.S. Open," *Journal of Sport and Social Issues* 29 (August 2005): 338–57; Nancy E. Spencer, "Sister Act VI: Venus and Serena Williams at Indian Wells: 'Sincere Fictions' and White Racism," *Journal of Sport and Social Issues* 28 (May 2004): 115–35; Mary G. McDonald, "Reading Althea Gibson: Revealing the Workings of Whiteness," paper presented at the thirty-first annual convention of the North American Society for Sport History, May 2003; Jennifer H. Lansbury, " 'The Tuskegee Flash' and 'The Slender Harlem Stroker': Black Women Athletes on the Margin," *Journal of Sport History* 28 (Summer 2001): 233–52; Doris Corbett and William Johnson, "The African-American Female in Collegiate Sport: Sexism and Racism," in *Racism in College Athletics: The African American Athlete's Experience*, ed. Dana Brooks and Ronald Althouse (Morgantown, W.Va.: Fitness Information Technology, 1993), 179–204; Cindy Himes Gissendanner, "African-American Women and Competitive Sport, 1920–1960," in *Women, Sport, and Culture*, ed. Susan Birrell and Cheryl L. Cole (Champaign, Ill.: Human Kinetics, 1994), 81–92.

29. Pamela Grundy, *Learning to Win: Sports, Education, and Social Change in Twentieth-Century North Carolina* (Chapel Hill: University of North Carolina Press, 2001).

30. Aram Goudsouzian, " 'Ba-ad, Ba-a-ad Tigers': Crispus Attucks Basketball and Black Indianapolis in the 1950s," *Indiana Magazine of History* 96 (March 2000): 5–43; Randy Roberts, *"But They Can't Beat Us": Oscar Robertson and the Crispus Attucks Tigers* (Champaign, Ill.: Sports Publishing, 1999).

31. Thomas Hauser, *Muhammad Ali: His Life and Times* (New York: Simon and Schuster, 1991). Additional scholarly accounts on Ali include Frederic Cople Jaher, "White America Views Jack Johnson, Joe Louis, and Muhammad Ali," in *Sport in America: New Historical Perspectives*, ed. Donald Spivey (Westport, Conn.: Greenwood, 1985), 145–92; Elliott J. Gorn, ed., *Muhammad Ali: The People's Champ* (Urbana: University of Illinois Press, 1995); Gerald Early, ed., *The Muhammad Ali Reader* (New York: Weisbach, 1998); Michael Ezra, "Main Bout, Inc., Black Economic Power, and Professional Boxing: The Cancelled Muhammad Ali/Ernie Terrell Fight," *Journal of Sport History* 29 (Fall 2002): 413–37. Journalist David Remnick conducts a comparative analysis of the careers of Sonny Liston, Floyd Patterson, and Muhammad Ali

in *King of the World: Muhammad Ali and the Rise of an American Hero* (New York: Random House, 1998).

32. Jeffrey Sammons, *Beyond the Ring: The Role of Boxing in American Society* (Urbana: University of Illinois Press, 1988). See also Jeffrey Sammons, "Rebel with a Cause: Muhammad Ali as Sixties Protest Symbol," in *Muhammad Ali*, ed. Gorn, 154–80.

33. Mike Marqusee, *Redemption Song: Muhammad Ali and the Spirit of the Sixties* (New York: Verso, 1999); Mike Marqusee, "Sport and Stereotype: From Role Model to Muhammad Ali," *Race and Class* 36 (April–June 1995): 1–29.

34. Harry Edwards, *The Revolt of the Black Athlete* (New York: Free Press, 1969), 8. Edwards also deals with the black athlete revolt in "The Olympic Project for Human Rights: An Assessment Ten Years Later," *Black Scholar* 10 (March–April 1979): 2–8; Harry Edwards, "Reflections on Olympic Sportpolitics: History and Prospects, 1968–1984," *The Crisis*, 1983, 20–24; Harry Edwards, *The Struggle That Must Be: An Autobiography* (New York: Macmillan, 1980); Harry Edwards, "The Black Athletes: Twentieth-Century Gladiators for White America," in *Sport Sociology: Contemporary Themes*, ed. Andrew Yiannakis, Thomas D. McIntyre, Merrill J. Melnick, and Dale P. Hart (Dubuque, Iowa: Kendall/Hart, 1976), 167–72. For a comprehensive review of *The Revolt of the Black Athlete*, see Michael E. Lomax, "Revisiting *The Revolt of the Black Athlete*: Harry Edwards and the Making of the New African-American Sport Studies," *Journal of Sport History* 29 (Fall 2002): 469–80.

35. See William J. Baker, *Sports in the Western World* (Totowa, N.J.: Rowman and Little-field, 1982); John A. Lucas and Ronald A. Smith, *Saga of American Sport* (Philadelphia: Lea and Febiger, 1978); Benjamin Rader, *American Sports: From the Age of Folk Games to the Age of Spectators* (Englewood Cliffs, N.J.: Prentice-Hall, 1983); Roberts and Olson, *Winning Is the Only Thing*; Joan Paul, Richard V. McGhee, and Helen Fant, "The Arrival and Ascendance of Black Athletes in the Southeastern Conference, 1966–1980," *Phylon* 45 (December 1984): 284–97; John Behee, "Race Militancy and Affirmative Action in the Big Ten Conference," *Physical Educator* 32 (March 1975): 3–8; Robert L. Green, Joseph R. McMillan, and Thomas J. Gunnings, "Blacks in the Big Ten," *Integrated Education* 10 (May–June 1973): 32–39; Douglas Hartmann, "The Politics of Race and Sport: Resistance and Domination in the 1968 Olympic Protest Movement," *Ethnic and Racial Studies* 19 (July 1996): 548–66; Ron Briley, "It Was Twenty Years Ago Today: Baseball Responds to the Unrest of 1968," in *Baseball History: An Annual of Original Baseball Research*, ed. Peter Levine (Westport, Conn.: Meckler, 1989), 81–94.

36. David K. Wiggins, "'The Year of Awakening': Black Athletes, Racial Unrest and the Civil Rights Movement of 1968," *International Journal of the History of Sport* 9 (August 1992): 188–208, reprinted in David K. Wiggins, *Glory Bound: Black Athletes in a White America* (Syracuse, N.Y.: Syracuse University Press, 1997), 104–22; David K. Wiggins, "'The Future of College Athletics Is at Stake': Black Athletes and Racial Turmoil on Three Predominantly White University Campuses, 1968–1972," *Journal of Sport History* 15 (Winter 1988): 304–33, reprinted in Wiggins, *Glory Bound*, 123–51. See also David K. Wiggins, "Prized Performers, but Frequently Overlooked Students: The Involvement of Black Athletes in Intercollegiate Sports on Predominantly White University Campuses, 1890–1972," *Research Quarterly for Exercise and Sport* 62 (June 1991): 164–77.

37. Donald Spivey, "Black Consciousness and the Olympic Protest Movement, 1964–1980," in *Sport in America*, ed. Spivey, 239–62; Donald Spivey, "The Black Athlete in Big-Time Intercollegiate Sports, 1941–1968," *Phylon* 44 (June 1983): 116–25.

38. Amy Bass, *Not the Triumph but the Struggle: The 1968 Olympics and the Making of the Black Athlete* (Minneapolis: University of Minnesota Press, 2002).

39. Douglas Hartmann, *Race, Culture, and the Revolt of the Black Athlete: The 1968 Olympic Protests and Their Aftermath* (Chicago: University of Chicago Press, 2003).

40. Gerald W. Scully, *The Business of Major League Baseball* (Chicago: University of Chicago Press, 1989); Lomax, "'Curt Flood Stood Up for Us'"; Sarah K. Fields, "Odd Bedfellows: Spencer Haywood and Justice William O. Douglas," *Journal of Sport History* (forthcoming). For a historical assessment of the various court challenges that led to the labor revolution in professional team sports, see Paul Staudohar, *Playing for Dollars: Labor Relations and the Sports Business* (Ithaca: Cornell University Press, 1996). See also Charles P. Korr, *The End of Baseball as We Knew It: The Players Union, 1960–1981* (Urbana: University of Illinois Press, 2005).

41. Neil A. Wynn, "Deconstructing Tyson: The Black Boxer as American Icon," *International Journal of the History of Sport* 20 (September 2003): 99–114. See also Jack Lule, "The Rape of Mike Tyson: Race, the Press and Symbolic Types," *Critical Studies in Mass Communications* 12 (June 1995): 176–95; John M. Sloop, "Mike Tyson and the Perils of Discursive Constraints: Boxing, Race, and the Assumption of Guilt," in *Out of Bounds: Sports, Media, and the Politics of Identity*, ed. Aaron Baker and Todd Boyd (Bloomington: Indiana University Press, 1997), 102–22.

42. Gerald Early, "Mike's Brilliant Career: Mike Tyson and the Riddle of Black Cool," in *Traps: African American Men on Gender and Sexuality*, ed. Rudolph P. Byrd and Beverly Guy-Sheftall (Bloomington: Indiana University Press, 2001), 250–58.

43. David L. Andrews, ed., *Michael Jordan, Inc.: Corporate Sport, Media Culture, and Late Modern America* (New York: State University of New York Press, 2001). See also David L. Andrews, "The Fact(s) of Michael Jordan's Blackness: Excavating a Floating Racial Signifier," *Sociology of Sport Journal* 13 (June 1996): 125–58; Cheryl L. Cole, "American Jordan: P.L.A.Y., Consensus, and Punishment," *Sociology of Sport Journal* 13 (December 1996): 366–97.

44. David K. Wiggins and Patrick B. Miller, eds., *The Unlevel Playing Field: A Documentary History of the African American Experience in Sport* (Urbana: University of Illinois Press, 2003). Wiggins has also compiled a collection of essays that examines the lives of twenty prominent African American athletes who competed behind segregated walls, in predominantly white organized sports, or both; see David K. Wiggins, ed., *Out of the Shadows: A Biographical History of African American Athletes* (Fayetteville: University of Arkansas Press, 2006).

45. Alan M. Klein, *Sugarball: The American Game, the Dominican Dream* (New Haven: Yale University Press, 1991). See also Alan M. Klein, "Culture, Politics, and Baseball in the Dominican Republic," *Latin American Perspectives* 22 (Summer 1995): 111–30; Alan M. Klein, "Trans-Nationalism, Labor Migration, and Latin American Baseball," in *The Global Sports Arena: Athletic Talent in an Interdependent World*, ed. John Bale and Joseph Maguire (London: Cass, 1994), 183–205; Alan M. Klein, "Headcase, Headstrong, and Head-of-the-Class: Resocialization and Labelling in Dominican Baseball," *Arena Review* 14 (May 1990): 33–46; Alan M. Klein, "Baseball as Underdevelopment: The Political-Economy of Sport in the Dominican Republic," *Sociology of Sport Journal* 6 (June 1989): 95–112; Alan M. Klein, "American Hegemony, Dominican Resistance, and Baseball," *Dialectical Anthropology* 13 (December 1988): 301–12.

46. Rob Ruck, *The Tropic of Baseball: Baseball in the Dominican Republic* (Westport, Conn.: Meckler, 1991).

47. Alan M. Klein, "Baseball Wars: The Mexican Baseball League and Nationalism in 1946," *Studies in Latin American Popular Culture* 13 (1994): 33–56; Alan M. Klein, *Baseball on the Border: A Tale of Two Laredos* (Princeton: Princeton University Press, 1997).

48. Samuel O. Regalado, *Viva Baseball!: Latin Major Leaguers and Their Special Hunger* (Urbana: University of Illinois Press, 1998). See also Samuel O. Regalado, "'Dodgers Beisbol Is on the Air': The Development and Impact of the Dodgers Spanish-Language Broadcasts, 1958–1994," *California History* 74 (Fall 1995): 280–89; Samuel O. Regalado, "'Image Is Everything': Latin Baseball Players and the United States Press," *Studies in Latin American Popular Culture* 13 (1994): 101–14; Samuel O. Regalado, "Baseball in the Barrios: The Scene in East Los Angeles since World War II," *Baseball History* 1 (Summer 1996): 47–59. Regalado has

also studied women's softball among Japanese Americans; see Samuel O. Regalado, "Incarcerated Sport: Nisei Women's Softball and Athletics during Japanese-American Internment," *Journal of Sport History* 27 (Fall 2000): 431–44. See also David LaFrance, "A Mexican Popular Image of the United States through the Baseball Hero, Fernando Valenzuela," *Studies in Latin American Popular Culture* 4 (1985): 14–22.

49. David Maraniss, *Clemente: The Passion and Grace of Baseball's Last Hero* (New York: Simon and Schuster, 2006).

50. Jorge Iber, "On-Field Foes and Racial Misconceptions: The 1961 Donna Redskins and Their Drive to the Texas State Football Championship," *International Journal of the History of Sport* 21 (March 2004): 237–56; Jorge Iber, "Mexican Americans of South Texas Football: The Athletic and Coaching Careers of E. C. Lerma and Bobby Cavazos, 1932–1965," *Southern Historical Quarterly* 55 (April 2002): 616–33.

51. Jorge Iber and Samuel O. Regalado, eds., *Mexican Americans and Sport: A Reader on Athletics and Barrio Life* (College Station: Texas A&M University Press, 2007).

52. For more on black nationalism, see Wilson Jeremiah Moses, *The Golden Age of Black Nationalism, 1850–1925* (New York: Oxford University Press, 1978); Wilson Jeremiah Moses, ed., *Classical Black Nationalism: From the American Revolution to Marcus Garvey* (New York: New York University Press, 1996); John H. Bracey Jr., August Meier, and Elliott Rudwick, eds., *Black Nationalism in America* (Indianapolis: Bobbs-Merrill, 1970). For an examination of the link between black nationalism and the Black Power movement, see Harold Cruse, *Rebellion or Revolution?* (New York: Morrow, 1968). For an account that links economic black nationalism to the Nation of Islam, see Juliet E. K. Walker, *The History of Black Business in America: Capitalism, Race, Entrepreneurship* (New York: Macmillan, 1998). I draw extensively from William Van Deburg's excellent work on the Black Power movement to devise an analytic framework to examine this linkage; see William Van Deburg, *New Day in Babylon: The Black Power Movement and American Culture, 1965–1975* (Chicago: University of Chicago Press, 1992). See also Solomon P. Gethers, "Black Nationalism and Human Liberation," *Black Scholar* 1 (May 1970): 43–50.

53. Recent works on basketball include Andrews, *Michael Jordan Inc.*; Todd Boyd and Kenneth L. Shropshire, eds., *Basketball Jones: America above the Rim* (New York: New York University Press, 2000).

54. James Edward Miller, *Baseball Business*, 127.

55. Although the works are impressionistic, recent scholarly attention has been given to the life of Sonny Liston; see Nick Torches, *The Devil and Sonny Liston* (Boston: Little, Brown, 2000); Thom Jones, *Sonny Liston Was a Friend of Mine* (Boston: Little, Brown, 1999). For an excellent essay on Sugar Ray Robinson, see Daniel Nathan, "Sugar Ray Robinson, the Sweet Science, and the Politics of Meaning," *Journal of Sport History* 26 (Spring 1999): 163–74. Some other recent works on the African American sporting experience include Daniel Buffington, "Contesting Race on Sundays: Making Meaning out of the Rise in the Number of Black Quarterbacks," *Sociology of Sport Journal* 21 (March 2005): 19–37; David J. Leonard, "The Next M.J. or the Next O.J.? Kobe Bryant, Race, and the Absurdity Of Colorblind Rhetoric," *Journal of Sport and Social Issues* 28 (August 2004): 284–313; Billy Hawkins, "Is Stacking Dead?: A Case Study of the Stacking Hypothesis at a Southeastern Conference (SEC) Football Program," *International Sports Journal* 6 (Summer 2002): 146–60; Thomas B. Jones, "Caucasians Only: Solomon Hughes, the PGA, and the 1948 St. Paul Open Golf Tournament," *Minnesota History* 58 (Winter 2003–4): 383–93; James H. Rigali and John C. Walter, "The Integration of the American Bowling Congress: The Buffalo Experience," *Afro-Americans in New York Life and History* 29 (July 2005): 7–44. Recent attention has been given to Oscar De La Hoya; see Fernando Delgado, "Golden but Not Brown: Oscar De La Hoya and the Complications of Culture, Manhood, and Boxing," *International Journal of the History of Sport* 22 (March 2005):

196–211; Greg Rodriquez, "Boxing and Masculinity: The History and (Her)Story of Oscar de la Hoya," in *Latino/a Popular Culture*, ed. Michelle Habell-Pallán and Mary Romero (New York: New York University Press, 2002), 256–62. Tim Elcombe examines Jack Scott's "Oberlin Experiment" in "Reformist America: 'The Oberlin Experiment'—The Limits of Jack Scott's 'Athletic Revolution' in Post-1960s America," *International Journal of the History of Sport* 22 (November 2005): 1060–85.

Sports and the
Racial Divide

1

New Orleans, New Football League, and New Attitudes

The American Football League All-Star Game Boycott, January 1965

—*Maureen Smith*

Within the tattered pages of a January 1965 issue of *Sports Illustrated*, an article written by San Diego Chargers All-Pro tackle Ron Mix described an event that has previously been overlooked by both sport and civil rights historians.[1] No African American athlete had ever been reported to be involved in a Freedom Ride or any civil protests.[2] Reading through Mix's two-page account of a historic and successful boycott by a group of all-star African American football players, one is struck by the political consciousness of the black athletes, evident in their comments. Art Powell of the Denver Broncos stated, "We know we aren't going to change these people. But neither are they going to change us. We must act as our conscience dictates." The Buffalo Bills' Ernie Warlick felt that a "definite action must be taken" in part because no change had resulted from a smaller protest originating from an Atlanta pool hall incident.[3]

Mix was unconvinced the walkout would be effective and wondered about African Americans living in New Orleans who couldn't just leave the southern city. He wondered if the players "were spurred on to this sacrifice because they felt guilty for having escaped the suffering of their Southern brother" and if the boycott was their opportunity to "take a stand, to carry their share of the work." He poignantly asked, "Was this their Freedom Ride? Their Birmingham jail?" Mix, therefore, made a direct comparison between the protest of the footballers with the nonviolent direct actions taken by members of Congress of Racial Equality (CORE) and the Freedom Ride of 1961 and the Southern Christian Leadership Conference (SCLC) and Martin Luther King, Jr., in Birmingham in 1963. In King's "Letter from Birmingham Jail," the civil rights leader penned, "Nonviolent direct action seeks to create such a crisis and foster such a tension that a community which has constantly refused to negotiate is forced to confront the issue."[4] The walkout of the African American athletes served as the first example in professional athletics where a group of athletes were able to use the nonviolent direct action methods used by those working in the struggle for civil rights and have their action result in the relocation of the game, as well as a discussion of New Orleans and the city's violation of recent civil rights legislation.[5]

This chapter explores the walkout by twenty-one African American football players and the subsequent relocation of the game within the context of an American society wrought with racial conflict.[6] A particular focus will be on the evolving race consciousness within the context of an emerging professional football league seeking legitimacy. The American Football League (AFL) was struggling to compete with the established and powerful National Football League (NFL), and the boycott occurred at a tenuous time when a possible merger of the two leagues was being discussed. Moreover, the AFL had been gaining in popularity in large part because of the talent and excitement the African American athletes were showcasing on the playing field. Five questions will serve to guide the narrative: at a time when boycott movements, sit-ins, and marches were becoming common practices in the civil rights struggle, how were these black athletes able to successfully have the game relocated to a new city by simply stating they would not play; why were they willing to go the lengths of a boycott when they faced losing pension funds, as well as retaliation from owners and fans; how important was it that several of them came from historically black colleges and universities; what role did the city of New Orleans play in this event; and what type of consequences did the players face for their participation in the boycott? As African Americans struggled to acquire civil rights through several collective and individual actions, African American athletes faced discrimination on playing fields across the country. Whereas the Civil Rights Movement gained momentum, this small group of African American athletes used sport as a platform for their own protest of discrimination in American society, setting a precedent for hundreds of

African American athletes who would make similar use of sport in the latter half of the 1960s.

The Rise of the American Football League[7]

To understand the events surrounding the boycott, it is necessary to discuss the early history of the American Football League. On August 14, 1959, Texas oilmen Lamar Hunt and Kenneth S. (Bud) Adams announced the formation of the AFL. Hunt was the son of Texas oilman H. L. Hunt, who was considered the richest man in the U.S., with a net worth of $2 billion in 1954 and an after tax income of $54 million a year. Hunt was the youngest of six children, and the foundation for his wealth was a trust established by his father in 1935. Adams was the son of the chairman of the board of the Phillips Petroleum Company. In 1947, Adams incorporated the Ada Oil Company, an energy company engaged in oil and gas exploration, marine and land transportation, and the marketing of crude oil and petroleum products. Hunt and Adams were thwarted in their efforts to obtain NFL franchises. The AFL would have franchises in eight cities: Boston, Buffalo, Dallas, Denver, Houston, Los Angeles, New York, and Oakland. AFL owners selected Joe Foss as the league's commissioner. Foss served two terms in the South Dakota House of Representatives, and in 1954 was elected governor, an office he held for two terms. Foss's first task was to sell the league to the American public, and he worked diligently to accomplish this. He logged over 200,000 miles in his first year on the job, appearing before local Kiwanis and Rotary clubs, at sports banquets, and at almost every convention that would invite him.

The relationship between the AFL and the NFL was an antagonistic one. Charging that the NFL was trying to put them out of business, the AFL filed a $10 million antitrust suit against the senior circuit. Although the AFL lost the suit, this animosity led both leagues to engage in destructive competition over the acquisition of college talent. In 1960, for example, the Houston Oilers signed Louisiana State University Heisman Trophy winner Billy Cannon to a contract that reportedly brought him $100,000, plus lavish incentives. The AFL paid top money and won a substantial number of college stars that included Don Floyd of Texas Christian, Johnny Robinson of LSU, and Joe Namath of the University of Alabama for an unprecedented $400,000.[8]

It was within this context that African American players were afforded new opportunities to play professional football in the U.S. Historian Charles Ross notes that in 1959 only fifty African American athletes played in the fourteen-team NFL, most from predominantly white colleges and universities.[9] The new league needed talent and recruited African American players from historically black colleges and universities, as well as from predominantly white colleges and universities.[10] In fact, of the players involved in the boycott, several of them were among the league's leaders in a myriad of statistical categories. For example, running back Cookie Gilchrist led the league in rushing touchdowns for four consecutive years from 1962 to 1965. Wide receiver Lionel Taylor led the league in receptions in 1960, 1961 (with a league high 100 catches), 1962, 1963, and 1965, finishing second in the league in 1964. Receiver Art Powell had a stellar 1963 campaign leading the league with 1,304 receiving yards and sixteen touchdown receptions. During the AFL's first season (1960), seven of the eight teams had at least one African American player on the team.[11] By the start of the 1964 season, more than forty African Americans were on the eight AFL rosters.[12]

In mid-January 1965, the AFL announced plans to remain an eight–team league for the upcoming year, but noted that it had thirty-eight applications from thirteen cities (including New Orleans) for expansion teams. They had recently signed a new five-year $36 million television contract with NBC, in addition to a $6.7 million deal with NBC for the championship and all-star games.[13] In the week leading up to the All-Star Game, Buddy Diliberto of the *New Orleans Times-Picayune* reported the AFL needed to sign only 37 percent of their draft picks to maintain parity with the NFL. He followed up with a report that the AFL had already signed 56 percent of the players drafted in the first five rounds. Season ticket sales for the 1965 season increased in all eight cities, with Buffalo doubling from 10,000 to 24,000, Denver more than tripling from 6,361 to 22,287, and the New York Jets surpassing their opponents, 13,000 to 35,000 for the highest in the league. Commissioner Joe Foss saw the increase in season ticket sales as "another yardstick by which progress of the league can be measured." Season tickets sales in 1964 had increased 16 percent, but jumped to 56 percent in 1965.[14] The AFL presented a formidable challenge to the NFL and was making successful strides toward a merger of the two leagues. The boycott would in many ways reveal the collective power of the African American athletes, but would also publicize the strength of the young league in solidifying themselves as capable and competent partners to the NFL.

The Boycott

William N. Wallace of the *New York Times* called the players' walkout "a boycott without precedent in professional sports."[15] Several events during the week preceding the All-Star Game led to the protest. African American all-stars were refused service at nightclubs and confronted nightclub doormen brandishing guns. Several players were stranded at the airport for up to three hours because no taxis would pick them up, while others were refused taxi service around the city. One taxi driver took some of the players to the wrong side of town, "frequented by queers and twilighters."[16] Other players recounted statements directed at them. Abner Haynes, for example, was in an elevator with a crowd of whites, who were heard saying "It's a shame to see these niggers going and coming like they have a right to be in here." Another player, hanging his coat near a white woman's coat, overheard the comment, "Look at them, they just jump around like monkeys in the zoo."[17] The players were led to believe that they would not encounter such incidents and were quite surprised by the reception they received.

On January 10, 1965, the African American players from both teams met at the Roosevelt Hotel, the headquarters for the East All-Star team, and discussed their treatment and possible responses to the treatment. The players included at least one from each AFL team: Ernie Ladd, Earl Faison, Frank Buncom, and Dick Westmoreland of the San Diego Chargers; Cookie Gilchrist, Ernie Warlick, Elbert Dubenion, and Butch Byrd of the Buffalo Bills; Bobby Bell, Mack Lee Hill, Abner Hayes, Junious "Buck" Buchanan, and Dave Grayson of the Kansas City Chiefs; Willie Brown of the Denver Broncos; Clem Daniels and Art Powell of the Oakland Raiders; Larry Garron and Houston Antwine of the Boston Patriots; Sherman Plunkett and Winston Hill of the New York Jets; and Sid Blanks of the Houston Oilers.[18] After a long discussion about the treatment they had received, the twenty-one African American All-Star players from the American Football League decided to boycott the All-Star Game in New Orleans scheduled for January 16, 1965.[19] Arguing that the city and its citizens discriminated against them, the African American players voted 18-3 to boycott the game and informed Commissioner Joe Foss of their decision.[20]

Several sources recognized Ernie Warlick of the Buffalo Bills as the spokesman for the group. Warlick stated, "The majority ruled. We felt we couldn't compete 100 percent under the circumstances. . . . This came as a complete surprise to us. We were led to believe that we could relax and enjoy ourselves in New Orleans just like other citizens."[21] Warlick further expressed his belief that collective action was an important step for the players, as well as the AFL. He stated, "The American Football League is progressing in great strides and the Negro football players feel they are playing a vital role in the league's progression and have been treated fairly in all cities throughout the league."[22] Two other players identified as being instrumental in starting the discussion of the issue were San Diego Charger teammates, Ernie Ladd and Earl Faison.[23]

Efforts to convince the players to stay by the New Orleans branch of the NAACP were unsuccessful and at least one player was angered by their intervention.[24] Commissioner Foss found the situation regrettable, but agreed the players had adequate reasons for the walkout. Foss felt he had "no recourse but to back the players, because they are members of the AFL family. . . . You have 20 members of your ballclubs pull out and that doesn't leave you anything to do but cancel the game."[25] In addition to the commissioner, the players had the support of the American Football League Players Association. Days after the walkout, the players association met and unanimously voted in support of the walkout.[26] Mix, the author of the *Sports Illustrated* article that detailed the protest, despite his reservations about the action, wrote, "This time you're wrong, but your cause is just and we're with you."[27] The successful outcome of the athletes to collectively protest the discriminatory treatment was realized when Commissioner Foss decided to relocate the game to Jeppeson Stadium in Houston, Texas.

Reactions from the New Orleans Sports and Cultural Activities Foundation, the organizing committee for the game, were not initially critical of the AFL, Commissioner Foss, and the decision to relocate the game. In a statement to the press, David Dixon, head of the New Orleans committee, questioned the action taken by the players, calling it preemptory. Dixon indicated that the New Orleans committee felt no bitterness toward the league or Foss.[28] Local civic leaders of both races informed the players that their "militant" actions would hinder progress in New Orleans and "would greatly retard efforts by men of good will, of both races, to achieve harmony in the most difficult problem of our times." The committee expressed concern that the players refused to negotiate or compromise and referred to the recent integrated Sugar Bowl as evidence that the city could handle integrated sport without incident.[29] Dixon did acknowledge the recent racial struggles in the city and admitted that the loss of the AFL All-Star Game was a "grievous injury on a city that has struggled sincerely not only to comply with the provisions of the Civil Rights Act of 1964, but before that to reach a voluntary accommodation of the races."[30] In a statement from the Citizens Special Committee, made up of New Orleans business and civic leaders, the group highlighted the "extraordinary progress in race relations" the city had made and felt the AFL incidents should not influence the good name of New Orleans.[31]

The City of New Orleans

Just two weeks earlier, on New Year's Day 1965, New Orleans had successfully hosted Syracuse University and Louisiana State University in the first integrated Sugar Bowl since 1956. African American sport columnist Sam Lacy believed that the integration of the Sugar Bowl would "go down in athletic and sociological history as stupendously significant" and was pleased to see the racial barriers that had previously "plagued" the "extravaganza" open to "all races, colors, and creeds," as players and spectators.[32] One newspaper noted the Syracuse team had eight African American players on the roster and that it would be the "first time so many Negroes have seen action in the lineups at the Sugar Bowl." It marked the first Sugar Bowl game with integrated seating.[33] A 1956 Louisiana law had prohibited interracial athletic contests and required segregated seating. The law also mandated separate eating facilities, waiting rooms, toilets, and interracial participation in a variety of "activities involving personal and social contact."[34] A federal district court invalidated the sport segregation policy and the United States Supreme Court upheld the ruling in May 1959.

In 1963, New Orleans lost over $9 million when the American Legion Convention changed location due to the southern city's racial policies. That same year, the Pelicans, a minor league baseball team in the Southern League, moved to Little Rock, Arkansas, because of restrictions on integrated rosters and spectator seating.[35] In January 1964, the Supreme Court invalidated the segregated seating policy.[36]

Historian Adam Fairclough notes that while there were few African Americans participating in nonviolent direct action in New Orleans during the early 1960s, sometimes numbering only twenty picketers, the protests in other southern cities did have an impact on New Orleans. Largely dependent on tourism, New Orleans's white businessmen were sensitive to the potential for civic demonstrations and disruptions.[37] As a city, they were struggling with how to apply and enforce the recently enacted 1964 Civil Rights Act. In the months preceding the scheduled AFL football All-Star Game, as well as the immediate months that followed, the Ku Klux Klan was still a menacing and violent presence throughout Louisiana.[38]

In their response to the AFL boycott, the national and local newspapers and editorials varied in their interpretations of the walkout, some blaming the players, but few holding the city accountable. One exception was channel WWL-TV, operated by Loyola University in New Orleans, who commented, "Either we are going to compete in this world of ours—as other cities are competing oh, so successfully. Or we close ourselves off from the rest of America and remain the petty, provincial capital of limited opportunity and dubious culture which some seem to enjoy."[39] Commissioner Foss expressed doubt that New Orleans was ready for the big league. "If they can't treat big leaguers with the dignity and respect they deserve, then the city will have to suffer the consequences."[40] New Orleans Mayor Victor Schiro felt the players did "themselves and their race a disservice by precipitous action. . . . We are a very cosmopolitan and tolerant city, but we are also a southern city, and there are times when personal reaction is unpredictable. . . . It seems to me the players who walked out on us should have rolled with the punches."[41] Schiro went further when he predicted, "If these men would play football only in cities where everybody loved them, they'd all be out of a job today."[42]

Mayor Schiro's "roll with the punches" comment was widely criticized by African American newspapers. Marion E. Jackson writing for the *Birmingham World* wondered how a player could roll with the punches when he was "getting his brains beat out?"[43] Geraldo M. Ebanks of the *Cincinnati Herald* wondered if the mayor would have rolled with the punches if he had been "similarly treated" and concluded that he would not have because "racial prejudice—especially when politically oriented—is degenerative."[44] James D. Williams, writing for the editorial page of the *Washington Afro-American*, disagreed with the mayor's "turn the other cheek" philosophy noting that it only resulted in the other cheek being slapped. Williams understood that Schiro believed the boycott would hurt race relations, but poignantly asked whose race relations would be hurt. He suggested that had the players accepted the treatment white residents could believe New Orleans was a "progressive and liberal southern city."[45] A *Call and Post* editorial felt the mayor was suggesting that the footballers should have "meekly overlooked and acquiesced to racial discrimination against them" and recommended that "if any rolling is in order today, New Orleans and other southern cities persisting in Jim Crow practices will have to 'roll with the punches' of our country's binding and determined new Civil Rights Act."[46] In *The Afro-American*, Sam Lacy recalled, "My grandfather and yours 'rolled with the punch' and their grandfathers before them did the same. . . . Today's grandfathers of the future are asking why it is that colored people are destined to be the only ones in this country showing the Christian attitude of turning the other cheek."[47]

The decision by Commissioner Foss to remove the All-Star Game had a profound impact on the city of New Orleans. The response of New Orleans and its citizens indicate the tremendous loss they felt losing the game, but also revealed their refusal to view the decision by the players to leave their city as valid. Most refused to recognize that the city was still in violation of the 1964 Civil Rights Act and were unwilling to place the boycott within the larger racial struggle plaguing the nation. To these New Orleanians, sport was to be the level playing field that their city was not.[48]

African American Footballers as Civil Rights Activists

It was more than conceivable that the black all-star athletes were impacted by the larger Civil Rights Movement and that this contributed to their success in having the game relocated.[49] The players did not ask Commissioner Foss to relocate the game and were fully prepared to not participate in the All-Star Game. That the game was relocated rather than canceled was a tribute to both their talent and number (they accounted for close to 40 percent of the two all-star teams). Still, why were they willing to go to the lengths of boycott when they faced lost pension funds and retaliation from owners and fans? The revenue from the game would have been contributed to the players' pension fund. To avoid any legal action, the league was forced to pick up the costs of transportation, hotels, and meals, which the New Orleans committee had been contracted to pay. The game was moved to a much smaller venue, which virtually guaranteed a loss. Assistant Commissioner Milt Woodard thought the New Orleans game would have been the league's "big pay day" for the players' pension fund, making up for the previous three All-Star Games hosted in San Diego. According to one press account, the ABC television contract worth $75,000 would still go to the players' pension fund. Woodard felt a sellout was the only opportunity for the league to break even.[50] Reporter Sam Lacy commented that while the league might suffer at the turnstiles, they learned a valuable lesson that their talented players yielded tremendous power when acting as one unit. Lacy was perhaps giving the players more credit than they deserved.[51] Still, to the players the money issue was significant. Prior to the game, running back Cookie Gilchrist indicated that the $250 difference between the bonuses for the winning and losing teams was enough to take the "game out of the fun and frolic class," saying that the extra money would just cover his "incidental expenses."[52]

One explanation for the players' willingness to engage in direct action is their collective experiences as African Americans who routinely faced discrimination in society and in athletics. A majority of the players had experienced numerous acts of discrimination in both sport and society. Abner Haynes of the Kansas City Chiefs, after moving into the all-white Glenview Homes in Dallas, faced verbal abuse and other slights.[53] Five of the players who suited up for the San Diego Chargers and New York Jets had faced similar indignities when they were refused entrance to the poolroom at the Atlanta Hilton hotel prior to a preseason game designed to test the Atlanta area for an expansion team. Marion Jackson of the *Birmingham World* wondered if the Atlanta experience didn't plant the "seeds of the rebellion" and noted that the Chargers-Jets game would not have occurred without the intervention of a civic counselor.[54] Despite their exploits on the football field, these African American athletes faced the same indignities endured by their parents' generation.

Certainly the racial consciousness of the players prior to the trip to New Orleans played a critical role in the decision to take action against the discrimination. Moreover, the players had seen other African American citizens take action in the form of Freedom Rides, marches, sit-ins, and other collective efforts to combat racial discrimination. These players were simply taking action and used similar tactics in the unchartered territory of professional sport. Before Muhammad Ali refused to be drafted into the United States Army, before Olympians Tommie Smith and John

Carlos raised their black-gloved fists in the Mexico City air, and before a number of black athletes at predominantly white colleges and universities protested racial discrimination, the AFL players acted in unison to protest their treatment and the racial policies of New Orleans.[55] Of significance was their decision to act as a collective unit.

African American newspapers nationwide recognized the collective effort and compared the players' protest with other civil rights protests in their reports on the incidents and related editorials. Equally significant was the support the players received from the AFL, Commissioner Joe Foss, and the players association. Columnist Cal Jacox, of the *Norfolk Journal and Guide*, championed the players' efforts: "Right or wrong, it took courage for the players to make the decision and then follow it through to the end. . . . Though the vote wasn't unanimous they stuck together and were 21 strong when the trek elsewhere began. . . . And this alone is a major accomplishment. . . . Their togetherness is a sign of the times and further indication that the Negro athlete is becoming increasingly aware of his responsibilities in the fight against bigotry."[56] Bill Nunn, Jr., echoed Jacox's sentiments in his *Pittsburgh Courier* column:

> The Negro athletes who refused to bow in the face of segregation in New Orleans last week are to be commended. While there have been scattered instances of black athletes taking firm steps against the injustices of jim crow before, never has such universal admiration for a large group been so widespread. To a man, the individuals who put principle above playing in a football game, have shown that courage can pay big dividends. When the 21 Negroes decided that they would not perform in a city where they weren't accepted as citizens, they had no idea of the repercussions they might face. Despite this, they went ahead and made their move.[57]

Nunn's colleague at the *Courier*, Wendell Smith, stated the sports world and nation should "bow low and long to the players who refused to tolerate New Orleans bigotry." Smith saluted Commissioner Foss for his support and praised the AFL for not hesitating to act or trying to "smooth things," recognizing that the players' concerns were valid.[58] Sam Lacy, writing for the *Afro-American*, compared the players to "the sit-inners, the Freedom Riders, and the Washington Marchers."[59] In an editorial for the same paper, the players were applauded for standing up the city's violation of civil rights laws, noting that the players "acted like college graduates who have been the backbone of the student demonstrations. Suddenly, we are even more proud of them as star football players and as advocates of freedom."[60] Sheep Jackson and his *Call and Post* readership hailed the players for having the "guts to stand up and be counted."[61] A *Norfolk Journal and Guide* editorial used the AFL game as an example of the dollar being an effective weapon for fighting discrimination.[62] Cliff Smith, seeing the bigger picture for his *Houston Forward Times* readers, realized that "what began with Jackie Robinson in Brooklyn, now embraces all sports throughout the land."[63]

Eight of the twenty-one players had attended historically black colleges and universities, while Sid Blanks, who attended Texas A & I, had been the first African American athlete to compete in the Lone Star Conference. Ernie Ladd, Willie Brown, and Buck Buchanan all attended Grambling and played for legendary coach Eddie Robinson. Buchanan was the first player from Grambling to be a number one pick in the AFL and NFL, ultimately choosing the AFL because of the league's young attitude.[64] Mack Lee Hill attended Southern University, Ernie Warlick attended North Carolina College, Dick Westmoreland attended North Carolina A & T, Winston Hill attended Texas Southern, and Clem Daniels went to Prairie View.

Coach Robinson, in his autobiography *Never Before, Never Again*, alludes to student-athletes at Grambling who were involved in the Civil Rights Movement during college. He points out that this generation of student-athletes were profoundly affected by the activism of their fellow students, as well as by the numerous protests, bombings, deaths, and other struggles related to the Civil Rights Movement.[65] Regardless of whether these African American athletes attended an HBCU or a predominantly white college, many of these black athletes attended schools in the southern region of the nation, making them keenly aware of the racial issues and tensions of the decade. Several southern colleges were finally opening their doors to African American students in the face of violent protests by white Americans. Many of them were one of only a few African Americans on their team and attending their colleges. These efforts at integration garnered great national attention in the media and most African American students during this time period would have been cognizant of the struggles facing them at predominantly white colleges and universities. Cookie Gilchrist, the only player who did not attend college, had played football in the Canadian Football League and was very outspoken on the issue of race. Gilchrist pointed out that his north-of-the-border experiences opened his eyes to the racial inequities in the United States and identified himself as not the "run-of-the-mill Negro athlete who accepts the crumbs offered."[66]

Many factors discussed earlier contributed to the players' decision to walkout, such as their prior encounters with racial discrimination. Still, one of the most significant factors in the decision to relocate the game in response to the boycott was the number of players involved and the AFL's reliance on these twenty-one players. In an All-Star Game that represented the best of the AFL's talent, the twenty-one players equaled close to 40 percent of the league's athletes.[67] Moreover, beyond the All-Star Game, the league needed the players to continue to put an exciting and quality product on the field that could compete with the NFL for attendance, recruiting college players, television revenue, and eventually a partnership with the already established league. The boycotting players were successful in large part because they were viewed as a valuable commodity.

The majority of the athletes did not suffer any repercussions beyond the loss of pension revenue. Though one owner wanted to establish a punishment for future incidents, the other owners voted him down.[68] The players received support from the league commissioner and the players association.[69] In essence, the AFL needed their talent to present a legitimate challenge to the NFL and any hopes of a merger with the already established league. The player pension fund was hurt by the boycott with fewer tickets sold in Houston, and the league covered the costs of relocating the game.[70] Someone hinted that whites were boycotting the game because of the walkout, to which an unidentified player responded, "I wouldn't care if we had to play to the empty seats, I would still do the same thing."[71] A sellout for Jeppesen Stadium had been expected, but what was not expected was twenty-two miles per hour gusts of wind and forty degree weather. Attendance for the relocated game, which the West won handily 38-14, was only 15,446.[72] Two of the boycotting athletes, Clem Daniels and Art Powell, scored touchdowns for the winning team.

Three players were traded before the start of the 1965 season. Within a week of the All-Star Game, Abner Haynes was traded from the Chiefs to the Denver Broncos. Described as a "flashy" halfback, Haynes did request a trade at the end of the season. He believed the trade also had to do with the walkout. "I believe what really forced the trade was my stand about the treatment of colored players in New Orleans. . . . I still think we were right in pulling out." Haynes indicated that ownership felt that other

African Americans on the team would be influenced by his presence.[73] Dave Grayson was traded to the Oakland Raiders.[74] Cookie Gilchrist was traded from the Buffalo Bills to the Denver Broncos. Gilchrist was still in the good graces of the AFL, evident by his selection for an AFL press tour during the summer of 1965.[75] Six of the players, Art Powell, Butch Byrd, Ernie Ladd, Dave Grayson, Bobby Bell, and Gilchrist were named to the 1965 All-Star team, making them eligible for the All-Star Game.[76] A majority of the players continued to have successful careers, with three earning a home in the Pro Football Hall of Fame.[77]

Popular Culture Depictions and Memory

Sport historians have attributed much of the activism of black athletes in the 1960s to the examples set by Muhammad Ali, but the All-Star Game boycott comes prior to much of Ali's activism. Moreover, as an individual athlete, Ali was not required to conform to the same "team" codes of established behaviors. There is an absence of literature related to the boycott despite the increased interest and attention of scholars to the time period.[78] Harry Edwards mentions it briefly in his book *The Revolt of the Black Athlete*, as does Ed Grover in his year-by-year history of the league, but neither offers an analysis of the incident.[79] The Pro Football Hall of Fame in Canton, Ohio, has a small exhibit addressing the integration of professional football.[80] The Pro Football Hall of Fame Archives contain very little on the event, but the exhibit does address it briefly in a video exhibit. A brief video clip addresses the boycott and credits the African American players (and implicitly the National Football League, although at the time the two leagues were clearly separate and the NFL had no involvement with the players who walked out of New Orleans) with changing two racial laws in New Orleans.[81] There is no evidence to support the video's claim that two racial laws had been legislated prior to the game. Of interest in the National Football League's depiction of the boycott is their alignment toward a position that reveals the league to be an agent of change in the Civil Rights Movement. This is an especially important manipulation of the events in part because the NFL makes no effort to distinguish between the two leagues. By claiming the history of the challenging league as their own, as opposed to a force that acted upon the established league, the NFL sets up an image of the league as being an institution that actively promoted racial equality rather than maintaining the divide. Even the AFL did little to remind their fans of the incident. In a review of the 1964 season, no mention was made of the incident.[82] It is noted that the All-Star Game was played in Houston, moved from previous years in San Diego.[83] In a short review of important dates, the invitation from New Orleans to host the game was noted on July 1, 1964, and the player walkout was listed on January 10, 1965.[84] At the time, it was clear the AFL was not interested in promoting the incident. Within weeks of the incident, newspapers no longer referred to the walkout, nor did these same newspapers recall the boycott in the following years as African American athletes protested college and professional athletics.

While Muhammad Ali and the image of Tommie Smith and John Carlos have been commodified to represent the era of civil rights activism in sports, no such image exists for this meaningful event. Moreover, there is no reference to the walkout in the growing literature on the activism of African American athletes during the 1960s. In an era when other African Americans fought for equality using any number of methods, the actions of these African American professional athletes provide a profound example of the power of the collective and the willingness to sacrifice for the goal of creating change—and the powerful platform sport can provide for such expressions of consciousness.

Notes

1. Ron Mix, "Was This Their Freedom Ride?" *Sports Illustrated*, 25 (January 18, 1965): 24–25. An edited version of Mix's article appeared in the *New Orleans Times-Picayune* on January 14, 1965, II, 13, under the title, "Mix Tried to Avert Walkout." Because he had a Juris Doctorate degree, Mix was nicknamed "The Intellectual Assassin" for his physical play.

2. Boxer Floyd Patterson accompanied retired baseball player Jackie Robinson to a Birmingham meeting. See Gilbert Rogin, "Meeting in Miami," *Sports Illustrated*, 21 (March 13, 1961): 18. NBA player Bill Russell discussed the 1963 March on Washington. See Russell's autobiography, *Go Up for Glory* (New York: Coward-McCann), 205–6. Russell also visited Jackson, Mississippi, at the request of Charlie Evers, brother of Medgar, in July 1963. He conducted basketball clinics despite the racial turmoil in the southern city. He also discusses this trip in *Go Up for Glory*, 211–13.

3. Warlick was referring to an incident the San Diego Chargers encountered in Atlanta prior to a preseason game in August 1964. The Chargers were staying at the Atlanta Hilton and the African American players were asked not to enter the poolroom. The players protested, but Coach Sid Gilliam talked with the players and was able to persuade them to not protest. Barron Hilton, owner of the Chargers, owned the hotel. See "Scorecard," *Sports Illustrated*, 24 (September 7, 1964). Also see *Birmingham World*, January 16, 1965. *Birmingham World* sportswriter Marion Jackson wrote that the "seeds of rebellion may have been planted in Atlanta" and reported that he was surprised that the walkout did not occur in Atlanta.

4. Martin Luther King, Jr., "Letter from Birmingham Jail," April 16, 1963.

18 Maureen Smith

5. For more on Martin Luther King, Jr., the SCLC, and the Civil Rights Movement, see David A. Adler, *Martin Luther King, Jr.: Free At Last* (New York: Holiday House, 1986); Martin Luther King, Jr., Papers Project Staff, *A Guide to Research on Martin Luther King, Jr., and the Modern Black Freedom Struggle* (Stanford, CA: Stanford University Libraries, 1989); Peter J. Albert and Ronald Hoffman, eds., *We Shall Overcome: Martin Luther King, Jr., and the Black Freedom Struggle* (New York: Pantheon, 1990); Martin Luther King, Jr., *The Autobiography of Martin Luther King, Jr.* (New York: Intellectual Properties Management, 1998); Martin Luther King, Jr., *The Papers of Martin Luther King, Jr.* (Berkeley: University of California Press, 1992); Adam Fairclough, *To Redeem the Soul of America: The Southern Christian Leadership Conference and Martin Luther King, Jr.* (Athens: University of Georgia Press, 1987); David J. Garrow, *Bearing the Cross: Martin Luther King, Jr., and the Southern Christian Leadership Conference* (New York: W. Morrow, 1986); idem., ed., *We Shall Overcome: The Civil Rights Movement in the United States in the 1950's and 1960's* (Brooklyn, N.Y.: Carlson, 1989); Greg Moses, *Revolution of Conscience: Martin Luther King, Jr., and the Philosophy of Nonviolence* (New York: Guilford, 1997); Flip Schulke, *The Making of Martin Luther King and the Civil Rights Movement* (New York: New York University Press, 1996).

6. Several newspapers initially reported that twenty-two athletes were involved in the boycott, but after looking through subsequent reports and the All-Star Game media guide, only twenty-one athletes were involved. The twenty-second player may have been fullback Matt Snell of the New York Jets. Snell was the AFL Rookie of the Year and selected to play in the game, but missed the game due to a military service call. Boston Patriots Larry Garron, another African American player, replaced him.

7. For more on the American Football League, see Bob Collins, Chet Nelson, and Jackie Kutsko, *From Striped Socks to Super Bowl and Beyond* (Colorado Springs, CO: Pikes Peak, 1980); Ed Fowler, *Loser Takes All: Bud Adams, Bad Football, and Big Business* (Atlanta: Longstreet, 1997); Larry Fox, *The New England Patriots* (New York: Atheneum, 1979); Ed Grover, *The American Football League: A Year-by-Year History, 1960–1969* (Jefferson, NC: McFarland, 1997); Jack Horrigan and Mike Rathet, *The Other League: The Fabulous Story of the American Football League* (1970); John Lombardo, *Raiders Forever* (Lincolnwood, IL: Contemporary Books, 2001); Joe McGuff, *Winning It All* (Garden City, NJ: Doubleday, 1970); George Sullivan, *Touchdown! The Picture History of the American Football League* (New York: Putnam, 1967). These books primarily recount teams in the league and the history of the league with little analysis of the league. They are all geared toward a popular readership.

8. For a comprehensive account on the signing war for college talent, see Michael E. Lomax, "Conflict and Compromise: The Evolution of American Professional Football's Labour Relations, 1957–1966," *Football Studies* 4 (2001): 5–39.

9. Charles K. Ross, *Outside the Lines: African Americans and the Integration of the National Football League* (New York: New York University Press, 1999), 140.

10. Grover, *The American Football League*, includes several accounts of incidents where African American players were recruited heavily from both the AFL and NFL, sometimes being "kidnapped" by a reporter to miss a signing deadline. The AFL used several tactics to attract players to their league.

11. Ross, *Outside the Lines*, 149.

12. Number of African American players in Ross, *Outside the Lines*, 165–78. Ross lists every African American player, the teams they played for, and the years they played. He does not differentiate between AFL and NFL and there is at least one error in his list. Moreover, the list only includes players who began play by 1962. It is, however, one of the few compiled lists with this information. During 1964, eleven of the twenty-two NFL All-Star rookies were African American; the AFL selected six African American rookies.; see *Pittsburgh Courier*, January 2, 1965.

13. Jack Hand, "AFL to Study Requests for Added Franchises," January 15, 1965, Football Hall of Fame Archives. Jack Horrigan, ed., *Official American Football League Guide* (St. Louis, MO: Sporting News, 1965), 76.

14. Jack Horrigan, "News and Notes From American Football League," July 18, 1965. Also see Horrigan, ed., *Official American Football League Guide*, 11.

15. *New York Times*, January 12, 1965.

16. *Afro-American*, February 6, 1965. Sam Lacy commented on the nightclub doormen and their guns in his column printed in the *Afro-American*, January 23, 30, 1965. Also see *Birmingham World*, January 16, 1965.

17. *Houston Forward Times*, January 23, 1965; also see *Cleveland Plain Dealer*, January 11, 1965; Ben Thomas, "AFL Cancels All-Star Tilt," January 11, 1965, Football Hall of Fame Archives; "AFL Visits Houston Year Early," January 12, 1965, Football Hall of Fame Archives; *New York Times*, January 11, 1965.

18. *New Jersey Afro-American*, January 16, 1965.

19. Although Mix states that there were twenty-two African American players, he only listed eight names, and other articles related to the topic consistently name twenty-one players.

20. The three players that voted to stay and play were Sid Blanks, Winston Hill, and George Byrd. See *Houston Forward Times*, January 23, 1965. For another account of what occurred in Room 990, see *New Orleans Times-Picayune*, January 11, 1965.

21. *Cincinnati Herald*, January 30, 1965.

22. *Denver Blade*, January 21–27, 1965. Also see *Norfolk Journal and Guide (National Edition)*, January 16, 1965.

23. The leadership of Ladd and Faison is according to players Abner Hayes, Clem Daniels, and Art Powell, who met with Lloyd C. A. Wells of the *Houston Forward Times*; See *Houston Forward Times*, January 23, 1965. Bill Nunn also mentioned Cookie Gilchrist as one of the leaders of the players' group. See *Pittsburgh Courier*, January 23, 1965; "Gilchrist has always been a player who has believed in standing up for his rights . . . whenever possible he has always taken a firm stand against racial injustices."

24. *Houston Forward Times*, January 23, 1965. Wells identified Abner Haynes as the player who was angered by the efforts of the local NAACP to encourage the players to stay.

25. *Norfolk Journal and Guide*, January 16, 1965; *New Orleans Times-Picayune*, II, p. 4. Roesler mentions that a few white players expressed disappointment that the game would not be played, but he does not identify the players.

26. *Milwaukee Sentinel*, January 15, 1965. For one account of Joe Foss and his decision, see *Pittsburgh Courier*, January 23, 1965. For more on the players association decision, see *Afro-American*, February 6, 1965. See also Hand, *New Orleans Times Picayune*, January 15, 1965. Boston Patriot Tom Addison, president of the Players Association, was quoted as saying "we came to a new understanding concerning the relations of men. The association was at the time of the incidents in New Orleans in sympathy with the Negroes, but through lack of communications was unable to assemble enough information to take a stand." The meeting included ten black players, with at least one from at each of the eight teams. According to Sam Lacy, three white players on the Buffalo Bills had "figured in recent civil rights contributions." Lacy identified the three players as Jack Kemp, Daryl Lamonica, and Wray Carlton. No other newspapers mentioned this. Lacy's source was Chuck Burr, publicity director of the Bills, who spoke with him about the team's reactions to the walkout. Burr did not identify the three players. See *New Jersey Afro-American*, January 16, 1965. Lacy also recalled a conversation he had with Foss and Lamar Hunt two years prior about his concerns for the potential of racial incidents should New Orleans be awarded a team.

27. Mix, "Was This Their Freedom Ride," 25.

28. Dixon was still very interested in attracting a football team for New Orleans and his initial response to the cancellation was one that did not challenge the AFL and their decision. Within days, Dixon would be more forthcoming. On January 16, 1965, Dixon was reported to have commented, "I would not at this time seek an audience or accept one from the AFL owners. But I am going to talk with Commissioner Foss and some of the owners. I have no idea of giving up the fight for professional football in New Orleans. I was crushed when all this

happened, but I've bounced back lots sooner than I thought I would." See *New Orleans Times-Picayune*, January 16, 1965.

29. *New Orleans Times-Picayune*, January 12, 1965. *Times-Picayune* sportswriter Bob Roesler did not include the names of any of the local civic leaders involved in the discussion. Also see *Afro-American*, January 23, 1965.

30. *New York Times*, January 12, 1965.

31. Ibid.

32. *Afro-American*, January 16, 1965. An integrated Sugar Bowl track meet was hosted the same weekend. See *Afro-American*, January 9, 1965. The Orange Bowl hosted a similar track meet, see *Afro-American*, January 9, 1965.

33. *Washington Afro-American*, December 29, 1964; *Houston Informer*, January 2, 1965. For a commentary on the economics of integrating the game, see *Birmingham World*, January 16, 1965. In a response to an editorial written by the white-owned newspaper in St. Louis, the *St. Louis Argus* published an editorial rebutting many of the newspaper's criticisms of the AFL players. One of the newspaper's point of evidence was that the African American players from Syracuse University did not complain about any discrimination during their Sugar Bowl trip making the athletes appear "meek and docile." The *Argus*, however, contended that the Syracuse team did refuse to train for the game in Mississippi, opting for Florida instead, thus showing the collegians to have some resolve. See *St. Louis Argus*, January 15, 1965.

34. Adam Fairclough, *Race and Democracy: The Civil Rights Struggle in Louisiana, 1915–1972* (Athens, GA: University of Georgia Press, 1995), 205.

35. *New Orleans Call and Post*, January 23, 1965. Sam Lacy also recalled that New Orleans had lost American Medical Association conference, been bypassed for NFL franchise, and reiterated the move of the Pelicans to Little Rock in the Southern League. *New Jersey Afro-American*, January 30, 1965.

36. For more on the history of integrating southern bowl games, including the Sugar Bowl in New Orleans, see Charles H. Martin, "Integrating New Year's Day: The Racial Politics of College Bowl Games in the American South," *Journal of Sport History*, 24 (Fall 1997): 358–77.

37. Fairclough, *Race and Democracy*, 336.

38. See ibid., 351–57; 373. Fairclough provides a number of Klan incidents, including integration efforts by CORE, in Bogalusa, Louisiana, in the months preceding and following the relocated football game. Between March and July 1965, the Klan was believed to be responsible for a dozen explosions in New Orleans.

39. *New Orleans Call and Post*, January 23, 1965.

40. *Pittsburgh Courier*, January 23, 1965.

41. *Cincinnati Herald*, January 30, 1965.

42. *Afro-American*, January 23, 1965.

43. *Birmingham World*, January 16, 1965.

44. *Cincinnati Herald*, January 30, 1965.

45. *Washington Afro-American*, January 16, 1965. For as much as the game's relocation hurt New Orleans, the selection of Houston aided the Texas city in their quest to be viewed as worthy.

46. *Call and Post*, January 30, 1965.

47. *Afro-American*, January 23, 1965.

48. The walkout appeared to dash any hope of New Orleans being awarded an expansion franchise in the AFL. However, less than a year later, the city was awarded the sixteenth NFL franchise team, despite no evidence that race relations had improved. What ultimately guaranteed the city's entrance into professional football was their ability to garner public support for the construction of a domed stadium. Only two weeks prior, the NFL and AFL had made the decision to merge the two leagues into one and the awarding of the New Orleans franchise marked the first joint action of the merged leagues. See *New York Times*, February 18, November 2, 1965; *New Orleans Times-Picayune*, November 2, 14, 1965.

49. In the years preceding the game, several incidents had occurred, including the 1963 March on Washington, the bombing of a Birmingham church which killed four girls, the Freedom Rides, a number of sit-ins, and the forced integration of schools.

50. *New Orleans Times-Picayune*, January 13, 1965; *New York Times*, January 13, 17, 1965.

51. *Afro-American*, January 23, 1965.

52. *New Orleans Times-Picayune*, January 9, 1965. *New York Times*, January 12, 1965. *New York Times* sportswriter William Wallace stated that the winning team would receive $700, while the losing team would get $500. It is ironic to note that the game was relocated to a city that had previously endorsed segregated seating five years earlier. See the introduction regarding Houston's Jeppensen Stadium's segregated seating policy.

53. *Dallas Express*, January 16, 1965. Reported the same day the newspaper printed the story about the All-Star Game being moved to Houston.

54. *Birmingham World*, January 16, 1965.

55. For more on protests and actions taken by black athletes during 1968 see Amy Bass, *Not the Triumph but the Struggle: The 1968 Olympics and the Making of the Black Athlete* (Minneapolis: University of Minnesota Press, 2002). For an excellent article detailing protests of black athletes during 1968, see David K. Wiggins, "'The Year of Awakening,': Black Athletes, Racial Unrest and the Civil Rights Movement of 1968," *International Journal of the History of Sport* 9 (1992): 188–208.

56. *Journal and Guide (Norfolk, Virginia)*, January 23, 1965.

57. *Pittsburgh Courier*, January 23, 1965. Nunn also notes that four of the players did not vote for the walkout, two for fear of their jobs, but that all went along with the vote. Nunn also cited Ernie Warlick and Cookie Gilchrist as leaders of the actions.

58. *Pittsburgh Courier*, January 23, 1965.

59. *Afro-American*, January 23, 1965.

60. *Afro-American*, January 23, 1965.

61. *Call and Post*, January 23, 1965.

62. *Norfolk*, January 30, 1965. The other example the paper noted was the recent decision by several school boards, city councils, local, and state agencies to sign non-discrimination pledges so they could continue to receive federal grants.

63. *Houston Forward Times*, January 16, 1965.

64. Grover, *The American Football League*, 233. It was a great source of pride for African Americans to have attended HBCUs and then achieve success in professional sports. Several black-owned newspapers often reported when black athletes made all-star teams, and noted which black players had attended HBCUs. For example, see *Pittsburgh Courier*, January 2, 16, 1965; *Houston Forward Times*, January 16, 1965; *Washington Afro-American*, December 29, 1964.

65. Eddie Robinson with Richard Lapchick, *Never Before, Never Again: The Stirring Autobiography of Eddie Robinson, the Winningest Coach in the History of College Football*, (New York: St. Martin's, 1999). See Chapter 5, "Family, Fame, and Civil Rights, 1955–69," 105–40.

66. Grover, *The American Football League*, 130.

67. According to statistics from the 1964 season, several of the twenty-one players involved in the boycott were ranked in the top ten for pass receiving, rushing, and interceptions. See Jack Horrigan, "News and Notes from American Football League," December 24, 1964.

68. Minutes of the sixth annual meeting of the AFL, January 13–16, 1965. Held at Shamrock Hilton Hotel, Houston, Texas. Available in the archives at the Football Hall of Fame, Canton, Ohio. Minutes address finances of the All-Star Game and note that the boycott was ill advised. The issue was tabled, p. 3. Day 2 of the meetings; the minutes show that there was a vote that the proceeds from game would go to the league. Payment was to be made to New Orleans for all-star expenditures. Three owners (Hunt, Adams, and Werblin) were selected to study the issue, p. 8. Day 3, p. 9; Dave Dixon believed that incidents were not isolated, but that players acted nastily. Dixon still wanted New Orleans to be considered for expansion. Owners issued a statement on p. 13 that "any city that hosts pre-season, all-star or any other games to be

investigated for discriminatory practices." The players association issues this same statement, see *New Orleans Times Picayune*, January 15, 1965. The owners asked Foss to send the letter to players indicating their responsibilities and penalties if they do not play and that any decision must include proper authorities. No comment on if the action was taken, p. 18. Bob Roesler reported that one owner wanted to fine and suspend players. See *New Orleans Times-Picayune*, January 16, 1965.

69. *Norfolk Journal and Guide*, January 16, 1965; *New Orleans Times-Picayune*, January 16, 1965.

70. *Times-Picayune*, January 13, 1965.

71. *Houston Informer*, January 23, 1965.

72. Attendance for the 1964 All-Star Game in San Diego was only 20,016. *Times-Picayune*, January 9, 1965; *Houston Informer*, January 23, 1965; *New Jersey Afro-American*, January 23, 1965.

73. *Washington Afro-American*, January 23, 1965.

74. Player trades were noted in Horrigan, ed., *Official American Football League Guide*, 56.

75. Al Ward, "News and Notes from American Football League," September 22, 1965.

76. Al Ward, "News and Notes from American Football League," December 16, 1965.

77. Bobby Bell, Willie Brown, and Buck Buchanan earned entrance into the Pro Football Hall of Fame.

78. Three years later, Jack Olsen authored a five-part series in *Sports Illustrated* that focused on the black athlete in America. See Olsen, "The Black Athlete—A Shameful Story," *Sports Illustrated*, 28 (July 1, 8, 15, 22, 29, 1968).

79. Harry Edwards, *Revolt of the Black Athlete* (New York, NY: Free Press, 1969); Grover, *The American Football League*, 145.

80. The exhibit is approximately five feet wide, seven to eight feet tall with some photos and text. The exhibit is on the integration of professional football and includes reference to the boycott.

81. A recently released DVD, *Inside the Vault: Volumes 1–3 (1960–1970)*, produced by NFL Films and Warner Home Video (2003), addresses the boycott as "the game that never happened."

82. Horrigan, ed., *Official American Football League Guide*, 11.

83. Ibid., 11.

84. Ibid., 75–76.

2

Battles for Control over Muhammad Ali's Career and Image

—Michael Ezra

On January 12, 1966, Muhammad Ali called a press conference to announce the formation of a new corporation that would promote his fights. The organization was named Main Bout, Incorporated, and its biggest stockholders were prominently positioned within the Nation of Islam. Since the company controlled the ancillary rights to Ali's title bouts, it would reap most of their revenues, which would come from closed-circuit television broadcasts. Ali envisioned that Main Bout would become the foundation of a larger economic organization designed to create employment and wealth for blacks.

Main Bout's creation, which threatened to shake up professional boxing's power structure, brought on widespread resistance. Reporters feared a takeover of the sport by the Nation of Islam. Government officials questioned whether the organization should be allowed to make money within their jurisdictions. Motion picture concerns, which owned most of the venues equipped to show closed-circuit fights, refused to do business with the Nation. Ali's opposition to the Vietnam War, which surfaced a month after Main Bout's formation, heightened public antipathy towards the new corporation. The resulting backlash made Main Bout vulnerable to a boycott of its first promotion.

Main Bout's story fits into several historical contexts. It reflected the economic nationalism that marked the programs of Booker T. Washington and Marcus Garvey. Like these leaders, and like many of his contemporaries in the Civil Rights Movement who were beginning to stress the importance of economic power, Ali believed that financial empowerment was central to black independence and autonomy. The resistance faced by Main Bout illustrated a key theme in African American business history. Black business development in the United States has lagged disproportionately because of undercapitalization and a lack of government support. Main Bout, like thousands of black-run enterprises before it, encountered these problems.[1]

Main Bout exemplified the Nation of Islam's economic tradition. Ali's plan to cultivate a black-controlled promotional network that included independent theater owners, public relations people, and job programs came from the Nation's economic collectives. Although the groups were not formally tied, it seems likely that Main Bout enriched the Nation of Islam. Main Bout's largest two stockholders were members of the organization and Ali tithed a portion of his purses to it.

This chapter seeks to locate Main Bout within these economic contexts to address the major inquiries of this essay: how have the battles for commercial control of Muhammad Ali's career affected his cultural symbolism; how have the narratives, which have defined Ali's image, reflected the ideas of those who control the Ali industry and those who oppose that control? Main Bout's takeover of the job of managing and promoting Ali from the all-white Louisville Sponsoring Group, for example, engendered for some people new ways of perceiving the fighter. Even though two of Main Bout's five board members were white, this transfer of control to Main Bout had racial overtones that were reflected in press coverage and public reception of Ali. Sometimes this process resulted in a positive understanding of the heavyweight champion; other times it caused people to despise him.

The central argument of this essay is that Muhammad Ali's image has always been produced and shaped by financial arrangements. Throughout his public life, Ali has had to balance his own sense of self with the desires of those who have had a stake in the Ali industry. Some critics have positioned this process as an unfortunate by-product of Ali's concurrent rise as an American icon and corporate pitchman near the end of the twentieth century. However, this essay argues that it has been happening since the beginning of his career. Those who have lamented Ali's decline from revolutionary political hero to product pusher have ignored the consistent influence of economics on his symbolism and cultural significance.

To illustrate the dynamic between commercial and cultural control of Muhammad Ali, this essay will explore three periods of his career: his six years with the Louisville Sponsoring Group, his creation of Main Bout, and his three-and-a-half years away from boxing following his 1967 conviction on draft evasion charges. These analyses will highlight the intertwining of economic concerns and Ali's cultural meanings, and will set the stage for an understanding of Ali's current image as a product of this intersection.

The Louisville Sponsoring Group

After his gold medal victory at the 1960 Olympics, managers and backers offering to finance his professional career in exchange for a percentage of the profits he was sure to generate besieged Cassius Clay. The fighter was conflicted. He knew that wealthy whites had the capital necessary to guide his career properly, but he also wanted blacks to have an important role in his development. Newspaper reporters commented on this process, sometimes giving advice about whom he should select. Their concerns reflected how image-makers took cues on how to perceive Clay from the choices he made about the economic control of his boxing career.

Clay's first suitor was Billy Reynolds, the Louisville metals magnate. Reynolds and Joe Martin, the policeman who had introduced the adolescent Clay to boxing, received the fighter in New York following his Olympic victory. There, they offered him a $10,000 signing bonus and a guaranteed ten-year contract at $3,600 a year. The annual figure could rise according to Clay's earnings, which he and Reynolds would split equally. The contract also called for Martin to train the fighter, as he had done through much of Clay's amateur career. Money, said Reynolds, was not the issue. It was his love of sport, sense of civic pride, philanthropic feelings towards Clay, and need for a hobby that caused him to pursue this opportunity.[2]

Despite the lobbying efforts of Louisville sportswriters who wrote articles urging Clay to take the offer, he turned Reynolds down. As he explained in his autobiography, the fighter felt that Reynolds would not treat him fairly. Clay had once worked at Reynolds's estate. It was unpleasant. He was subjected to racial slurs and accused of theft. The experience made him suspicious of Reynolds. He felt that the man who was wining and dining him in New York "didn't seem to be the real Mr.

Reynolds. He seemed more real when I sat on his porch eating with the dogs."[3]

While Clay's refusal of Reynolds did not make waves at the time, the press turned retrospectively to it as a way of perceiving Ali's draft resistance. One Louisville newspaper asked: "Why would any normal Kentucky boy who wanted to get ahead in boxing turn down a millionaire benefactor with the generosity, affluence, and connections of William Reynolds? When he turned down Reynolds we should have realized how twisted and misguided was Black Cassius, this same young man we Kentuckians once loved and respected so much. This was the turning point."[4] The editorial locates Ali's demise with his rejection of white control over his career and illustrates how economic concerns affected his image.

Throughout his career, Clay was willing to work with and accept help from whites. While the fighter considered a wide range of offers from potential backers, Louisville's elite were using their influence to put together his professional debut and, in the words of one, to "put a little money in the kid's pocket." Mayor Bruce Hoblitzall spearheaded a task force that included business leaders, boxing insiders, and community organizations. They organized a charity boxing show that would benefit an area children's hospital while paying Ali a $2,000 purse. Both Louisville's black and white press agreed that this was "quite a chunk of money for a fellow [in] his first fight," "very generous," and "a terrific payday." Area newspapers lent support, running half-page ads. Governor Bert Combs waived the State Fairgrounds rental fee for the event. A grocery chain sold tickets and provided free parking. Through direct solicitations, businesspeople canvassed their friends and sold 1,500 top-priced tickets. Civic leaders brought in Wilma Rudolph, the track-and- field star, to drum up publicity for the promotion. All of this caused the *Louisville Times* to remark that Clay's career would begin "amidst probably the greatest fanfare ever drummed up for a six-round bout." In short, Louisville's political and economic elite banded together to lend their support to Cassius Clay while he searched for a permanent management team. As a charitable event, the fight did amazing business, pulling in 6,200 people who paid over $12,000 to see it. The promotion made clear that control over Cassius Clay's career could mean millions to whomever gained it.[5]

Although he benefited from whites during this period, Clay was determined to employ blacks in key positions whenever possible. Following his Olympic victory, he told a reporter, "First thing I do when I get home is to see a lawyer to plan pro connections. I need an old head to help this 18-year-old boy avoid mistakes." He hired Alberta Jones, the Howard University graduate and first black woman admitted to the Kentucky bar, as the sole negotiator of his first contract. For his debut, Clay chose as his manager of record former amateur opponent and Louisville resident George King. And as he had done on-and-off throughout Clay's amateur days, Fred Stoner trained the fighter. By employing Stoner in his professional debut, Clay sent the message to Billy Reynolds that he was not interested in hiring Joe Martin as his trainer and therefore was not interested in taking on Reynolds as his manager. Alberta Jones would later deliver Clay's formal rejection of Reynolds's offer. Although on the surface Clay's operation seemed to be white-dominated, its core was black. Later in his career, when Clay determined Stoner to be inadequate to guide him professionally, he made former light-heavyweight champion Archie Moore his trainer. Eventually, Clay would hire Angelo Dundee, an Italian American, as his permanent trainer.[6] But Ali's career began with blacks in key positions, and when he had the ability to make that possible, he often did. For Ali, black power meant using his boxing career to employ and enrich other African Americans. Even if the promotion of his professional debut was white, the people working closest with Ali to prepare for it and to capitalize from it were black.

Clay's choice of Stoner over Martin culminated years of rivalry between the two trainers and showed how the fighter's career could sometimes become a battleground for power between blacks and whites. In his autobiography, he describes Martin as less competent but more connected than Stoner. "Martin's strict rule was that there be no association with Stoner," he wrote. But this caused a dilemma for Clay. Martin's connections allowed him to book fighters on a local television show called *Tomorrow's Champions*, which paid Clay four dollars per appearance. Stoner could not get his fighters on television. His gym lacked the facilities and equipment of Martin's. He lacked connections to wealthy backers and sponsors like Billy Reynolds. Because "[most] of Martin's boys were white, and most of those he tried to seriously recruit were white," Clay enjoyed privileges that Louisville's black amateurs did not. Nevertheless, as his career progressed, Clay decided that he had to switch trainers, "even if it meant cutting off a good source of income." The reason was simple. Despite all the accouterments of Martin's operation, "the boys from Stoner's gym were better boxers than those at Martin's." Even during his amateur days, Clay's career became a site where power struggles with racial overtones developed. The choice for the young fighter was clear. Even if it meant giving up certain privileges, Clay chose to learn his craft with a black trainer among other black fighters. Although granting control over his boxing career to whites produced short-term gains, Clay felt that long-term autonomy and excellence would come from his participation in black-led structures. His choice of Stoner over Martin reflected this philosophy, as would his formation of Main Bout and refusal to be drafted.[7]

Based on a recommendation by Alberta Jones (who received $2,500 "for all she has done for us—and she did plenty," said Clay), Clay agreed in October 1960 to sign a six-year contract with the Louisville Sponsoring Group, a syndicate of eleven white men from his hometown. Members of the Louisville Sponsoring Group were rich; seven were millionaires and three were heirs to family fortunes worth millions. The eleventh member, Bill Faversham, assembled the organization, was its managing partner, and served as its primary press contact. The agreement gave the Louisville Sponsoring Group the rights to the first six years of Clay's professional career. The first two years of the contract were guaranteed at $4,000 a year, but for four years afterwards, the Louisville Sponsoring Group gained the annual option to terminate or renew the agreement at a minimum of $6,000 a year. Since the contract called for Clay to receive half of his purses, his salary would rise if his fight earnings were more than double the guaranteed amounts listed above. After six years, the option to renew or terminate shifted to Clay. Clay also received a $10,000 signing bonus from the Louisville Sponsoring Group. The syndicate released a statement following their negotiations with the fighter: "Each of the 10 members of the group has admiration for Cassius Clay as a fine young man. . . . The principle purpose of the group is to provide hometown support for Cassius's professional career and to aid him in realizing the maximum benefits from his efforts." The arrangement with the Louisville Sponsoring Group held many advantages for the young fighter. The syndicate had money to hire first-rate trainers and sparring partners, pay for food and medical care, and insure that Clay would not be hustled into dangerous matches prematurely. It managed Clay's finances. It put 15 percent of his earnings into a trust fund that could not be reached by the fighter until his thirty-fifth birthday. It made sure Clay's taxes were paid in full and on time. The group also shielded him from organized crime and paid all of his living expenses.[8]

Numerous biographies about the fighter have presented the Louisville Sponsoring Group in a favorable light. Thomas Hauser, whose 1991 book sold over 150,000 copies, made the *New York Times* best-seller list, and became the foundation for the fighter's reemergence as a beloved icon, described Clay's deal with the Louisville Sponsoring Group as "fair and generous for its time." John Cottrell, the British journalist, wrote, "Clay the unproven professional was entirely happy to put himself in the hands of these eleven fairy godfathers, and there was an atmosphere of complete trust." Claude Lewis, one of Clay's first biographers, heaped praise on the syndicate in his 1965 book: "There are eleven sponsors in the group, and at a time when the boxing world is beclouded by underworld dickering, misappropriated funds, government investigation, and a general sorrowful malaise, they present an uplifting sight. . . . Not only does their private wealth insure Clay that he will never end up broke through any fault of theirs, but they surround him with a substantial moral and ethical environment, a rare commodity in boxing these days." For forty years, biographers of Cassius Clay/Muhammad Ali have portrayed the Louisville Sponsoring Group positively. Their praise reflects contemporary coverage of the partnership, which generally positioned Clay as the beneficiary of his dealings with white backers.[9]

In their praise of the Louisville Sponsoring Group's management of Clay's finances, however, writers ignored evidence that the fighter had a clear sense of his own worth, an awareness of the economic pitfalls that had felled many of his pugilistic predecessors, and an understanding of what to do with his newfound money. After signing his contract, he told a *Louisville Courier-Journal* sportswriter, "The first thing I'm doing with that $10,000 my sponsors gave me is putting aside $3,000 for Uncle Sam. . . . There's a lot of things I want to be in this fight game, but I sure don't want to be a Joe Louis. That is, I don't want to have the income tax troubles Joe Louis has had." The young fighter could account for all the money from his signing bonus and professional debut. When the reporter questioned this, Clay called his parents. "Mother," he said, "we'll have to get out the checkbook. I want to show this man I'm no spendthrift." While it is impossible to tell whether Clay's career would have run smoothly without the Louisville Sponsoring Group, it is certain that he was not a financial dimwit at the mercy of his backers. To portray the group as the fighter's financial savior is to ignore the possibilities of Clay's financial acumen.[10]

Throughout their tenure as Clay's managers, the Louisville Sponsoring Group encouraged this portrayal of themselves not only as his financial savior but also as a moral guiding force. A 1963 *Sports Illustrated* feature described the group of millionaires as "Innocent of prizefighting's bad old ways." Their motivation for managing Clay was also described in this manner. One member claimed, "All we want to do is see that Cassius winds up rich." Another said, "One motive is to do something for boxing at a time the sport needs help." A third added, "We think we can keep him out of the financial trouble Joe Louis got into—which made me sick to see." There was also talk by group members about profiting from Clay's career, but "the official line" was, "We are behind Cassius Clay to improve the breed of boxing, to do something nice for a deserving, well-behaved Louisville boy and, finally, to save him from the jaws of the hoodlum jackals." Although the description of Clay as well behaved was telling, others painted a different picture. "If anybody is the boss of this boy," said Angelo Dundee, "it's the contract. In all my years I've never known a fighter getting such a break as this." Generally, however, the Louisville Sponsoring Group portrayed themselves as motivated by philanthropy, as spiritual and financial guides to a young man who needed help.[11]

What reporters did not know was that Clay was already a member of the Nation of Islam, and it was that organization, and the influence of his parents, which provided ethical guidance for him. Blacks, not whites, were at the center of Clay's moral universe. During a 1962 lunch meeting with a newspaper reporter, Clay responded to the writer's ordering a ham sandwich with a lecture on trichinosis. He claimed to no longer eat pork. He wore a dark suit with a white shirt and bow tie, standard garb for Nation members. Another sportswriter called Clay "a personable young man [with] a moral code that demands admiration." The fighter thought so, too. "I've never been locked up. I've never been cautioned in the ring for holding or hitting low or nothing," he noted. "I live by the Bible. My mother and father taught me to live right. No stealing, no cussing, no drinking, no smoking." It was blacks that made Clay the way he was, not the Louisville Sponsoring Group. Later in Clay's career, with the formation of Main Bout, the Nation of Islam would not only supplant the Louisville Sponsoring Group as the fighter's moral savior, but also as his financial one. The bad press that followed this transition illustrated the relationships between commercial control of Clay's career and the resulting cultural images of him.[12]

Although Cassius Clay, by then called Muhammad Ali, was essentially finished with the Louisville Sponsoring Group when his contract with them expired and he formed Main Bout in 1966, he got in a parting shot against the organization in his autobiography. Some members were described as telling racist jokes. Others were called cold and mean. Still others were portrayed as cheap. A decade later, Ali was angry that reporters had championed the Louisville Sponsoring Group as anything more than capitalists: "Every newspaper account I read described the event in the holiest light, with ten white angels tending charity in the jungle. Not as the good, hard, common-sense business deal that it was." Biographer David Remnick, describing Ali's autobiography, notes, "Ali's early financial backers, the Louisville Sponsoring Group, were portrayed as a bloody-minded band of white businessmen who regarded their charge as little more than a property to exploit."[13]

Rise and Fall of Main Bout, Inc.

At a press conference in January 1966, Muhammad Ali announced that he had formed a new corporation, Main Bout, Inc., to manage the multimillion dollar promotional rights to his fights. "I am vitally interested in the company," he said, "and in seeing that it will be one in which Negroes are not used as fronts, but as stockholders, officers, and production and promotion agents." Although racially integrated, Main Bout was led by the all-black Nation of Islam. Its rise to this position gave blacks control of boxing's most valuable prize, the world heavyweight championship. Main Bout embraced historical cooperative strategies of black economic empowerment endorsed by Booker T. Washington, Marcus Garvey, and Malcolm X. Muhammad Ali envisioned Main Bout as an economic network, a structure that would generate autonomy for black people.[14]

From the beginning, Main Bout encountered resistance. Initially, it came from white sportswriters, but about a month after its formation, Ali's draft status changed to 1-A, meaning he had become eligible for military service in the Vietnam War. He responded by publicly opposing the war. In response, politicians nationwide joined the press in attacking Main Bout. The political controversy surrounding Ali made it easier for Main Bout's economic competitors—rival promoters, closed-circuit television theater chains, organized crime—to run the organization out of business. Money and politics were important elements of white resistance to Main Bout, but we must also consider the organization's potency as a black power vehicle, and its symbolic meaning to the larger American public.

Several important black leaders have embraced capitalism as a black power strategy. At the turn of the twentieth century, Booker

T. Washington modeled his Tuskegee Institute as a center for black economic development and investment. Eschewing political protest in favor of business opportunities, Washington argued, "Brains, property, and character for the Negro will settle the question of civil rights." As biographer Louis Harlan explained, "Washington offered to trade black acquiescence in disfranchisement . . . in return for a white promise to allow blacks to share in . . . economic growth." Washington also helped found the National Negro Business League. The organization endorsed "buy-black" campaigns and the creation of nationwide investment trusts that would provide capital to upstart businesses.[15]

Marcus Garvey positioned commerce as the central site through which his political, economic, and cultural programs for black liberation would come together. In 1919, he founded the Negro Factories Corporation. To capitalize on it he offered a million dollars worth of stock exclusively to blacks at five dollars a share. At its peak in the early 1920s, Garvey's Universal Negro Improvement Association (UNIA) and its allied corporations operated three grocery stores, two restaurants, a printing plant, a steam laundry, and a clothing manufacturing department. The UNIA owned buildings and trucks, published a newspaper, and employed 1,000 black people in the United States. Garvey's eventual demise as a race leader resulted from his lack of capital and government support. Garvey was deported following a conviction, wrongful in the eyes of many, that he had used the mails to defraud his investors. Garvey faced the two major problems that have limited black business success in America, according to historian Juliet Walker: "While the government has failed blacks, blacks have not failed themselves. . . . If black financial achievements seem inconsequential, it is not that blacks have failed to save, but that the capital available for saving has been unconscionably circumscribed by race. . . . In America, government support, both direct and indirect, is critically important for business success."[16]

According to a biographer of Elijah Muhammad, the Nation of Islam's longtime leader, "The most pertinent source of the Nation's form of nationalism was the Universal Negro Improvement Association." Muhammad, who had been a corporal in Chicago's UNIA chapter, felt that capitalism was a key site for black power. The Nation of Islam's constituency was made up largely of the underclass, whose major concern was poverty. Throughout the organization's history, Muhammad and his followers founded urban-based businesses like bookstores and bakeries, as well as agrarian enterprises. "There has never been a leader of our people who went all-out to set up an economic plan for our people," he wrote. To achieve independence, blacks must "work collectively and harmoniously . . . . If there are six or eight Muslims with knowledge and experience of the grocery business—pool your knowledge, open a grocery store." In 1964, Nation of Islam spokesman Malcolm X asserted, "the black man himself has to be made aware of the importance of going into business." In various cities, Nation of Islam mosques were business centers used not only to worship, but also to develop small business enterprises. By the 1960s, the Nation of Islam had developed into an $80-million empire that included sizable real estate and land holdings, restaurants, dry cleaners, its own bank, newspapers, and personal health care products.[17]

Throughout the Civil Rights Movement, organizations like Martin Luther King's Southern Christian Leadership Conference (SCLC) and the Student Nonviolent Coordinating Committee (SNCC) merged political action with economic goals. According to movement veteran Julian Bond, the campaign had an economic underpinning from the beginning. "When [SCLC] people were boycotting the Montgomery buses," Bond noted, "they didn't just want the front seats, they wanted bus driver jobs. When we [SNCC] were demonstrating at lunch counters in Atlanta, we didn't just want to sit at the lunch counters, we wanted jobs in the store." In a May 1965 newspaper editorial, SNCC Chairman John Lewis wrote about the movement's increasing focus on black economic power: "In 1960 we were demanding the right to eat a hamburger at any lunch counter. It took us three years to discover that we could not afford the hamburger and that we needed money." According to Lewis, political and economic power was inseparable. "Money means economic power," he continued. "In order to get and to maintain economic power we have to bargain. Bargaining means political power. So it took us three years to understand that political power insures the stability of economic power." Appearing on national television a year later, Lewis's successor Stokely Carmichael also underscored the relationships between politics and economics. "As I see the problem in this country it is an economic problem in terms of black people being forced, being exploited," he said. "We are property-less people in this country. We are property-less and we have to seek to redress that and the only means open to us now are political means. So we grasp that political power now, and then we see . . . how we can work with that political power to then achieve economic power." SNCC's 1965 campaign to form an independent black political party in Lowndes County, Alabama, coincided with its proposal for a Poor People's Land Cooperative in that area. As part of its backing of the Mississippi Freedom Democratic Party's challenge of the white-supremacist Mississippi Democratic Party in 1964, SNCC proposed a Mississippi Farm League to "Give Negroes economic, and therefore political power. A union of farmers will give Negroes economic autonomy. . . . As a strong organization it can give its members protection and effectively lobby for policies beneficial to them."[18]

Muhammad Ali's formation of Main Bout had the potential to put increased economic power into the hands of blacks. At the press conference introducing Main Bout, Ali told reporters the company would control the ancillary rights to his fights, starting with a multimillion-dollar March 29 match in Chicago against Ernie Terrell. Main Bout's ownership of these ancillary rights gave them access to the vast majority of revenues from Ali's bouts. The ancillary promoter had the rights to live and delayed telecasts, radio broadcasts, fight films, and any further transmission or distribution of a bout. The local promoter, on the other hand, produced the live event and ran its on-site ticket sales. The major monies from big-time boxing matches during this period, including Ali's, came from closed-circuit television. Because seating at and revenue from the hundreds of closed-circuit theaters nationwide outnumbered that which could be generated at the arena where a given fight took place, such bouts usually had closed-circuit television takes much larger than from other sources.

Main Bout had five stockholders. Herbert Muhammad, son of Nation of Islam leader Elijah Muhammad, was its president. John Ali, the Nation of Islam's National Secretary, was Main Bout's treasurer. Together, they shared 50 percent of its stock and half of its board's six votes. The closed-circuit television operator Michael Malitz and his attorney Bob Arum were Main Bout's vice-president and secretary, holding 20 percent of Main Bout's stock and one vote each. Jim Brown, the professional football player and Main Bout's vice-president in charge of publicity, controlled one vote and 10 percent of the company. Malitz and Arum were Main Bout's sole white members. They came up with the idea for the enterprise while promoting a 1965 fight in which Jim Brown served as their broadcaster. Malitz and Arum asked Brown to carry to the champion a proposal for a company that would allow Ali to control the finances for his fights and potentially increase black participation in their production. Brown passed the idea to Ali. Ali and the Nation of Islam approved the measure and Main Bout was the result.[19]

Like Muhammad Ali, Jim Brown emphasized Main Bout's potential for black economic uplift. He told a reporter, "Our goal is to use the money that we make—and hope to make in future ventures—to support the founding of businesses by Negroes. At first, we'll have to count basically on small businesses." That summer, several months after Main Bout's formation, Brown retired from professional football and founded the Black Industrial and Economic Union (BIEU). Although Main Bout was not formally connected to the BIEU, their goals were similar. Both wanted to increase black economic power in the United States. Muhammad Ali recognized this, and in 1967, he donated $10,000 to Brown's group.[20]

Some white newspaper reporters were alarmed. Syndicated *New York Daily News* columnist Gene Ward claimed, "Any way one sizes up this take-over of the heavyweight title by the Black Muslims . . . the group which advocates violence as the major weapon of racial war . . . the fight game is going to be the worse for it. This could be the death blow." Eminent sportswriter Jimmy Cannon asserted, "The fight racket has been turned into a crusade by the Muslims. . . . This is a fete to celebrate a religion that throws hate at people." Doug Gilbert of the *Chicago American* added, "the Muslims own Clay . . . they have what amounts to a hammerlock on all that's lucrative in boxing." Reporters also compared Main Bout unfavorably to the Louisville Sponsoring Group.[21]

Although Main Bout had critics within the black press, several writers welcomed its creation. Cal Jacox, the *Norfolk Journal and Guide* sports editor and syndicated columnist, challenged the white press to cover Main Bout fairly. According to Jacox, "Boxing is in an uproar. It seems that pro football star Jim Brown has joined a group that will promote Cassius "Muhammad Ali" Clay's title bout with Ernie Terrell and includes members of the Black Muslim sect among its officers; now, because of this alliance, the alarmist[s] are crying all over the place." Jacox assessed the fears of some white sportswriters, "They are saying that the Muslim philosophy will dominate Main Bout, Inc., and with this domination, they contend will come—via Cassius as the heavyweight champion—complete control of boxing." But to Jacox, this was not the issue. Main Bout's most important functions were outside professional boxing. "Jim Brown, in rebuttal, explained that the sole purpose of the new organization is to use its profits to generate capital for Negro businessmen," he continued, "and that explanation is good enough for this corner. And, from here, it should probably be sufficient for the critics, who are way off base in castigating the project before they've given it a chance to reveal its program to the public."[22]

In February 1966, less than a month after Main Bout's formation, the United States Selective Service reclassified Muhammad Ali as draft-eligible for the Vietnam War. When reporters called Ali for comment, he signified his political and religious opposition to the Vietnam War. In a telephone interview with Tom Fitzpatrick of the *Chicago Daily News*, Ali claimed that he had seen "lots of whites burning their draft cards on television. If they are against the war, and even some congressmen are against the war," Ali asked, "why should we Muslims be for it?" According to Ali, the war violated the principles of the Nation of Islam. "Let me tell you, we Muslims are taught to defend ourselves when we are attacked," he added. "Those Vietcongs are not attacking me. All I know is that they are considered Asiatic black people and I don't have no fight with black people." Ali warned that his reclassification would incite the worldwide Muslim community: "I don't want to scare anybody about it, but there are millions of Muslims around the world watching what's happening to me."[23]

A common supposition was that the Nation of Islam had manufactured Ali's draft resistance only to protect its investment in the upcoming fight with Terrell. After that, claimed these reporters, Ali would drop his shenanigans and join the Army. To save their profits, Jimmy Cannon assured readers, "The Black Muslims will shut up Clay." The editorial boards of Chicago newspapers voiced their antipathy to Ali and the Nation of Islam. The *Chicago American* claimed to be "sorry for Cassius Clay . . . he is as innocent as a puppet compared to the gang of fanatics that now owns and operates him. In fact, he is a puppet." The *Chicago Tribune* asserted, "The Black Muslims have ordered [Ali] to appeal as a conscientious objector." These writers disputed the sincerity of Ali's position and his understanding of the issues surrounding it.[24]

In Chicago, Ali's draft resistance and an escalating distrust of Main Bout unleashed furious attacks by local newspapers and politicians who called for banning his match with Terrell. The *Chicago Tribune* found it "deplorable that so many Chicagoans are unwittingly encouraging [Ali] by their interest in a fight whose profits will go largely to the Black Muslims." Charles Siragusa, the Illinois Crime Investigating Commission's executive director, felt that "it is an insult to the people of this state to permit a man like Clay who swears allegiance to an admitted cult of violence to reap a harvest of cash from the very citizens he has insulted with his whining attempts to avoid the draft." Aided by the local press, white city and state politicians formed a full-fledged assault against the match within a matter of days.[25]

After weeks of such resistance, Illinois Attorney General William Clark declared the match illegal. Citing possible inconsistencies in the licensing procedures for Ali and Terrell and a widely ignored rule that any corporation promoting a boxing or wrestling event had to have at least fifty people in it, Clark advised the Illinois State Athletic Commission to "adjourn their meeting and to so advise the participants" that their promotion was finished in Chicago. While Clark's legal claims were legitimate, such rules had always been loosely enforced, if not ignored. Almost certainly, Ali's draft resistance and Main Bout's affiliation with the Nation of Islam brought increased scrutiny over the licensing and promotion of his fight with Terrell. Chicago Mayor Richard Daley backed the decision: "The attorney general has issued an opinion holding the fight illegal. All state officials are bound by the opinion of the attorney general." The Illinois State Athletic Commission, which had final say on sanctioning the fight, acquiesced and cancelled the match. The *Chicago Tribune* praised Daley and Clark for intervening.[26]

Main Bout's association with the Nation of Islam combined with Ali's draft resistance to engender nationwide opposition to his title fight with Terrell. Unwelcome in Chicago, Main Bout shopped the contest around the United States with little success. In each city, local boxing people greeted Main Bout with interest, but state and local government officials rejected them. Main Bout's Bob Arum explained, "I got calls from promoters all over the country wanting to hold the fight, even from Huron, [South Dakota]." However, said Arum, "the day after a promoter would call me, the governor of his state or the mayor would announce there'd be no Clay fight in his town or state." Promoters in Louisville, for example, completed negotiations with Main Bout and the Kentucky State Athletic Commission agreed to sanction the bout. Influenced by local veterans groups, however, members of the Kentucky State Senate announced the next day that they would block the fight. In Pittsburgh, promoters inquired about hosting the match. The next day, Pennsylvania legislators moved to bar it. After local promoters and the Maine State Athletic Commission announced their interest in sponsoring the contest, Governor John Reed rebuffed them. Promoters in South Dakota, Rhode Island, Oklahoma, and Missouri also asked about holding the bout in their states, but were blocked. The pattern was clear: as soon as the news broke that area boxing people were interested in the fight, local or state officials opposed them. With the contest less than a month away, Main Bout had yet to secure a site.[27]

Main Bout finally got approval to hold the fight in Toronto and was forced to find a substitute opponent, Canadian heavyweight George

Chuvalo, when financial reasons caused Terrell to withdraw from the bout. By then, however, the promotion had gone bust. A month earlier, the Associated Press had predicted gross receipts of over $4,000,000 and a minimum purse of $450,000 for Ali. The day after Main Bout announced that they had signed Chuvalo, however, the Associated Press reported that the fight's gross would be approximately $500,000. Although there had been radio broadcasts of all of Ali's previous title matches, only a handful of the fight's forty-two sponsors agreed to support the bout. The radio broadcast had to be cancelled. Critics of Main Bout, Ali, and the Nation of Islam proposed a boycott of the closed-circuit broadcast. In Miami, a 2,700-member American Legion post said that it would picket any theater that showed the fight. No Miami sites broadcast Ali versus Chuvalo. Some sportswriters asked readers to stay away from the bout. Eddie Muller, the *San Francisco Examiner*'s boxing writer, chastised any theater operators who "might take it upon themselves to accept the TV firm's promotion and make a quick dollar." Referring to a proposed local boycott of the fight, Muller commented, "If every state follows California's action perhaps it'll be a complete nationwide blackout, which is as it should be."[28]

The most crippling blow to the promotion, by far, was its abandonment by closed-circuit television theater chains. Main Bout had contracted 280 North American closed-circuit television venues to broadcast the Terrell fight, but only 32 sites ended up showing the match against Chuvalo. Several cities that normally hosted Ali title fights in at least one area venue, including Cincinnati, Milwaukee, Kansas City, and Minneapolis-St. Paul, did not screen the bout. California's two biggest boxing promoters announced that they would meet with theater owners to make sure that no venues in California showed the March 29 contest. When Main Bout approached Ray Syufy, owner of twenty-one drive-in theaters in Northern California, to televise the match, it was turned down, although Syufy admitted the company had made him a "lucrative offer." In total, the fight was shown in only two California venues, both of them independent theaters. By contrast, Ali's previous bout was shown in thirteen Los Angeles area theaters alone. In New York, seven Loews' theaters withdrew 13,000 seats from the closed-circuit pool. Ernie Emerling, the firm's public relations vice-president claimed, "Too much silly-shallying over the site didn't leave us enough time to print tickets and advertise; we should have had six to eight weeks." Later, New York's RKO theater chain canceled their offer to show the fight in ten area locations. While twenty-five New York City venues with a seating capacity of 80,000 had shown Ali versus Patterson, only five New York City theaters with a seating capacity of

11,000 hosted Ali versus Chuvalo. In Chicago, Ed Seguin, representing the Balaban and Katz chain of theaters, reported that his firm would not show the fight "because of all the uncertainty over where, and whether, it was coming off." Both the B&K and Warner theater chains canceled their arrangements with Main Bout nationwide.[29]

The Ali-Chuvalo fight was financially disastrous, although fans saw an excellent boxing match that Ali won by fifteen-round unanimous decision. The closed-circuit telecast sold about 46,000 tickets for $110,000. This gross take was twenty to forty times below closed-circuit revenues from each of Ali's three other championship fights. The $150,000 on-site, live gate was also lower than for each of Ali's previous title bouts. Furthermore, Ali's $60,000 purse was approximately a tenth of those for each of his previous title matches and at least three times less than for any fight of his championship career. The Associated Press summarized, "Theater-television of last night's Cassius Clay-George Chuvalo heavyweight title fight proved a resounding dud, as expected." Eddie Muller crowed, "Forming the Main Bout, Inc. organization was a costly mistake. Whoever put money into the firm must wind up broke. There's no way, as far as we can see, of the organization recouping." The fiasco illustrated Main Bout's lack of control over the terms of Ali's fights.[30]

Black observers identified racism and a possible criminal conspiracy as reasons for the financial failure of the Ali- Chuvalo fight. "There are some reports of possible court action or civil rights agencies may be looking into the cancellations of the closed-circuit television showings to ascertain if there was any overt racial discrimination involved," according to Clarence Matthews of the *Louisville Defender*. "What columnists have tried to do is thwart the Black Muslims through castigation of Clay," Marion Jackson wrote in the *Atlanta Daily World*. "It seems as though the Black Muslims for the first time [have] projected a Negro group—Main Bout, Inc., in control of a nationwide closed circuit telecast." *Muhammad Speaks* accused white reporters of hiding their racism through so-called patriotic attacks on Ali. "Outbursts over [Ali's] military draft status were [a] means of killing two birds with one red, white, and blue stone" and an "attempt to smear" Main Bout, according to the newspaper. The newspaper also wrote: "Strong denunciations against an avalanche of hypocritical attacks against World Heavyweight Champion Muhammad Ali by sections of the white press and super-patriotic politicians continued to grow here in the Negro communities as increasing numbers of black leaders supported the right of the young Muslim champion to express his views on military service in Viet Nam without being subjected to a vicious boycott to prevent him from practicing his profession." The most strident response came from Moses Newson of the *Baltimore Afro-American*. Newson praised Main Bout for surviving "in face of the most vicious and concentrated 'kill them off' campaign ever joined in by the press, the Mafia, and politicians." He asserted that white "reporters, broadcasters, and others who tried to kill the fight scribbled and spouted bitter reams to a degree that they actually need to offer something more lest they themselves might be thought part of an unholy alliance that includes racists, hypocrites, and mobsters." On Capitol Hill, Main Bout's Jim Brown, in a press conference with Harlem Congressman Adam Clayton Powell, contended, "The ostensible reason" for the boycott "is because of Clay's so-called unpatriotic remarks about the draft, but that's just an excuse [to destroy Main Bout]." Powell vowed to have the U.S. Department of Justice and the Equal Employment Opportunity Commission investigate the situation, although it was unclear whether he did so.[31]

Following the Chuvalo fight, Main Bout remained Ali's promoter, with mixed financial results. Muhammad Ali's conviction on draft evasion charges in June 1967, however, ended Main Bout's run after only seventeen months and seven fights, and it is difficult to assess the company's impact on black economic power. Ultimately, Main Bout's collapse stemmed from its lack of government support and capital. State athletic commissions nationwide unanimously refused to license Ali immediately following his indictment in May 1967. If any state athletic commission had sanctioned an Ali fight, he would have fought there. Following his conviction, Ali stayed out of prison on appeal, but his passport was invalidated, eliminating his chances of fighting abroad. Realizing Ali, the organization's major source of capital, was finished, Arum, Malitz, and Brown left Main Bout to form their own company, Sports Action, Inc., which would promote the tournament designed to replace Ali as heavyweight champion. The Nation of Islam and Ali were frozen out of professional boxing. For the next three-and-a-half years, Ali did not fight professionally.[32]

Ali and Black Economic Uplift

Ali's exile from professional boxing is the basis of his iconic status today. He stood up for his principles while sacrificing material gain. Ali's heroism comes from his giving up millions of dollars and the world heavyweight championship. Being a race man stems from his decision to promote racial uplift over personal enrichment. Moreover, during his tenure with the Louisville Sponsoring Group and his stint under Main Bout, financial considerations largely shaped Ali's cultural image.

Veterans of the Civil Rights Movement, both at the time and now, have linked Ali's impact to his material sacrifice. Julian Bond said, "I admired him all the more, because of all the people who spoke out against the war, he had the most at risk." An antiwar hero in his own right, Bond invoked Ali during speaking engagements and press conferences. Bond told the National Conference of Negro Elected Officials during a 1967 speech that it would be "an excellent idea" to award Ali the Nobel Peace Prize: "A man like Muhammad, much more so than the others, has made a sacrifice most of us could not make if we wanted to, but Muhammad Ali is a man who has the respect and adulation of millions of peoples the world over and has an economic potential to which most people never come close. But he has sacrificed this voluntarily by following his conscience and his religious beliefs. He should have international recognition as a devoted man in the pursuit of peace."[33]

Martin Luther King admired Ali for the same reasons. King was particularly impressed that Ali "is giving up even fame. He is giving up millions of dollars in order to stand up for what his conscience tells him is right." Ali's refusal to be inducted into the armed forces and King's first public denunciation of the Vietnam War both happened during April 1967. Around that time, King met with the champion while in Louisville for an SCLC board meeting. A press conference followed and King told reporters, "As Muhammad Ali has said, we are all victims of the same system of oppression."[34]

Prominent black nationalists and civil rights activists, like CORE National Director Floyd McKissick and SNCC's Bob Moses, also supported Ali and praised his economic sacrifice. "I am saddened that you were forced to choose between your conscience and an unjust punishment," wrote McKissick in an open letter to the champion. "Your dilemma dramatizes to me, as a Civil Rights leader, that the Civil Rights Movement has, in fact, accomplished pathetically little." The CORE leader praised Ali for "[sacrificing] so much for a principle" because "your decision was made with full knowledge of its implications."[35] Moses said similarly, "what made people in the civil rights movement take Ali seriously was the idea that he was jeopardizing his actual status. Titles were on the line."[36]

One of the key issues for federal courts to consider while Ali appealed his draft evasion conviction was whether or not to allow him to work. Since stateside government officials would not license Ali, he sought permission to travel abroad to fight. Federal judges, however, used Ali's race leadership to rationalize their denial of his request. Ali had reason to believe that he would be able to find work overseas. Almost immediately following his conviction, the European Boxing Union announced, "In our view the case is still pending because Clay has appealed his conviction. Our feeling is that any decision should be postponed until his appeal is acted on." The Japanese Boxing Association also said they would sponsor an Ali bout. United States District Judge Joe Ingraham, citing Ali's appearance at a Los Angeles antiwar rally, denied any change in Ali's travel status. "The defendant appears to be ready to take part in anti-government, anti-war activities," accused Ingraham. He added, "the government has been especially generous in allowing him to travel throughout the continental United States." In this case, Ali's cultural and political image created a lack of government support, which in turn affected his earning status.[37]

Ali's utilizing earnings for black economic uplift bolstered his claims to be a race man. In early 1967, the United Negro College Fund (UNCF) announced the champion had become the largest single black contributor to the organization by way of a $10,000 donation. Said Ali: "Although I myself never had the opportunity to go to college, I give to the United Negro College Fund this $10,000 out of my love, admiration, and respect for their 34,000 dedicated students to help in some small way so that the seeds of immortality hidden within each one of them may be nourished and developed to their fullest capacity. To me, they are all 'The Greatest.'" When asked why he had been fighting so frequently during this period, Ali told reporters that he wanted to earn more money to donate to black education.[38]

Ali's creation of Main Bout, Inc. generated opportunities for blacks to become involved in the promotion and production of his fights. He also offered to use Main Bout to generate income for black colleges, a move the UNCF was unable to coordinate. UNCF President Dr. Stephen Wright told reporters, "We were offered the opportunity to participate in the closed-circuit television broadcast of the Ali-Terrell title bout [rescheduled for February 1967] for the fund's own profit." This offer built on Ali's standing policy of paying for telecasts of his bouts to be shown at black colleges. Six schools had accepted Ali's giveaway, at an estimated cost to Main Bout of $4,500 per closed-circuit installation, to see his November 1966 title defense in Houston against Cleveland Williams. Ali pledged to donate a large portion of the receipts from that bout not only to black colleges, but also to area veterans' hospitals. When Ali visited the city's Booker T. Washington High School, he stressed that education was central to black power. "I have a million dollars, but I can't spell. . . . Take your opportunity in high school," he said. After preaching at the local Nation of Islam mosque, he asserted, "The Negro will never be recognized, never be able to socialize without an education. To do it he needs money. . . . Because of our tax setup I can give 30 percent of my fight [revenues] toward educating the 22 million Negroes."[39]

There are more examples of Ali's attempts to merge boxing and racial uplift. In June, just days before Ali's conviction, Michigan State Athletic Commissioner Chuck Davey announced that his state would host an Ali fight to benefit black charities. Ali promised not to defend his championship, take any purse, or donate any of the earnings to the Nation of Islam. Said Davey, "He hasn't had his day in court yet, so I don't think I can pass judgment before he's had his day in court." The fight, however, never materialized. Speaking at CORE's annual convention, Ali offered to help southern blacks by staging a benefit bout against the boxer who emerged victorious in the tournament designed to replace him as heavyweight champion. "Here before all the newsmen and television cameras," he said, "I challenge the winner of that tournament and promise to give every penny to feed people in Mississippi and throughout the South." He estimated that such a bout would raise $1 million "or more with no trouble." When Ali tried to follow through, he was unable to get authorization from uncooperative state boxing commissions. California State Athletic Commissioner Jules Berman, after questioning the fighter and denying him a license to fight in California, told reporters, "We all have religion, but my country comes first." *Baltimore Afro-American* sports columnist Sam Lacy called the decision "just about as scurvy as anything the high-handed American political machine has done to its own needy."[40]

Ali knew that growing numbers of people were looking at him as more than an important symbol, but as a leader, and he sensed that his philanthropy and growing bond with black colleges were crucial to this growing importance. In an interview, Ali expressed a goal of giving "$100,000 to a Negro scholarship fund." Claiming that black colleges across the South had asked him for contributions, and that he had just donated over $150,000 to the Nation of Islam, Ali said that he wanted to fight five times in 1967. "I'm a race man," he said. "It means more to me than personal gain or showing my teeth. If I end up with a quarter in my pocket I can look at myself and say I helped thousands of people."[41]

Constructing a New Image

Muhammad Ali's primary image-maker during the 1990s was Thomas Hauser. In addition to authoring several books about Ali, Hauser appeared on television and in documentaries as his spokesperson.[42] One Ali biographer wrote at the end of the decade, "The foundations for the current Ali renaissance were laid by the publication of Thomas Hauser's biography." Hauser claims that Ali's "public profile had dropped after his retirement from boxing. Thereafter, if Ali appeared at an event, those in attendance were excited but he wasn't on the national radar screen." With Hauser as his mouthpiece public interest in Ali began to rise.[43]

Hauser's relationship with Ali began in 1988, when the Ali camp through the champ's best friend Howard Bingham contacted him. It was Ali's wife, Lonnie, "who wanted a book that would place Muhammad in context, not just as a fighter but also as a social, political, and religious figure." After Hauser completed his manuscript, he traveled to the Ali family farm in Michigan to meet with Ali, Lonnie, and Bingham, and read to them aloud the finished draft. "By agreement," recalled Hauser, "there was to be no censorship. The purpose of our reading was to ensure that the book would be factually accurate." If there were things in the book that Ali and his wife objected to and Hauser felt that it was necessary to leave such things in the book, a rebuttal paragraph in Ali's words would be placed alongside the offending material. Hauser retained editorial control over the book and its release.[44]

Although the book has become the seminal text in the study of Ali's life and is indispensable to our understanding of him, there have been some observers who have questioned its accuracy. It was subject to the typical limitations of authorized biographies, and perhaps also by Hauser's admiration for Ali. Howard Cosell wrote, "My theory is that Hauser has gotten too close to his subject and is too enamored of Ali to write a completely honest and objective book."[45]

From the beginning of their collaboration, Hauser has crafted an image of Ali as a humanitarian and a figure of racial healing and tolerance. One book, *Healing: A Journal of Tolerance and Understanding*, is positioned as "part of a multi-dimensional, international campaign to combat bigotry and prejudice." Another book, *Muhammad Ali and Company*, contains essays by Hauser on subjects like Ali's trip to Iraq to convince Saddam Hussein to forestall the Persian Gulf War, Ali's visiting high schools to promote racial understanding, and Ali's trip to the United States Holocaust Memorial Museum.[46]

What is surprising about this attempt to make Ali into a figure of racial healing is that his public actions, which have gone largely unreported by Hauser, seem to defy that portrayal. Other contemporary observers have told stories that throw into question the idea that promoting tolerance and understanding is a top Ali priority, regardless of how he is positioned in this manner. Professional wrestler Ric Flair discusses a 1995 trip he took with Ali to North Korea: "Because of the ravages of Parkinson's disease, it was difficult to understand Muhammad Ali when he spoke. But at one function, we were sitting at a big, round table with a group of North Korean luminaries when one of the guys started rambling on about the moral superiority of North Korea, and how they could take out the United States or Japan any time they wanted. Suddenly, Ali piped up, clear as a bell, 'No wonder we hate these motherfuckers.'" The point here is not that Ali is hateful, but that when he has input over his own image, it varies from that offered by those who would make him into a figure of tolerance and racial healing.[47]

Perhaps the most important factor in Hauser's positioning of Ali as a figure of racial brotherhood has been his distancing of Ali from his past with the Nation of Islam. This started with a passage in Hauser's biography of Ali: "Elijah Muhammad's death marked a turning point for the Nation of Islam, and foreshadowed a significant change in Ali's public pronouncements on race. In the past, the public and private Ali had seemed almost at war with each other over whether white people were evil. Now Ali was able to say openly, 'I don't hate whites. That was history, but its coming to an end.'" Five years later, in the book *Muhammad Ali in Perspective*, Hauser wrote:

> Meanwhile, Ali's religious views were evolving. In the mid-seventies, he began studying the Qur'an more seriously, focusing on Orthodox Islam. His earlier adherence to the teachings of Elijah Muhammad—that white people are "devils" and there is no heaven or hell—was replaced by a spiritual embrace of all people and preparation for his own afterlife. In 1984, Ali spoke out publicly against the separatist doctrine of Nation of

Islam spokesman Louis Farrakhan, declaring, "What he teaches is not at all what we believe in. He represents the time of our struggle in the dark and a time of confusion in us, and we don't want to be [associated] with that at all." Ali today is a deeply religious man.

While this focus on Ali's denunciations of the Nation of Islam is not the same as excluding his association with the organization from the historical record, they create the same effect that Ali's membership in the Nation of Islam is irrelevant to his cultural significance today.[48]

Most of Ali's biographers, regardless of their opinions about the fighter's influence on American society, have denounced the Nation of Islam. *Sports Illustrated* writer Mark Kram asserted that Ali "was no more a social force than Frank Sinatra. . . . Seldom has a public figure of such superficial depth been more wrongly perceived, by the right and the left." Hauser, on the other hand, believes, "With the exception of Martin Luther King, no black man in America had more influence than Ali during the years when Ali was in his prime." While they may disagree on Ali's legacy, both agree the Nation of Islam negatively impacted the world. In Kram's *Ghosts of Manila*, Herbert Muhammad was described as a hypocrite more interested in food and sex than religion. The Nation of Islam is portrayed as lecherous, sucking every penny it could from Ali's earnings. In *Muhammad Ali: His Life and Times*, Hauser tries to distinguish between the public Ali who berated whites as devils and the private Ali who employed white men like Angelo Dundee, Ferdie Pacheco, and Gene Kilroy in trusted positions like trainer, doctor, and aide-de-camp, respectively. The Nation of Islam under Elijah Muhammad prevented Ali from being himself, writes Hauser, especially in his attitudes towards race.[49]

One of the ways Ali's biographers have attacked the Nation of Islam is through their criticisms of Ali's 1975 autobiography, *The Greatest: My Own Story*. The most detailed assault on *The Greatest* was by Hauser, who felt the book was biased and inaccurate. Although it could be argued that Hauser's portrait of Ali is itself glorified and based on careful collaboration between Ali and the author, he criticizes *The Greatest* for the same reasons:

> In 1976, Random House had published the Ali "autobiography," written by Richard Durham. Given Ali's popularity, the book had enormous potential but it was plagued by problems from the start. Ali was uninterested in the project, and spent relatively little time with Durham. Indeed, he never read

his "autobiography" until after it was published. Moreover, even though Durham was an editor for *Muhammad Speaks*, before any material was submitted to Random House, each page had to be approved and initialed by Herbert Muhammad.

Hauser's methodological criticism of *The Greatest* serves a twofold purpose: to establish his own work as the definitive authorized biography of Ali and to disparage the Nation of Islam's influence on him.[50]

Other biographers have made similar comments. David Remnick, in his best-selling *King of the World*, describes *The Greatest* this way:

> [The Nation of Islam] selected as ghostwriter Richard Durham, the editor of the Nation of Islam's newspaper, *Muhammad Speaks*. Durham was not himself a Muslim—his politics were, if anything, Marxist. Durham was a talented writer, but at the same time he was obligated to do for Ali what Parson Weems had done for George Washington. Just as Weems had described a mythical Washington chopping down cherry trees and hurling coins across the Potomac to highlight moral purity and awesome physicality, Durham made Ali out to be a champion fueled almost solely by anger and racial injustice.

Mark Kram had similar misgivings, calling it "a screed of misdirection and fantasy that, along with the film of the same title, is in part responsible for the Ali myth." Mike Marqusee, in *Redemption Song: Muhammad Ali and the Spirit of the Sixties*, is milder in his criticism. According to Marqusee, "The accuracy of the book is disputed by most chroniclers of Ali's life today, and Ali himself claims to have read it only after it was published . . . it rarely sounds like Ali." Importantly, however, Marqusee also notes, "it is the last expression of the radical and angry Ali, thanks probably to its writer, Richard Durham, a black nationalist." By refuting the accuracy of *The Greatest*, these authors refute the influence of the Nation of Islam on the essential Ali. All of these authors claim that *The Greatest* is more the product of the minds of Richard Durham and Herbert Muhammad than of Muhammad Ali. By doing this, they free Ali from the Nation of Islam, which puts him into a position to be cast as a figure of racial brotherhood.[51]

At least one author, Gerald Early, has challenged these portrayals of *The Greatest*. He calls it "a work that has been undeservedly dismissed." The book should not be looked at "as a true or 'authentic' picture of the fighter, but as a tactical or strategic representation of his politics and his political

image." Early provides methodological information the other authors
do not, and these facts bolster the book's credibility. Toni Morrison, the
great writer, was its editor. Richard Durham supplied Morrison with a
box of audiotapes from "an enormous number of conversations" Ali had
with numerous interviewers. From those tapes, Morrison constructed the
book, which was then submitted to Herbert Muhammad for approval.
This process suggests that much of *The Greatest* came from Ali rather than
Nation of Islam mythmaking.[52]

Statements about the accuracy of *The Greatest* are commentaries
about the essential nature of Muhammad Ali. In many ways, *The Greatest*
is a chronicle of the battles for commercial control over Ali. The book
criticizes whites like Billy Reynolds and Joe Martin who tried to exert
influence on Ali's career. When white authors challenge the accuracy of
The Greatest they legitimize their own attempts to shape Ali's cultural
image. They also alter Ali's legacy by distancing him from the Nation of
Islam. As his autobiography, *The Greatest* was Ali's grandest attempt to
take control over his own image making. Those who dismiss it try to take
that power out of Ali's hands and put it into their own.

Control over Ali's image shifted early in the twenty-first century.
Thomas Hauser no longer writes about Ali the way he once did. According
to Hauser, "The relationship between Muhammad and myself has not
changed. . . . The relationship between me and the people surrounding
Muhammad has changed." While Hauser will not publicly discuss
specifics, it seems that Lonnie Ali, the fighter's wife, no longer wants him
to be Ali's primary spokesman.[53]

Perhaps as a result of this, Hauser began to report things that about
Ali's life he had previously overlooked or bypassed in earlier writings. At
a December 2001 fund-raiser to benefit the Muhammad Ali Institute for
Peace and Conflict Resolution, Ali stepped up to the dais and asked the
crowd, "What's the difference between a Jew and a canoe?" The answer:
"A canoe tips!" Another disparaging joke about Hispanics followed. In a
piece for an internet boxing website, Hauser described the incident and
commented, "Ali sometimes speaks and acts without considering the
implications of his words and conduct. . . . Muhammad Ali leads best
when he leads by example and by broad statements in support of tolerance
and understanding among all people. To ask more of him . . . is looking
for trouble." While this does not contradict Hauser's previous positioning
of Ali as a figure of racial healing, it provides nuance and detail that is
missing from his earlier work.[54]

Hauser also wrote an article in November 2003 expressing concern over what he calls "the lost legacy of Muhammad Ali." In this piece, Hauser decries the erasure of important truths from our historical memories of Muhammad Ali, most notably his relationship with the Nation of Islam and his racially tinged disparagement of fighters like Joe Frazier. "Sanitizing Muhammad Ali and rounding off the rough edges of his journey," he writes, "is a disservice both to history and to Ali himself. Rather than cultivate historical amnesia, we should cherish the memory of Ali as a warrior and as a gleaming symbol of defiance against an unjust social order when he was young." Furthermore, Hauser writes, "corporate America 'rediscovered' Ali. And since then, there has been a determined effort to rewrite history. To take advantage of Ali's economic potential, it has been deemed desirable to 'sanitize' him. And as a result, all the 'rough edges' are being filed away from Ali's life story." Hauser also claims that Ali has become complicit in this process, citing a televised 2002 interview. When asked about politics and terrorism, Ali responded, "I dodge those questions. I've opened up businesses across the country, selling products and I don't want to say nothing and, not knowing what I'm doing, not being qualified, say the wrong thing and hurt my business." Hauser concludes, "It's hard to imagine Muhammad Ali in the 1960s withholding comment on the war in Vietnam for fear of jeopardizing his business interests."[55]

One could say, however, that Hauser was guilty of the same thing while he served as Ali's primary image-maker. Since that has changed, so has his willingness to emphasize Ali's relationship with the Nation of Islam, his tendency towards racial humor and offensive language, and other factors about his life that might not be palatable to mainstream audiences. Hauser's relationship with Ali illustrates the intimacies between commercial control of the Ali industry and the cultural transmission of his image.

Conclusion

In recent years, many people have come to the same conclusion about the amendment of Muhammad Ali's cultural image. They lament what they see as Ali's transformation from a defiant and oppositional leader to a cuddly and nonthreatening pitchman, one whose symbolic shift provides whites with an opportunity for self-congratulatory pronouncements of racial advancement. These critics have identified correctly that economic factors are crucial to Ali's slide towards mainstream affection. Their charge is that the real Ali has been sequestered, and that his history has become sanitized.[56]

They blame several forces for this: Ali's health problems, his wife Lonnie's protection of his image, faulty historical memory, and corporate co-optation. They are right to say that Ali and the people who surround him have capitalized from this recent outpouring of mainstream support. We are inundated with images of Ali, and at times when the commercial benefits of presenting him as a hero are maximized. His now-famous lighting of the Olympic torch was orchestrated by a television network. He can be counted on annually to appear in several first-run endorsements during the Super Bowl, when commercials are as much a part of the show as the game itself, and when advertising costs reach unparalleled heights. To be certain, the makers of Muhammad Ali's image have an important investment to protect. The more popular he is, the more money they stand to gain.

But what these critics fail to consider is that there has always been an intimate relationship between Ali's cultural image and the motives of those who have commercial control over him. In their lamentations for what they believe to be the exorcism of the essential Ali, they have ignored that Ali has never been in total control over the manufacture of his image. That image has always been for sale, if not by Ali then by others who would stand to profit from it. Even when Ali sacrificed personal wealth by fighting the draft, it would be wrong to think that nobody capitalized from his decision. Politicians discussed his case, and presumably earned support from their constituencies by criticizing him. Newspaper reporters, many of whom vilified him, wrote about his case. Television networks and Main Bout's promotional rivals profited from the abundance of boxing matches that could be made in the wake of Ali's dominance of the heavyweight division. One does not need to sanitize Muhammad Ali to profit from his image. There has been profit in making Ali into an antagonist; there has been profit in making him into a hero. The lamentation of his rise to iconic status as the product of corporate repackaging ignores this. It rests on the false premise that the essential Ali was the one who was suspended from boxing for three-and-a-half years. What is often overlooked is that particular image of Ali was also based on commercial considerations, both by Ali and those who would profit from his exile. While it is fair to say that both Ali's cultural image and commercial control over his career have changed over the years, the relationship between those factors has not. It is less important to try to identify Ali's actual meanings than it is to understand the forces engaged in their production.

Notes

1. John Bracey, August Meier, and Elliot Rudwick, *Black Nationalism in America* (Indianapolis: Bobbs-Merrill, 1970); Wilson J. Moses, *The Golden Age of Black Nationalism* (New York: Oxford University Press, 1978); August Meier and Elliot Rudwick, *Along the Color Line: Explorations in the Black Experience* (Urbana: University of Illinois, 1976); Sterling Stuckey, *Slave Culture: Nationalist Theory and the Foundations of Black America* (New York: Oxford University Press, 1987); David Levering Lewis, *W. E. B. Du Bois: Biography of a Race, 1868–1919* (New York: Henry Holt, 1993); Tony Martin, *Race First: The Ideological and Organizational Struggles of Marcus Garvey and the Universal Negro Improvement Association* (Westport: Greenwood, 1976); Rodney Carlisle, *The Roots of Black Nationalism* (Port Washington: Kennikat, 1975).

2. David Remnick, *King of the World: Muhammad Ali and the Rise of an American Hero* (New York: Random House, 1998), 105; *Louisville Courier-Journal*, September 6, 7, 11, October 9, 1960; Muhammad Ali with Richard Durham, *The Greatest: My Own Story* (New York: Random House, 1975), 52–60.

3. *Louisville Times*, September 20, 1960; Ali with Durham, *The Greatest*, 52–58.

4. Quoted in Ali with Durham, *The Greatest*, 53.

5. *Louisville Courier-Journal*, October 1, 6, 16, 20, 23, 28, 29, 30, 1960; *Louisville Times*, October 11, 29, 31, 1960, March 4, 1961.

6. Cassius Clay quoted in *Louisville Courier-Journal*, September 7, 1960; *Louisville Courier-Journal*, October 6, 20, 1960; *Louisville Defender*, August 12, November 25, 1965, August 12, 1966; Ali with Durham, *The Greatest*, 52–58; Remnick, *King of the World*, 107; *Louisville Times*, November 12, 1960; *Los Angeles Times*, November 14, 1962; Thomas Hauser, *Muhammad Ali: His Life and Times* (New York: Touchstone, [1991] 1992), 33–36.

7. Ali with Durham, *The Greatest*, 40–51.

8. Interview with Gordon Davidson (attorney for the Louisville Sponsoring Group), April 4, 2000; notes in author's possession. Cassius Clay quoted in *Louisville Courier-Journal*, November 2, 1960; Huston Horn, "The Eleven Men behind Cassius Clay," *Sports Illustrated*, 23 (March 11, 1963), 62–70.

9. Hauser, *Muhammad Ali*, 30; John Cottrell, *Man of Destiny: Muhammad Ali, Who Was Once Cassius Clay* (New York: Funk and Wagnalls [1967] 1968), 46; Claude Lewis, *Cassius Clay* (New York: MacFadden-Bartell, 1965), 39.

10. Cassius Clay quoted in Ruby, *Louisville Courier-Journal*, September 7, 1960.

11. All quotes from Horn, "The Eleven Men behind Cassius Clay," 63–70.

12. *Los Angeles Times*, April 17, 23, 1962; Alex Haley, *The Autobiography of Malcolm X* (New York: Ballantine, [1964] 1992), 309–15; Remnick, *King of the World*, 125–35; Karl Evanzz, *The Messenger: The Rise and Fall of Elijah Muhammad* (New York: Pantheon, 1999), 196; *Louisville Courier-Journal*, September 14, 1997.

13. Remnick, *King of the World*, 89; Ali with Durham, *The Greatest*, 61, 67.

14. Much of this section of the essay is excerpted from my article "Main Bout, Inc., Black Economic Power, and Professional Boxing: The Cancelled Muhammad Ali/Ernie Terrell Fight," *Journal of Sport History* 29 (Fall 2002), 413–37. I thank the journal for allowing me to use the material. Muhammad Ali quoted in *Louisville Defender*, January 13, 1966.

15. Booker T. Washington quoted in Louis R. Harlan, *Booker T. Washington: The Making of a Black Leader, 1856–1901* (New York: Oxford University Press, 1972), 237; Louis R. Harlan, *Booker T. Washington: The Wizard of Tuskegee, 1901–1915* (New York: Oxford University Press, 1983), viii, 101; Louis Harlan in Raymond W. Smock, ed., *Booker T. Washington in Perspective: Essays of Louis Harlan* (Jackson: University Press of Mississippi, 1988), 100–102; August Meier, *Negro Thought in America, 1880–1915* (Ann Arbor: University of Michigan Press, [1963] 1968), 124–26.

16. Lawrence Levine, "Marcus Garvey and the Politics of Revitalization," in John Hope Franklin and August Meier, eds., *Black Leaders of the Twentieth Century* (Urbana: University of Illinois Press, 1982), 109–10, 127, 134–35; Juliet E. K. Walker, *The History of Black Business in America: Capitalism, Race, Entrepreneurship* (New York: Macmillan, 1998), xix.

17. Claude Andrew Clegg, *An Original Man: The Life and Times of Elijah Muhammad* (New York: St. Martin's, 1997), 70–71; Elijah Muhammad, *Message to the Blackman in America* (Newport News: United Brothers Communications, [1965] 1992), 40, 174; Malcolm X quoted in "The Ballot or the Bullet," reprinted in Henry Louis Gates Jr. and Nellie Y. McKay, eds., *The Norton Anthology of African-American Literature* (New York: W. W. Norton, 1997), 92; Walker, 273, 433.

18. Interview with Julian Bond, March 18, 2002; notes in author's possession. John Lewis, "SNCC's Lewis: We March for Us . . . And for You," *New York Herald-Tribune*, May 23, 1965, reprinted in *Student Nonviolent Coordinating Committee Papers*, Subgroup A; Series I: Reel 1: Item 37; Transcript of Carmichael's June 19, 1996, appearance on CBS's "Face the Nation" appears in *Student Nonviolent Coordinating Committee Papers*, Subgroup A: Series I: Reel 2: Item 58; Idem., Subgroup A: Series I: Reel 2: Item 52; Idem., Appendix A: Reel 70: Item 534A (Document dated August 7, 1964).

19. Although Main Bout had only five members, the organization was split into six voting shares in order to give the Nation of Islam 50 percent control. *Los Angeles Herald-Examiner*, January 10, 1966; Hauser, *Muhammad Ali*, 151–52; *New York Times*, January 9, 1966; *Chicago Daily News*, January 28, 1966.

20. Jim Brown quoted in *Chicago Daily News*, January 28, 1966; *New York Times*, January 9, 1966; *Montreal Star*, July 14, 1966; *Baltimore Sun*, July 15, 1966; *Louisville Courier-Journal*, July 22, 1966; *New York Post*, February 3, 1967.

21. *Chicago's American*, February 5, 13, 1966; *Miami Herald*, February 19, 1966; *Louisville Courier-Journal*, November 20, 1965; *Chicago Tribune*, February 21, 22, 1966; *New York Daily News*, March 1, June 4, 1966.

22. *New York Amsterdam News*, January 25, 1966, 25; *Cleveland Call and Post*, January 22, 1966.

23. Muhammad Ali quoted in *Chicago Daily News*, February 18, 1966.

24. *Los Angeles Herald-Examiner*, February 21, 22, 1966; *New York Herald-Tribune*, February 23, 1966; *Chicago Daily News*, February 22, 1966; *Chicago's American*, February 25, 1966; *Chicago Tribune*, February 25, 1966.

25. *Chicago Tribune*, February 19, 23, 1966.

26. *Chicago's American*, February 25, 26, 1966; *New York Herald-Tribune*, March 2, 1966; *Chicago Tribune*, March 3, 1966, 20.

27. *Detroit Free Press*, March 10, 1966; *New York Times*, February 27, March 1, 2, 1966; *Los Angeles Herald-Examiner*, February 28, 1966; *Baltimore Sun*, March 1, 2, 1966.

28. *New York Herald-Tribune*, March 2, 6, 1966; *Baltimore Sun*, March 16, 30, 1966; *New York World-Telegram and Sun*, March 10, 30, 1966; *San Francisco Examiner*, March 10, 12, 30, 1966; *Chicago Daily News*, February 9, 25, 1966; *Chicago Tribune*, March 15, 1966; *New York Times*, March 10, 1966.

29. *New York Herald-Tribune*, March 2, 17, 29, 1966; *Baltimore Sun*, March 30, 1966; *New York World-Telegram and Sun*, March 9, 30, 1966; *San Francisco Examiner*, March 8, 12, 1966; *Los*

Angeles Herald-Examiner, November 21, 1965, March 8, 1966; *San Francisco Examiner,* March 10, 19, 22, 23, 1966; *New York Daily News,* November 17, 1965.

30. *Baltimore Sun,* March 30, 1966; *San Francisco Examiner,* March 12, 25, 30, 1966; *New York Times,* March 30, 1966; *New York World-Telegram and Sun,* March 30, 1966; *New York Herald-Tribune,* March 2, 1966.

31. *Louisville Defender,* April 7, 1966; *Atlanta Daily World,* March 13, 1966; "Champ Ali on Threshold of New Achievements," *Muhammad Speaks,* April 5, 1966, 6; "Black Leaders Speak Out: Rage over Champ's View Reflect Viet Crisis," *Muhammad Speaks,* March 25, 1966, 7; *Baltimore Afro-American,* April 9, 1966; Jim Brown quoted in *Chicago Daily News,* March 10, 1966; *New York Herald-Tribune,* March 11, 1966, 20.

32. Ezra, "Main Bout, Inc.," 413–37.

33. Interview with Julian Bond, March 18, 2002; notes in author's possession. Julian Bond quoted in "Julian Bond Speaks on Need for Black Struggle against American Injustice," *Muhammad Speaks,* October 20, 1967, 27.

34. Martin Luther King quoted in "King Denounces U.S. Position on Viet: Praises Heroic Stand of Muhammad Ali," *Muhammad Speaks,* May 12, 1967, 2; Martin Luther King quoted in Mike Marqusee, *Redemption Song: Muhammad Ali and the Spirit of the Sixties* (London: Verso, 1999), 213.

35. Floyd McKissick quoted in *Pittsburgh Courier,* May 13, 1967. Also see "News from the Camp of the Champ," *Muhammad Speaks,* May 19, 1967, 9.

36. Interview with Bob Moses, February 12, 2002; notes in author's possession.

37. *Chicago Defender,* June 24, 1967; "Revenge-Filled White Christian Court Continues Persecution of Muhammad Ali," *Muhammad Speaks,* August 11, 1967, 2; *Baltimore Afro-American,* July 15, 1967, August 12, 1967.

38. Muhammad Ali quoted in *St. Louis Argus,* January 27, 1967; Shabazz Information Service, "Muhammad Ali Becomes Biggest Single Black Contributor to UNCF Charities," *Muhammad Speaks,* March 3, 1967, 20; *Louisville Defender,* February 9, 1967.

39. *New York Times,* February 6, 1967; *New York World Journal Tribune,* February 6, 1967; Stephen Wright quoted in Shabazz Information, 20; *Chicago Daily News,* October 25, 1966; *San Francisco Examiner and Chronicle,* October 30, 1966; *Houston Chronicle,* November 1, 1966; Muhammad Ali quoted in *Chicago Tribune,* November 16, 1966; Muhammad Ali quoted in *Houston Post,* February 8, 1967.

40. *Chicago Defender,* June 10, 1967; *Los Angeles Sentinel,* July 6, 1967; *Baltimore Afro-American,* July 22, 1967.

41. Muhammad Ali quoted in *New York Post,* February 3, 1967.

42. Thomas Hauser objects to being called Ali's "mouthpiece" or "primary spokesman." He would rather be described as "Ali's biographer and one of the conduits for transmitting his thoughts to the media and the public." Hauser also rejects the idea of himself as an "image maker." He claims that his writings on Ali are "about finding a way that Muhammad could use his extraordinary persona to the maximum extent possible to promote tolerance and understanding between all people and, most significantly today, between America and the Islamic world. Muhammad is uniquely able to contribute to this cause, which is far more important than selling athletic shoes. But you can't sell products for corporate America and, at the same time, sell hard truths to the world. The corporate 'image makers' won't allow it." Email correspondence with Thomas Hauser, September 27, 2004; notes in author's possession.

43. Marqusee, *Redemption Song,* 299; Thomas Hauser, "Ali: The Legacy," *Observer Sports Monthly,* November 2, 2003, http://observer.guardian.co.uk/osm/story/0,6903,1072751,00.html.

44. Neil Leifer and Thomas Hauser, *Muhammad Ali Memories* (New York: Rizzoli, 1992), n.p; Interview with Thomas Hauser, August 25, 2004; notes in author's possession.

45. Howard Cosell, *What's Wrong with Sports* (New York: Pocket Books, [1991] 1992), 266.

46. Muhammad Ali, Thomas Hauser, Richard Dominick, *Healing: A Journal of Tolerance and Understanding* (New York: Harpercollins, 1996), f.c.; Thomas Hauser, *Muhammad Ali and Company* (Norwalk: Hastings House, 1998), 3–41.

47. Ric Flair with Keith Elliot Greenberg, *To Be The Man* (New York: Pocket Books, 2004), 240.

48. Hauser, *Muhammad Ali*, 295; Thomas Hauser, *Muhammad Ali in Perspective* (San Francisco: Collins, 1996), 12.

49. Mark Kram, *Ghosts of Manila: The Fateful Blood Feud between Muhammad Ali and Joe Frazier* (New York: Perennial, [2001] 2002), 2, 36–52, 88, 95–103; Hauser, *Muhammad Ali*, 14, 294–96.

50. Hauser, *Muhammad Ali*, 343.

51. Remnick, *King of the World*, 89; Kram, *Ghosts of Manila*, 232; Marqusee, *Redemption Song*, 284–85.

52. Gerald Early, "Some Preposterous Propositions from the Heroic Life of Muhammad Ali: A Reading of *The Greatest: My Own Story*," in Elliott J. Gorn, editor, *Muhammad Ali: The People's Champ* (Urbana: University of Illinois Press, 1995), 71–72.

53. Interview with Thomas Hauser, August 25, 2004; notes in author's possession.

54. Muhammad Ali quoted in *Louisville Courier-Journal*, December 20, 2001, http://www.courierjournal.com/localnews/2001/12/20/ke1220015124341.htm; Thomas Hauser, "Ali as Diplomat: 'No! No! No! Don't!'" December 2001, secondsout.com.

55. Muhammad Ali quoted in Hauser, "Ali: The Legacy"

56. Ibid.

3

Bedazzle Them with Brilliance, Bamboozle Them with Bull

Harry Edwards, Black Power, and the Revolt of the Black Athlete Revisited

—Michael E. Lomax

On October 7, 1967, a group of African American athletes and Black Power activists, led by Harry Edwards, formed the Olympic Committee for Human Rights (OCHR). The formation of the OCHR was in response to an informal survey Edwards conducted to assess the attitudes of world-class athletes regarding the problems black athletes faced specifically and issues affecting the black community in general. A specific objective of the OCHR was to organize a boycott of the 1968 Olympic Games in Mexico City, Mexico. This organizational effort, called the Olympic Project for Human Rights (OPHR), was based on the supposition that African American's role in sports was intimately interdependent with the overall struggle for human rights in American society. Other plans, like organizing rebellions on college campuses and boycotting racist athletic clubs, were discussed, but the OPHR was the primary focus.[1]

A significant social movement that coincided with the formation of the OCHR was the Black Power Movement. Bayard Rustin once called Black Power an "attempt to provide psychological solutions to problems that are profoundly economic," a slogan without "a program." In his biography of Huey Newton, Hugh Pearson pondered the "price of black power in America," the cost of nationalism, stained with violence, and the advocation of separatism that brought the wrath of mainstream America upon their heads. The current reassessment of Black Power, and its range of cultural and social forms, has rekindled debates of thirty years ago. Was Black Power good or bad for Americans? Was it good or bad for America? To be sure, these questions are important, but they represent only one way to examine this complex, multifaceted, and fragmented movement/ ideology. William L. Van Deburg's groundbreaking work, *New Day in Babylon* looked beyond the despair and disillusionment toward Black Power's important cultural and psychological affirmation. Van Deburg reveals Black Power as a fundamental stage in the development of an African American political consciousness. More decisive for my purpose here is Van Deburg's important understanding that "Black Power was a freshly minted variant of the traditional African American freedom agenda." Harry Edwards's role in the revolt of the black athlete illustrates that "the civil rights movement" and the Black Power movement, often portrayed in very different terms, sprang from the same soil, confronted the same dilemmas, and reflected the same quest for African American freedom.[2]

This paper analyzes Harry Edwards's role in the black athlete revolt within the context of the Black Power Movement. Four questions will serve to guide the narrative: what were the forces that influenced Edwards to become a social activist; how did Malcolm X's impassioned rhetoric impact Edwards's ideology/philosophy; what were the forces that led to the creation of the OCHR; and how did the OPHR fall short of its stated objectives to link sports with the overall struggle for human rights in American society. The goal of this paper is to show how the formation of the OCHR exemplified Malcolm X's assertion for the need for black unity, self-determination, and the internalization of the black struggle that became more fully developed and institutionalized in the Black Power era.

Harry Edwards attempted to contextualize the black athlete revolt within the framework of the overall black liberation movement in America. The goals of the revolt were to obtain equality, justice, regain black dignity lost during three hundred years of slavery, and to attain basic human and civil rights guaranteed by the United States Constitution and the concept of American democracy. Infused with cultural pride and historical wisdom, oppressed black athletes would, with new confidence, begin to chart their own course in the sports world. The primary opposition Edwards faced, however, came from African American athletes. A significant number of African Americans, young and old, viewed sports as one of the few institutions that facilitated upward social mobility and served as a leveler of racial prejudice in American society. Edwards dealt with African American athletes who were not deeply concerned with altering the basic values of society or initiating fundamental changes. They merely hoped, through collective action, to win greater participation in the existing sporting institutions.

The Rise of a Social Activist

Harry Thomas Edwards was born on November 22, 1942, in St. Louis, Missouri. His father, Harry Sr., moved to East St. Louis, Illinois, and met his wife, Adelaide, to whom he proposed marriage in the winter of 1940. He worked on and off at several jobs, but trained primarily for a boxing career.[3] The Edwards family, consisting also of seven brothers and sisters, were essentially a respectable working-class family. Harry Sr. and Adelaide had dreams of a better life. They typified the World War II generation that desired a better life for their children. However, as the children grew older, their lives were marred by the abject poverty they endured. As Edwards explained, the children were "alone much of the time, malnourished most of the time, desperately in need of love and supervision all the time." They represented the permanent underclass that emerged in post–World War II America.[4]

Harry Edwards's father was responsible for his son's early involvement in organized sports. According to the younger Edwards, his father insisted upon it. His athletic ability was good enough to result in his transfer from the all-black Dunbar Junior High School to the predominantly white Hughes-Quinn Junior High School. From the beginning, however, Edwards's attitude toward sports was ambivalent. He found them to be "too demanding in terms of time, too confusing in terms of my priorities then; and utterly unrewarding relative to the physical and personal sacrifices necessary to be a member" of the junior high school football team. Despite his ambivalence, Edwards continued to participate in sports, primarily because of the high value placed on them by his friends, his teachers, and especially his father. Concern for academics extended as far as athletic eligibility.[5]

Edwards participated in football, basketball, and track and field at East St. Louis High School. Of the three sports, he put the majority of his effort and energy in track and field, throwing the discus. By his senior year in 1959, Edwards was one of the best discus throwers in the state of Illinois.

Despite his achievements, Edwards was classified as "hard to coach" and a problem athlete. Several scouts from colleges and universities stated that he had a bad attitude and that he was an academic risk. According to Edwards, one football coach from Indiana University indicated that he lacked the discipline necessary to succeed academically or athletically in college. This stereotypical labeling of Edwards served to reinforce his ambivalence and disillusionment towards organized sports.[6]

Yet it would be Edwards's athletic performance in track and field, his physical stature (6 feet 8 inches and 225 pounds), and the assistance of a local black attorney, Frank Summers, who helped him escape the hard streets of East St. Louis. A former athlete from Indiana University, Summers stressed the need for Edwards to persevere through the pressure placed on him. The white establishment expected him to fail, but he could not allow that to defeat him. Summers impressed upon Edwards that he had a brilliant mind and the potential to be a great athlete. These conversations left a lasting impression on Edwards. Summers stressed the need for Edwards to leave the Midwest. Edwards needed to be in an environment where he could grow and develop. He recommended that Edwards move to California and offered to buy him a train ticket and advance him five hundred dollars. The attorney considered the money an investment rather than a loan or gift. Upon his graduation from East Side High School, Harry Edwards boarded a train headed to Fresno, California, where he would live with his grandmother and attend the local junior college there.

It was at Fresno City College that Edwards developed an insatiable appetite for knowledge. This appetite was grounded in his aspiration to attend a four-year college, so he immediately set out to take the courses necessary to facilitate this transfer. Early efforts to establish the discipline necessary to handle college work were frustrating, but Edwards endured. By the fall of 1960, Edwards had accumulated a B-plus overall grade average, and according to his sociology teacher, "the beginnings of a solid intellectual perspective." Edwards excelled athletically also. By the end of the track season, he won a half of dozen watches, numerous trophies, and set new school, league, state, and national junior-college discus records. His success resulted in him receiving more than twenty-five scholarship offers across the country.[7]

In the fall of 1960, Edwards accepted an athletic scholarship to attend San Jose State College, now San Jose State University. He chose San Jose for two reasons. First, it was a northern California school; Edwards had not forgotten Frank Summers's impression of the Bay Area. Second, San Jose State's track and field program had a national reputation. World-class sprinters like Ray Norton, Bob Pointer, and later Tommie Smith, Lee Evans, and John Carlos attended there.

San Jose State had also acquired a reputation as a "party school," but according to Edwards, it was no place for blacks looking for a good time. African Americans were almost nonexistent on the campus. The majority of blacks at San Jose State were either athletes, or athletes who had used up their eligibility and were trying to graduate. Fraternities and sororities that excluded blacks from joining their organizations controlled campus social life, student government, and other student-centered activities. Social life was tough for blacks who could not travel north to Richmond, Oakland, or San Francisco.[8]

Although Edwards continued to excel academically and athletically, he had trouble dealing with the racism at San Jose State. His initial response was to smile and be accommodating, focusing on fulfilling his academic and athletic goals. Occasionally, he made efforts to talk to one of his coaches about the racism at the school, the demonstrations in the South, and relations between blacks and whites in general. The coach's response was to evade the subject and focus on other "important" issues, like team unity. According to Edwards, one coach—during a discussion on why blacks were excluded from fraternities—stated that he did not need to join a fraternity when he was in college. He added: "Some people need that sort of thing. But you're probably like me. You don't need it."[9]

To Edwards, having his coach turn his question around to imply that he was interested in joining a fraternity was "awfully shifty," but that was not the real issue. Edwards wanted to know why these fraternities excluded individuals from joining because of the color of their skin. More importantly, why did the university sanction this discriminatory behavior? Why didn't the university ban these fraternities? For the first time, Edwards began to question the status quo, which made many of his coaches feel uneasy around him. Moreover, it marked the start of Edwards's recognition of institutional racism that would later influence his social activism in the sports world.

Clearly Edwards's desire to strive academically armed him with the ability to think critically and begin to question the sports world's status quo. This led, however, to his alienating coaches and eventually led to the end of his athletic career in track and field. Edwards characterized his relationship with track coach Bud Winter as the worst personality clash he ever experienced and that an explosion was inevitable. By the spring of 1961, Edwards and Winter's relationship had collapsed, leading to that unavoidable explosion. As a school record holder, Edwards was elected co-captain of the track and field team. Among his responsibilities, Edwards would intercede with the coach on behalf of the athletes when problems arose. One case involved an unnamed black athlete who was a distance runner. His performance was mediocre at best, but he performed well in dual meets, practiced diligently everyday, and met any request the coaches made. In essence, this black athlete was a "team player."[10]

The athlete in question was recruited out of a junior college, but when he failed to live up to expectations, he was soon forgotten. According to Edwards, he was not provided the proper shoes to run in, though he was kept on the team. It was Edwards's position that any athlete on the team should be provided the proper equipment. When he approached Winter about this, their conversation degenerated from a discussion to an argument to an insult. It was unclear why Winter behaved the way he did. Undoubtedly, the track coach perceived that Edwards was challenging his authority. The incident resulted in Winter throwing Edwards off the track team and supposedly revoking his scholarship. As Edwards left Winter's office, however, he suggested that the track coach read the small print in his grant-in-aid contract. It stated his athletic scholarship would remain in force as long as he remained academically eligible to participate and maintained sports involvement. Since Edwards also played on the basketball team, Winter was in no position to revoke his scholarship.

Edwards continued to play basketball, but he focused more on academics. On the advice of his social work professor, Dr. Erv Tallman, Edwards changed his major from social work to sociology. Tallman suggested the switch of majors because of the concerns and interests he was developing. Edwards stated that his academic involvement provided him with the analytical depth to shape his perspectives on the sports and social situations at San Jose State and also increased his interests in the Civil Rights Movement. In June 1964, Edwards graduated from San Jose State "with distinction." One of his sociology professors nominated him for a Woodrow Wilson Fellowship. At the conclusion of the Woodrow Wilson essay and oral competitions, he was awarded a fellowship to be applied toward graduate study at any university in the United States or Canada. Edwards chose Cornell University and he also decided to forego any involvement with sport. He had received tryout offers from two professional football teams—the San Diego Chargers and the Minnesota Vikings—but he chose Cornell because the school's sociology department had an excellent reputation in research on race relations and social stratification.

Harry Edwards's insatiable appetite for knowledge, his experience as a collegiate athlete, and the racism he endured at San Jose State shaped his role as a social activist in the black athlete revolt of the late 1960s. The fact that he chose academics over athletics illustrated how Edwards rejected the status quo that led him to challenge the discriminatory behavior embedded within athletic institutions. Before he mounted this campaign against racism in sports, Harry Edwards traveled to New York where his political and social consciousness would be awaken by a black Muslim leader whose teachings influenced a generation of militants in the Black Power era.

The Rise of African American Militant

Harry Edwards enrolled at Cornell University at a time when NAACP activist Clarence Mitchell declared that President Lyndon Johnson had "made a greater contribution to giving a dignified and hopeful status to Negroes in the United States." Johnson committed his administration to the goal of "the full assimilation of more than twenty million Negroes into American life." The Civil Rights Act of 1964 desegregated public accommodations of every kind, in every city and state. Prompted by events in Selma, Alabama, the Voting Rights Act of 1965 had an even greater scope. Black expectations were heightened by the law's provision limiting the use of literacy tests as a suffrage qualification. Federal examiners were sent into the South with the full authority of the government to safeguard blacks' registration and voting privileges. Between 1964 and 1969, the percentage of black voters in the South soared. The left wing of the Civil Rights Movement applauded these legislative efforts, but this enthusiasm was tempered with a cynicism born from hard experience.[11]

Simultaneously, many African Americans were disillusioned with the political process, stemming from the notion that federal officers were not doing enough to ensure compliance with the directives included in the civil rights and war on poverty legislation. Skeptics claimed the Civil Rights Act created the illusion of progress for African Americans. Historian Manning Marable states that the Civil Rights Act increased the institutional, political, and vigilante violence against blacks across the South. As Johnson swung the Democratic Party toward the moderate tendency of the desegregation movement, white southern Democrats abandoned the party in droves. In January 1966, noncompliance was highlighted by the murder of Sammy Younge, a twenty-one-year-old college student and civil rights worker who was shot in the back of the head after demanding to use a whites-only restroom at a Tuskegee, Alabama, gas station. Moreover, the Johnson administration's growing commitment to Vietnam, combined with the uneasiness within the white liberal camp after the 1966 Watts riot, seemed to bode ill for increased funding of civil rights enforcement.[12]

Contributing to this sense of disillusionment was the growing dissatisfaction with the civil rights programs favored by black moderates. The movement of the early 1960s had spurred unprecedented federal interest in black America's attempt to gain equality before the law. However, its critics pointed out that nonviolent direct action had not eliminated nor reconstructed the black ghetto. If black Americans applauded the fact that southern brothers and sisters no longer were forced to sit in the back of the bus, they were also painfully aware that years of marches, speeches, and petitions had failed to end de facto segregation in the North. For some, the civil rights establishment had achieved only a series of partial, localized victories, and they spent a substantial amount of energy catering to the fears of their paternalistic white allies. To their critics, the moderates' program could do little to improve the daily lives of the impacted black masses because they failed to make significant inroads against two key components of black oppression—dependence and powerlessness.[13]

African American athletes also exhibited this sense of disillusionment. By the early 1960s, black athletes, free from the insecurity of the early years of integration, became increasingly outspoken against inequitable conditions. Several black athletes in Major League Baseball, like Henry Aaron and Bill White, voiced a variety of complaints that included mistreatment in the minor leagues, the hated spring training ritual, and the recurring problems in hotels. Cleveland Browns fullback Jim Brown was one of the most outspoken black stars in professional football. In 1964, Brown, who had a contract for over $50,000 a year, led the NFL in rushing with 1,466 yards. He stunned the white sports world by refusing to appear grateful for his fame and wealth. "I am not thankful to be here," Brown insisted. "If anything, I am more angry than the Negro who can't find work." A Cleveland sportscaster warned Brown that he was on the wrong track, criticizing American society and expressing sympathy for the Black Muslims. The announcer also told Brown that he admired him as a football player and never viewed him as a Negro. Such color-blind sentiments might have soothed African Americans just a few years earlier. It did not mollify Brown who retorted, "That's ridiculous! You have got to look at me as a Negro. Look at me man! I'm black!"[14]

Efforts were also made to boycott specific sporting events. In 1960, a black boycott of the Olympic Games in Rome, Italy, had been suggested as one way of protesting southern police's treatment of civil rights workers. In 1963, Dick Gregory, a black human rights activist, politician, and comedian, tried to organize a boycott of the Russian-American Track and Field Meet by black athletes. Although the boycott failed, it did give impetus to the notion of using amateur athletics to dramatize racial injustice. The following year former gold medal winner Mal Whitfield advocated that blacks boycott the 1964 Olympic Games in Tokyo, Japan. Whitfield challenged black athletes to act against racism. He argued that the black Americans' struggle would have repercussions throughout the world and serve as an example, particularly for Third World nations. However, black America was not ready to meet the challenge in 1964. In 1965, when black players arrived in New Orleans to compete in the American Football League (AFL) East-West All-Star game, they found the doors of the city's leading social clubs closed in their face. They quickly agreed to boycott the event, requiring AFL Commissioner Joe Foss to move the game to Houston.[15]

Despite their exploits on the field, black athletes still endured the same racial indignities their parents' generation had experienced. While some black professional athletes enjoyed high salaries and notoriety, they still experienced discrimination when they tried to purchase homes in the cities in which they performed. Their hard-earned success in the athletic arena did not bring the rewards off it. Yet this generation of black athletes refused to accept the status quo. Their youth had been marked by sweeping changes in the economy, in demography, and in American racial attitudes. Moreover, their outspokenness reflected this sense of disillusionment among African Americans by the mid-1960s.

It was within this context that Harry Edwards became more concerned with the overall progress of the African American struggle for racial equality. As he explained in his autobiography, a new militancy emerged that was "both fostered and fed by growing concerns, particularly among young blacks, that the gradualism of the established civil rights methods and leadership was too slow." These concerns led Edwards to confront his own political responsibilities and resulted in him making periodic weekend trips to New York City to Malcolm X's Muslim mosque. His trips to New York occurred at a time when Malcolm had established his Organization for African American Unity. Malcolm X had broken loose from the restraints of Elijah Muhammad and the Nation of Islam and made journeys to Africa and to Mecca. Historian Vincent Harding points out that Malcolm decided to look for ways to stand in solidarity with King and the Student Nonviolent Coordinating Committee (SNCC) and the troubled southern movement. Moreover, Edwards pointed out that these trips to New York changed his entire outlook on life, on black people, and on himself.[16]

Several factors contributed to this transformation that occurred in Edwards's life. First, as historian William Van Deburg points out, Malcolm X's impassioned rhetoric was "street smart," and it had an almost visceral appeal to a young black economically distressed constituency. He constantly urged this constituency to question the validity of their "school book-and-media-inspired faith" in an integrated American Dream. Edwards was one of many who responded. Without question, Edwards could relate to Malcolm's impassioned street-smart rhetoric given his poverty-stricken upbringing. More important, Edwards's experience in college athletics, combined with his desire to strive academically, had established a mindset to question the ideology surrounding the sporting culture.[17]

Malcolm X's efforts to convince blacks to reevaluate themselves represented the second factor. By stressing the need for blacks to reassess themselves, Malcolm X pointed the way to a psychological liberation. He told a *Village Voice* reporter, "The greatest mistake of the movement has been trying to organize a sleeping people around specific goals. You have to wake the people up first, then you'll get action." "Wake them up to their exploitation?" the reporter asked. "No," he explained, "to their humanity, to their own worth, and to their heritage." Regardless of how unorthodox a solution might be Malcolm X sought to find solutions to complex problems plaguing black people during this era. He spoke for the need for black unity and self-determination, for community control, and the internalization of the black struggle. Much of what Malcolm advocated foreshadowed the more fully developed and institutionalized Black Power sentiment. As SNCC coordinator Stokely Carmichael stated, Malcolm knew "where he was going, before the rest of us did."[18]

Finally, to Edwards, these were new and stimulating ideas, and they stirred a passion in him to legitimize and act upon deeply felt convictions.

His travel to New York served as a political and cultural awakening. Edwards, however, did not realize how influential Malcolm was on his life until after the Muslim leader's assassination. From that point on Edwards discontinued using the word Negro and decided, as Malcolm had often said, that "we must take pride in our *Blackness* [his emphasis], in ourselves, before we can do anything else."[19]

By the spring of 1966, Harry Edwards completed his master of arts degree in sociology at Cornell University, and spent the remainder of the year working several part-time jobs in the Bay Area. He returned to San Jose State in the fall of 1967 as a half-time instructor in the sociology department. Upon his return he found the plight of black students and athletes had essentially remained the same since his days as a college athlete. What was also disturbing was the lack of commitment by college administrators to alter the racial situation. That fall Edwards acted upon his "deeply felt convictions."

Near the end of the fall rushing week at fraternities and sororities, Edwards had a conversation with Ken Noel, a former nationally ranked middle distance runner who was pursuing a graduate degree in sociology. When Edwards was dropped from the track team in 1962, Noel was also suspended from San Jose City College for trying to organize a boycott among out-of-state basketball players. The boycott was in response to city college's failure to live up to promises made to lure athletes to their program. During their conversation, Edwards and Noel perceived the plight of black students on campus was a "group problem" that required collective action. In addition, a general lack of understanding of African American problems by the college administration further exacerbated blacks' experience at San Jose State.[20]

Their first move was to approach the administration with some "well-documented" complaints about the rampant racism on campus. According to Edwards, they accumulated documentation about racist practices in fraternities and sororities, in the athletic department, in student admission policies, and in housing. After attempting to see several administrators without success, Edwards and Noel were referred to Dr. Stanley Benz, the Dean of Students. After reportedly laughing in their faces, Benz stated, "where the tradition, desires, and interests of the white majority were concerned, the needs of a minority of black students were inconsequential."[21]

When the administration failed to address their concerns, Edwards and Noel felt they had no other alternative but to denounce the situation and demand redress publicly. They called for a rally against racism on the opening day of classes for the fall semester. The purpose of the rally centered around two objectives. First, athletics were as racist as any other areas of college life. Second, Edwards viewed sport as a power lever that brought the community and student body, as well as the administration, together into a pressure situation. He had watched, all too often, black people in the Civil Rights Movement demonstrating and picketing groups, organizations, and institutions of limited concern to people in positions of power. Therefore, Edwards decided to exploit something more central to the concerns of the entire local community structure—athletics. After all, what activity was of more relevance to a college than the first football game of the season? Further, what was of more immediate importance to a college administration than the threat of stopping a football game that had been contracted for a substantial amount of money? The rupture of such a business relationship could possibly lead to cancelling all future competition with that particular college or university.[22]

On September 18, 1967, the *San Jose Mercury* reported a list of demands Edwards constructed and the corresponding action that would occur if they were not met. He wanted the administration to inform Sigma Chi and all other groups that they must provide equal treatment or be barred from the campus. Other demands included eliminating closed-door sessions held by administrators or others empowered to alleviate Negro grievances; establishment of "machinery" which would keep student groups from functioning as racist organizations; assurances from athletic personnel that Negroes would be given the same treatment as their white counterparts in all areas, including social events; orders from President Robert D. Clark and Dr. Stanley Benz that housing near the campus discovered as discriminatory be denounced; and admission of more Negro students. In addition to the demands, the rally resulted in the creation of the United Black Students Association (USBA) and Edwards served as coordinator.[23]

Edwards outlined their protest strategy if these demands were not met. Black student protestors would picket the administration building and the physical education department. Next, they would picket fraternity row and then camp on their lawns. Finally, if the situation called for it, they would disrupt the opening football game against the University of Texas at El Paso (UTEP). They planned to march out onto the field after the kickoff and remain there. Moreover, Edwards revealed a fundamental tactic that would permeate the overall Black Power Movement. As he explained, "If anyone touched us, we would have sent him to the cemetery." In other words, black student protestors were prepared to defend themselves against threats of retaliation, a radical departure from the nonviolent direct action protest strategy.[24]

On September 19, San Jose State President Robert Clark ordered the athletic department and coaching staff to respond to charges of discrimination. Depicted as a "man of scholarship," character, and leadership, Robert Clark was inaugurated president in May 1965. In his short tenure he had garnered a reputation of dealing fairly with the tough professors' union movement and was respected by the faculty and other state college presidents. Edwards accused the athletic department of exploiting black athletes, excluding them from social activities, and practicing housing discrimination. "If there's a party for the athletes and the white boys go to it," Edwards explained, "you wind up in somebody's attic watching television and contemplating your toes." The indictment resulted in San Jose State Athletic Director Robert Bronzan conducting an inquiry into the charges of racial discrimination. Although he acknowledged the practice of discrimination in housing, Bronzan defended his department's practices, stating that the school's policy regarding the recruitment of minority students were "no different than any other school." What Bronzan failed to recognize was that this was the primary reason the rally was organized in the first place—to challenge the status quo.[25]

The following day spokespersons for several fraternities and sororities admitted with "unprecedented candor" that they practiced racial discrimination. However, they pleaded for time and a chance to "change the future" and declared that "we propose to integrate . . . we are integrating." Edwards made it clear the USBA would not make any compromises because the "law, ethics, [and] morality [were] on [their] side." He added that if the administration did not address the situation, "this college would have trouble." When the Dean of Students, Stanley Benz, pointed out that all 185 organizations at the college must sign antidiscrimination pledges, Edwards replied that was not enough.[26]

By the middle of the week, racial tension mounted. On September 21, the *San Jose Mercury* reported that President Clark canceled the opening football game between San Jose State and UTEP. The cancellation was in response to unnamed individuals and groups threatening to burn down Spartan Stadium. According to the *Mercury*, several "Soul Brothers" called Edwards to express their support of his proposed sit-in. They added that "something" could happen and that the "stadium could go."

Edwards emphasized to Clark that he might not be able to control all the individuals who may attend the game, resulting in its cancellation. After his meeting with Clark, however, Edwards indicated that he planned to follow through with a sit-in if the USBA demands were not met.[27]

In response to the proposed sit-in, both Clark and Bronzan addressed the USBA's demands. Bronzan proposed forming a special committee composed of six students, including at least three African Americans. White coaches could no longer demote a black athlete without clearing the action with the special committee. On campus blacks would handle the recruiting of future black students. Next, all fraternities and sororities were placed on immediate probation. Clark then established the nation's first college ombudsman position to "conduct a continuous and aggressive campaign against racial discrimination practiced by our students." He appointed J. Benton White, a white Methodist minister from Alabama, to the new job. Finally, Clark had other specific suggestions that included new rules for treatment of San Jose State athletes and devising new strategies for recruiting more minorities to the college. The USBA accepted the proposed changes.[28]

Reaction to Clark's response to the black student protest was mixed. Senator Clark L. Bradley (R-San Jose) denounced Clark's actions and called for an attorney general's investigation and prosecutions, if warranted. Bradley stated that Clark should have stood up to this "element." Senator Alfred E. Alquist (D-San Jose) stated that Clark's decision to cancel the football game was a wise one, but he added that Edwards's actions were "way off base." According to Alquist, the proper time for Edwards to protest against discrimination in housing would have been a year earlier, when property owners around the college were crying that their housing was only half full. What Alquist failed to recognize was at that time Edwards was attending college at Cornell.[29]

The severest criticism Clark received occurred a week after the campus unrest. State Superintendent of Public Instruction Max Rafferty accused the college president of submitting to blackmail when the latter canceled the football game. Rafferty added: "If I had to ask the President to call in the whole U.S. Marine Corps, that game would have been played." Governor Ronald Reagan characterized the cancellation as "appeasement" and stated that similar situations in the future warranted an increased presence of law enforcement to protect anyone attending the game. The governor also declared Edwards unfit to teach. In response, Edwards dismissed Reagan as a "petrified pig, unfit to govern."[30]

The cancellation of San Jose State's home opener with UTEP marked the first time a major college canceled an athletic event under the pressure of racial protest. Canceling the game did have economic consequences. According to Bronzan, postponing the game cost the college between $15,000 and $30,000. More importantly, the black student protest— that resulted in the cancellation of the game—illustrated a collective response among African Americans to demand redress to issues that affected them. By establishing this black coalition, the USBA, efforts were made to improve their conditions in an integrated setting. Harry Edwards and the USBA attempted to redistribute political power within the framework of the college and athletic infrastructure, without de-emphasizing integration. By linking athletics and community oppression and by pointing to the ways race had become imbedded in the college setting of postwar America, Edwards challenged the belief that integration alone represented a sufficient remedy for historical inequities. Throughout the protest, Edwards admitted the athletic department was not totally responsible for discrimination in housing. Rather, this behavior had been "institutionalized" and embedded within the college and athletic venue.[31]

To Harry Edwards, however, the San Jose State protest had been a lesson in learning how to use power. Power could be gained by exploiting the white man's economic and almost religious involvement in athletics. Sports were the only area of campus life where blacks could exercise any political leverage, but only if they were organized. An attack upon the sports institution was widely regarded as an assault upon the most central and preeminent values and beliefs of that society. Despite this consequence, the effectiveness of the San Jose State protest resulted in Harry Edwards's taking center stage in what would be termed "the revolt of the black athlete."

The Olympic Project for Human Rights

Occurring simultaneously with the San Jose State protest, calls for boycotting the Olympic Games resurfaced. On July 23, 1967, at the first annual Black Power Conference in Newark, New Jersey, a resolution was adopted urging blacks to boycott the Olympics and professional boxing matches. The resolution was in response to Muhammad Ali losing his heavyweight title after his refusal to be drafted into the U.S. Army. The proposal also called for boycotts of the products of commercial sponsors of all professional boxing matches. Speaking in support of the resolution, Dick Gregory pointed out the only way Ali could regain his title was for blacks to boycott all boxing matches and commercial sponsors nationally.[32]

Another event that contributed to the Olympic boycott fever were remarks attributed to San Jose State sprinter Tommie Smith. Smith was Edwards's student and a world record holder in the 200 meters. After competing in the World University Games in Tokyo, Japan, a Japanese news reporter asked Smith if there was a possibility that Negro athletes would boycott the 1968 Olympic Games. Smith replied that some athletes appeared to be in favor of it, but a boycott at that time was unlikely. It appeared, however, that his remarks were blown out of proportion. According to Smith, the next thing he knew the newspapers were reporting that he was leading a boycott.[33]

It was within this context that Harry Edwards made his initial steps to form the Olympic Committee for Human Rights. Several members from various black organizations attended the meeting. They included George Washington Ware, field worker for SNCC; Tommie Smith; Ken Noel; Jimmy Garrett, chairman of the Black Student Union at San Francisco State College; and Bob Hoover, political activist and counselor at San Mateo Junior College. The committee decided the best way to mobilize black athletes was to conduct a workshop and spell out formally the direction the Olympic boycott phase of the revolt would take. The Olympic boycott became the cornerstone of the Olympic Project for Human Rights. While other plans were proposed, like organizing rebellions at various college campuses, the Olympic boycott was their primary concern.

On November 22, 1967, the OCHR organized a workshop as part of the Western Regional Black Youth Conference, held in Los Angeles, California. Reportedly, fifty college athletes attended the workshop, but only five—Smith, Lee Evans, Lew Alcindor (known today as Kareem Abdul-Jabbar), Ode Burrell, and Ron Copeland—were of world class status. Efforts were made to maintain the secrecy of the proceedings. African American sportswriters were permitted to attend the workshop, but were prohibited to bring tape recorders, paper and pencils, and cameras into the meeting. The OCHR decided to make the mainstream press dependent upon their reports and interpretation of the workshop, rather than allowing them to observe the activities and thereby influence the proceedings by their presence.[34]

The fundamental underpinning of the workshop was to highlight the plight of blacks in America in a "world court," and link the black athlete revolt to the overall struggle for black liberation. As Edwards stated, the revolt of the black athlete had its roots and drew its motives from the first moment a black captive chose suicide rather than slavery. In more recent times, lynchings, murders, and beatings served to heighten black resistance, providing the movement with a new force and direction. By highlighting blacks' treatment in a "world court," Edwards sought to move the struggle for black liberation from the orbit of civil rights to the sphere of human rights. Sports, the Olympics in particular, served as the vehicle to facilitate this transition.[35]

Edwards began the workshop by outlining the OPHR's goals and objectives. During his discussion, Edwards asked two fundamental questions. Wasn't it time for black people to stand up as men and women and refuse to be used as "performing animals for a little extra dog food?" Wouldn't the 1968 Olympic Games serve as a good starting point? "Only then," Edwards added, "would the white man stop treating us like animals—especially if we are ready to do whatever is necessary to back up this move." The boycott was connected to two additional objectives: a refusal to take part in any event in which there were participants from South Africa and Rhodesia; and a boycott of events linked with the New York Athletic Club (NYAC) which, according to Edwards, restricted its membership to white Christians.[36]

Several athletes followed Edwards relating their experiences as athletes at major colleges and universities. Tommie Smith argued that he was not willing to sacrifice his manhood and dignity for participating in the games. While he recognized the significance of the Olympics, he added that if his sacrifice alleviated the oppression and injustice suffered by black people, he would be willing to participate in a boycott. High jump champion Ode Burrell took the floor and stated his unequivocal support of the boycott. The most moving and dynamic statement was made by UCLA star center Lew Alcindor. Alcindor related his experience of almost being killed by a police officer in Harlem in the summer of 1966. According to Alcindor, the policeman was shooting on the street where a substantial number of black people were either standing or walking by. This negligence on the part of this policeman made Alcindor recognize that "[blacks] don't catch hell because we aren't basketball stars or because we don't have money. We catch hell because we are black." Alcindor concluded: "This is how I take my stand—using what I have." In other words, the primary weapon that black athletes had to advance the struggle for black liberation was their athletic talent. Therefore boycotting the Olympic Games reinforced

Malcolm X's assertion to wake up the people that all was not right with the sports world, the supposed bastion of equal opportunity and upward social mobility.[37]

Sentiments to boycott the 1968 Olympic Games were not without opposition, however. "Deacon" Dan Towler, a former professional football player for the Los Angeles Rams, opposed the boycott. Towler highlighted the positive attributes sports provided for African Americans and how great a privilege it was for blacks to compete for America. His statements were greeted with a chorus of boos. Other blacks that came in an attempt to dissuade the athletes from supporting the movement left the meeting after witnessing Towler's fate.

More than two and a half hours after the meeting began, Edwards asked the athletes what they wanted to do. According to *Sports Illustrated* journalist Jonathon Rodgers, immediately shouts of "Boycott! Boycott!" rose from all parts of the room. Concurrently, a disruption occurred outside the church when the members were about to vote on the proposed boycott. Pro-Communist leftists tried to disrupt the meetings and take over the movement, but the security force in charge of policing the conference drove them off. The disturbance resulted in the OCHR altering its plans to call for an individual vote. Instead, they settled for a mass "Yea-Nay" vote, much like the House of Representatives or the Senate, because of the confusion outside.[38]

Although the OCHR believed it received the endorsement to mobilize the athletes it sought, statements made in the press painted a different picture. The *Washington Post* reported that veteran Olympian and world record holder Ralph Boston said the proposed boycott didn't make sense. Boston declared, "I don't think this would be the thing that very many people would go along with." Art Walker, America's best triple jumper, indicated that he would compete if he made the team. Walker was invited to attend the workshop, but chose not to. Charlie Greene, a six-time NCAA sprint champion from Nebraska, said, "It comes down to a matter if you're an American or if you're not. I'm an American and I'm going to run."[39]

Several former Olympians voiced their opposition to the proposed boycott. Novell Lee, a boxer who won the gold medal in 1952, stated that the people behind the boycott did not know what they were doing and that the young athletes were ill-advised. He added: "Athletics is the only field in which the Negro has been treated well." UCLA's 1960 Olympic decathlon champion, Rafer Johnson declared: "I think if an athlete has the ability to make the team, he should be allowed to go. The Olympic Committee and the Olympic organization always have been fair to the Negro." Jesse Owens became the most outspoken former Olympiad against the proposed boycott. Owens deplored "certain people" using the Olympics for political "aggrandizement." He added: "There is no place in the athletic world for politics."[40]

Athletes who reportedly supported the boycott elicited a mixed message. Approximately two hours after the workshop concluded, Tommie Smith reportedly said that Edwards's announcement might have been premature. Smith told a *San Jose Mercury* reporter that Edwards took it upon himself to make a statement and that he was not authorized to do so. However, Smith was still committed to the boycott. "I will not turn back from my decision," he reportedly said. "I will give anything for competition and gold medals. I will go so far as to give my right arm, but not my manhood." Lew Alcindor was uncertain whether he would participate on the Olympic basketball team or not. According to the *Los Angeles Times*, Alcindor disclosed that the boycott resolution did not bind him personally, since it was vote by acclamation. A central concern for Alcindor was how participation on the Olympic team would affect his eligibility. If the UCLA star dropped out for one quarter to play in the Olympics, he would be ineligible for the first nine games. The earliest Alcindor could return would be in January 1969.[41]

Resistance to the proposed Olympic boycott was not without precedence. Arguably, since the late nineteenth century black athletes who competed in the white sports world were both a reflection and extension of the accommodationist ideology, commonly attributed to Booker T. Washington. In other words, African American athletes emerged in the white sports world when blacks' cultural worldview was shaped by an economic ideology that emphasized the acquisition of wealth and middle class virtues. Through acquiring wealth and middle class respectability, blacks would, theoretically, earn acceptance into the mainstream of American society and prejudice would be eliminated. This compilation of ideologies functioned as an accommodation to the system of segregation and discrimination. For black athletes this meant making certain concessions to appease white prejudice. For example, because of the legacy of Jack Johnson, Joe Louis's promoters crafted his image to be acceptable to white norms and expectations. They went so far as to instruct Louis in maintaining proper hygiene, controlling his car driving, and other behaviors that might offend whites.[42]

African American entrepreneurs—particularly in the Negro Leagues—fostered the accommodationist ideology in the segregated sports world. From the outset, black businessmen recognized that in order to do business in America they had to negotiate with the white power structure. Negro National League (NNL) President Andrew "Rube" Foster advocated an economic philosophy that stressed black advancement through individual commitment by blacks to the gospel of work and wealth. This philosophy also promoted the need for black ballplayers to conduct themselves as gentlemen on and off the field. Hilldale Athletic Club magnate Ed Bolden promoted his ball club around the notion of "clean baseball." Like Foster, Bolden expected his players to behave in a gentlemanly manner. Foster's successor as NNL President, Charles Hueston, argued that sports, in the form of games, were essential in nation building, and baseball served as one of the "levelers of race prejudice" in America.[43]

However, by the 1960s a new generation of black athletes emerged who were no longer willing to accept the status quo. They refused to shun mounting injustices altogether and began to voice their opposition against discrimination and segregation. More important, integration alone and athletic performance did not address the issues black athletes confronted on predominantly white campuses: discrimination in housing, their experiences with white coaches, and their social environment outside the athletic arena.

Former black Olympians argued that sports provided better opportunities for African Americans than other areas in American society. However, their assertions don't hold water. Blacks benefited from the post–World War II economic boom, more than doubling their median income from 1940 to 1960. The northward migration of nearly three million African Americans brought gains in professional, white-collar, skilled, and semiskilled occupations. Whites competed with blacks for even the lowest-paid jobs during the Depression, but in the postwar years employment and salaries spiraled upward through the late 1940s and 1950s, easing fears that black gains would threaten white affluence and security. The two decades after World War II, the number of blacks in the armed forces almost tripled, from 107,000 in 1949 to 303,000 in 1967.[44]

In the 1960s, African Americans made major inroads in high-level federal government positions, and filled younger executive positions in growing numbers. Moreover, historically, blacks' economic well-being has traditionally improved during periods of labor scarcity: World War

I, the 1920s, World War II, and the Vietnam War. In other words, this was a period in which blacks had more job opportunities opened to them. Concurrently, this was an era when the integration of professional sports, like baseball and football, occurred at a snail's pace, only to increase somewhat with the advent of television and the rise of rival leagues.

The proposed boycott of the Olympic Games highlighted a gnawing dilemma regarding the opportunities sports provided for African Americans. On the one hand, economically speaking, sports did provide some semblance of upward social mobility. Even Edwards benefited from his athletic ability to pursue a career in academia. On the other hand, athletic success on the field, and the notoriety it brought, did not guarantee opportunities to buy housing in affluent areas, coaching jobs after their careers were over, or front office positions. Blacks did not fare well in product endorsements. The 1960s marked the start of star athletes, like Green Bay Packers halfback Paul Hornung, supplementing their incomes through product endorsements. According to *Time* magazine, Hornung earned $50,000 a year—$20,000 for playing football, the rest from endorsements (Wilson footballs and Jantzen sportswear), commercials, and personal appearances. When St. Louis Cardinals pitcher Bob Gibson won the Most Valuable Player in the 1964 World Series against the New York Yankees, no opportunities to endorse products were forthcoming. In an era when blacks made some inroads in professional baseball and football, neither sport had a black head coach or field manager. In the NFL only two blacks—Emlen Tunnell and Lowell Perry—served as assistant coaches in the postwar era, and in the NBA Bill Russell became a player-coach for the Boston Celtics.[45]

It is because of this mixed legacy that Harry Edwards sought to highlight the plight of black athletes in an international setting. It should be noted, however, that the boycott was not a rejection of integration into the mainstream of American society. Instead, the OPHR was a collective response by black athletes to dismantle the existing barriers to racial equality. Whites were not dissuaded to join the movement. According to the *New York Times Magazine*, white students assisted Edwards in developing and distributing literature to the black athletes. However, whites would be held at arms length and not be allowed to take over the movement.[46]

Despite this mixed response about the proposed Olympic boycott, the OCHR continued its efforts to mobilize the black athletes. They turned to Louis Lomax, a veteran civil rights activist and personal friend of Edwards, for advice and direction. Lomax helped Edwards draw up six demands that would best serve the ends the OCHR sought. Next, they decided to bring in as many recognized leaders as possible into the movement to strengthen the forces behind the OPHR. They contacted Dr. Martin Luther King, president of the Southern Christian Leadership Conference (SCLC) and Floyd McKissick, director of the Congress of Racial Equality (CORE). They purposely avoided organizations that were primarily "Negro oriented," like the Urban League and the NAACP.

On December 15, 1967, the OCHR held a press conference in the Americana Hotel in New York City. King, McKissick, and Lomax accompanied Edwards at the conference. Specific demands by the OCHR included the expulsion of the International Olympic Committee's (IOC) "racist" president Avery Brundage; appointment of a black member to the U.S. Olympic Committee (USOC) and an additional black coach to the U.S. team; a ban on competition between Americans and teams from apartheid states such as South Africa and Rhodesia; restoration of Muhammad Ali's heavyweight title; and desegregation of the New York Athletic Club. Each of the leaders delivered a short message in support of the movement. King declared that no one looking at the demands could ignore them in truth. McKissick stated that an athlete was on the field for two or three hours "then becomes a black man again and is subject to discrimination." Lomax characterized Ali's loss of the heavyweight title as "a total castration of the black people in this country."[47]

After the press conference, the OCHR retired to Lomax's suite to discuss additional strategies they might employ to maintain momentum. King suggested that an information booklet be sent to all those athletes who remained uncertain about the political or social relevance of the Olympic Project for Human Rights. The booklet outlined the goals of the proposed boycott, provided a justification for such action, and elaborated on the six demands. In addition, Lomax, King, and McKissick agreed to serve as formal advisors. Early in 1968, H. Rap Brown, chairperson for SNCC, pledged support for the OPHR. Support also came from Organization US's Ron Karenga and from scores of lesser-known black activists.

This early support in 1968 was instrumental in the OCHR's efforts to organize a boycott of the New York Athletic Club. A meet was to be held in the newly constructed Madison Square Gardens to commemorate the hundredth anniversary of the first indoor track in the United States. The central purpose of the boycott was *not* [my emphasis] to force the club to integrate blacks into its segregated organizational structure. Rather, the boycott served to regain some of the black dignity that athletes had compromised over several decades by participating for an organization that prohibited them from showering in their facilities. Concurrently, the OCHR sought to pressure the NYAC's board of directors to justify, explain, or clarify their policies.

External pressure to boycott the NYAC meet occurred on two fronts. First, the OCHR contacted several New York–based organizations and individuals. They contacted H. Rap Brown, Callis Brown of CORE, C. Summer (Chuck) Stone of the National Black Power Conference, Lincoln Lynch of the United Black Front, and Omar Abu Ahmed of the Black Power Conference. These individuals, through their organizations, took on the major responsibility of mobilizing black people to picket the meet. Marshall Brown, an Amateur Athletic Union (AAU) official, agreed to contact black athletes on the East Coast. He also contacted many of the schools and clubs that had traditionally competed in the meet to enlighten them about the boycott's goals and objectives. The OCHR took on the responsibility to contact athletes in the West and Midwest.[48]

Evidently their efforts paid dividends. The *New York Times* reported that the Public Schools Athletic League and the Catholic High School Association withdrew from the meet; many of these teams had African American runners. Villanova, one of the powerhouses of the East, withdrew from the meet. According to sportswriter Larry Merchant, CCNY's withdrawal from the meet was "a blow from which no major meet could ever hope to recover." Several prominent black athletes, among them Jimmy Hines, Earl McCullough, O. J. Simpson, Ralph Boston, and Mel Pender indicated they would not participate in the meet. Many of these athletes received intimidating phone calls, warning them that the OCHR could not insure their safety if they crossed the picket line. Arguably, threats to their safety and not the OCHR's goals and objectives influenced these black athletes' decision to boycott the meet.[49]

The OCHR sought to attract international attention to the boycott. Their task was made easier because several foreign teams were touring America's indoor track meets. They focused their attention on the Russian National track team. A telegram was sent to the Russian Embassy in Washington, D.C., to inform them that black people would protest the meet because of the racist exploitation by the sports establishment in America in general and the NYAC in particular. The OCHR told the Russian ambassador that they could not guarantee the athletes' safety if they crossed the picket line. The Russian team withdrew from the meet.[50]

Second, the New York Athletic Club endured external pressure from several organizations across the country. The *New York Times* reported that three major human relations agencies urged the AAU to withdraw its sanction of the club's track meet. Instead, Metropolitan AAU President Jerry Hardy reaffirmed the association's position of nonintervention into the NYAC's internal affairs. Fifty Notre Dame alumni encouraged their fellow alums to resign from the NYAC, unless the club explained its membership policies regarding nonwhites and non-Christians. The NAACP, the Urban League, and the Anti-Defamation League of B'nai B'rith pledged their support to the NYAC boycott. Clearly this intense pressure was becoming a public relations nightmare for the New York Athletic Club.[51]

Despite this intense external pressure, the NYAC staged its indoor track and field competition. Outside Madison Square Gardens, approximately 1,500 to 2,000 demonstrators surrounded the facility. Almost a hundred picketers noisily chanted, "Racism must go," as they marched on the sidewalk in front of the entrance. Inside, a reported crowd of 15,972 attended the meet. However, the *New York Times* reported there were many empty seats at the mezzanine level (the highest level); there were also clusters of empty seats throughout the gardens. The Gardens stopped selling tickets at 5 P.M. the preceding day because of a reported bomb threat. Undoubtedly, Garden officials took the threat seriously, since H. Rap Brown reportedly said the facility should be "blown up." Only nine African American athletes competed in the meet—five of them were from UTEP. The best known among them was world-class long jumper Bob Beamon. In his autobiography, Beamon stated that he crossed the picket line because he was just too homesick to pass up a trip to New York. In order to return home, he had to compete in the meet. In any event, performances were subpar, primarily because the athletes were unquestionably concerned for their safety.[52]

The New York Athletic Club boycott was an effective one. Undoubtedly, this external pressure brought upon the NYAC organizers was a direct result of the OCHR's efforts. Harry Edwards exhibited the ability to mobilize several Black Power organizations to support the Olympic Project for Human Rights' goals and objectives. But just when it appeared the OCHR had achieved a significant victory in its attempts to boycott the Olympic Games, the International Olympic Committee made an announcement that somewhat undermined their accomplishment.

On February 15, 1968, Avery Brundage announced at a press conference in Grenoble, France, that the IOC had decided to let South
Africa compete in the Mexico City games. Within hours of Brundage's
announcement, Ethiopia and Algeria announced their withdrawals
from the games, and several other countries followed suit. In response,
the OCHR issued a statement fully endorsing the black nations' actions.
They attempted to establish a "bond of communication" between black
America and black Africa based on mutual descent and the "problems
growing out of genocidal policies of certain white racist societies (e.g. the
United States, South Africa, Southern Rhodesia, etc.). Finally, the OCHR
would try to establish a second set of games to be held preferably in an
African nation. The games would supposedly be financed by a coordinated
effort around the world to raise funds to allow athletes to compete in the
true Olympic spirit. A fund- raising drive would be initiated in America
to support all athletes who qualified to participate in these "African
Games." In addition to the OCHR's efforts, Curt Canning, captain of the
Harvard University crew, and fellow white crew members announced the
formation of a group to support Edwards's OPHR, although they stopped
short of endorsing the boycott of the summer games.[53]

Concurrently, the American Committee on Africa (ACOA) issued
a statement signed by sixty athletes calling for America to boycott the
games unless South Africa was barred from competition. The ACOA was
made up of people like Senator Eugene McCarthy, actor Sydney Poitier,
Jackie Robinson, and Martin Luther King. They contended that the racist
policies in South Africa violated Olympic rules against discrimination and
political interference. Athletes who signed the statement included Jim
Bouton, Ruben Amaro, Haywood Dotson, a black basketball player from
Columbia University, Steve Mokone, a South African soccer player who
was attending the University of Rochester, and Kwaku Oheme-Frempong,
a Ghanaian on Yale University's track team.[54]

External pressure by the OCHR, the African nations, and the ACOA
forced the IOC to reverse its decision. On April 20, the IOC rescinded the
invitation to South Africa to participate in the Mexico City games. In June,
the Mexican organizing committee of the games ruled that because of a UN
Security Council resolution imposing sanctions on Rhodesia, it would deny
admittance to any person traveling on a Rhodesian passport. Therefore,
Rhodesia was also barred from participating in the Mexico City games.

On the surface, the IOC's reversal appeared to be a victory for the
Olympic Project for Human Rights. One of its mandates was to boycott any

event in which South Africa or Rhodesia participated. Previous scholars argued that the IOC's reversal drastically reduced the enthusiastic support for a boycott of the summer games—a valid assertion. What is often overlooked, however, is that the IOC's reversal diverted attention away from the OPHR's fundamental objective: that African American's role in sports was intimately interdependent with the overall struggle for human rights in American society. Moreover, Edwards overstated the supposed mandate the OCHR received at the November Black Youth Conference. In other words, this sense of unity among black athletes regarding the boycott movement was more stated than validated.[55]

Several factors highlighted this lack of unity among the black athletes regarding the Olympic boycott. Lack of economic residuals constituted the first factor. From the outset, the OCHR relied exclusively upon Harry Edwards's salary to finance the movement. The OCHR had to rely on volunteers to assist them in printing and distributing literature to black athletes throughout the country. Although Edwards made major inroads to Black Power organizations, they could not provide the economic support the OCHR needed.

The inability to influence public opinion in the media represented the second factor. The lack of economic resources further exacerbated the OCHR's attempts to convey their message in the media. Edwards admitted the OCHR was losing the struggle in the media, so the best way to counteract the lack of economic residuals was to go on the offensive. Edwards replaced his professorial attire with Black Power regalia—a black beret, sunglasses, a goatee, and combat boots. In addition, he began to espouse the fiery rhetoric commonly attributed to Black Power radicals that captured the white press's attention. He would refer to President Lyndon Baines Johnson, for example, as "Lynchin Baines Johnson." Black athletes who did not support the boycott effort were characterized as "Uncle Toms."[56]

Edwards sought to create "chaos" in the media, so neither the USOC nor the press knew whether the black athletes would boycott or not. For example, if one New York paper carried a comment by Lee Evans that he bolted the movement, a San Francisco paper may declare the track star denounced athletes who did not support the movement. Edwards also engaged in this activity. He once began a press conference by stating: "Ladies and gentlemen of the press, I have asked you here today in order to secure equal time and speak in your media—to answer myself." This tactic served to keep media attention on the OPHR, but at the same time, proved to be a mixed blessing. The white press focused primarily on Edwards's fiery rhetoric that tended to marginalize the OPHR's goals and objectives. Because of the absence of economic resources to mount an effective media strategy, Edwards's tactics were understandable.[57]

The OCHR's attempts to influence public opinion was further undermined by statements made by former and contemporary black athletes regarding the Olympic boycott. Former heavyweight champion Joe Louis stated that the black athletes would make a serious mistake if they decided not to represent America in the Olympics. Ralph Boston remained adamant in his opposition to the boycott. After the IOC's reversal, Tommie Smith and Lee Evans reportedly had a change of attitude about the boycott. Evans supposedly said that "this [the IOC's reversal] certainly changes my mind some about participation." Two of the staunchest supporters of the Olympic boycott were now having second thoughts.[58]

Jesse Owens continued his assault against the proposed Olympic boycott. Owens took the offensive in public lectures, in the press, and on radio and television. He acknowledged that black militants considered him "a member of the old school," but he insisted that they had no monopoly on suffering "a lot of injustices in our nation." Owens continued to advance the argument that sports have "bridged the gap of misunderstanding more . . . than anywhere else." Simultaneously, television made it easier for Olympic enthusiasts to oppose the boycott. On March 30, 1968, an independent sports network aired *Jesse Owens Returns to Berlin*, an hour-long documentary written and produced by Bud Greenspan. No fewer than 180 local television stations carried the film in the United States, and it aired concurrently in fifteen foreign countries.[59]

Owens's prime-time special reinforced his assault on the boycott movement. The 1936 Olympic Games had been brought alive in the public consciousness, and Owens drew comparisons between Berlin and Mexico City. "Then we had the Jewish problem and now we have a civil rights question," he reportedly told his audience. "The parallel is real because the social problem is a vital one to the Negro." However, as historian William Baker accurately points out, the boycott controversy in 1936 centered on Adolf Hitler's persecution of the German Jews. The Mexican government was of no concern to American blacks in 1968. Their complaints focused on their own society, not with foreigners.[60]

The expansion of the team sports industry constituted the third factor. Attempts to mount the black athlete revolt occurred simultaneously with challenges from rival leagues, particularly against the National Football League and the National Basketball Association. In 1960, the NFL faced its most serious challenge—the rise of the American Football League. Because of the antagonistic relationship between the two leagues, a bidding war for the top college talent resulted, leading to increased opportunities for blacks to play professional football. Concurrently, the NBA faced two challenges—the American Basketball League in 1960 and the American Basketball Association in 1967. Like football, a bidding war for players occurred, leading to increased opportunities to play professional basketball. Television also led to increased opportunities for blacks, as both football and basketball needed to place a better product on the field. In the 1960s, Major League Baseball added eight new teams to the American and National Leagues, bringing their total number of franchises to twenty-four.[61]

Increased opportunities, evidently, led to Edwards receiving "bribes" to call off the boycott. According to Edwards, he was offered money on two occasions, totaling over $125,000. One businessman offered him part-interest in a promotional scheme that included a travelogue magazine entitled, *Holiday at the Olympics*, to be distributed during an eight-month personal appearance tour of North and South America. The second opportunity called for Edwards to call off the boycott and publicize the purported role of an aspiring 1968 presidential candidate in "making [him] see reason." At the same time, sprinters "who couldn't catch a cold," and hurdlers "who couldn't catch a peanut with a bushel basket" were offered lucrative professional football bonuses if they participated and did well in the Olympics. Athletes were also offered flattering incentives to play major league baseball to steal scores of bases. John Carlos added: "The agents came out to our practices, and they tried to buy our allegiance by promising us that if we did not protest, we could get anything that we wanted. They reminded us that the NFL, Hollywood, big businesses, and other areas of the financial world would be available to us if we kept our mouths shut." These bribes were not without foundation, given the need for these professional sports to place a better product on the field to maximize their profits through television. Moreover, offering these inducements to sprinters and hurdlers to become flankers and split ends was understandable, due to former Olympic Gold medalist Bob Hayes's success with the Dallas Cowboys.[62]

The failure to gain support of African American female athletes constituted the fourth factor. Wyomia Tyus, holder of five world records and a gold medalist at the 1964 Olympic Games, stated that black male athletes never invited black female athletes to their meetings. Jarvis Scott, a 400-meter runner, claimed she supported the OPHR's objectives, but not the boycott. Scott added that she and other black women on the U.S. team "were most disappointed that our feelings were not brought out, while the men issued statements and held [press] conferences; finding out what we felt was only a last minute thing." Furthermore, concerns for their quest for human rights were either marginalized or ignored.[63]

The ideology of accommodation represented the final factor. Harry Edwards represented the post–World War II African American generation that was no longer willing to accept the status quo. They sought ways to eliminate existing barriers to racial equality by any means necessary. He was one of many black athletes who represented this sense of disillusionment that came to exemplify the Black Power Movement. Through a collective response among black athletes throughout America, Edwards attempted to bring international attention to their plight to illustrate that all was not well in the sports world. In this way, Edwards epitomized Malcolm X's assertion for the need for black unity and self-determination, for community control and the internalization of the black struggle that became more fully developed and institutionalized in the Black Power era. Instilled with cultural pride and historical wisdom, black athletes would, with a new confidence, begin to chart their own course in the sports world.

Efforts to dismantle the existing racial barriers, however, came in conflict with the ways black athletes were socialized to participate in sports in American society. In his autobiography, *The Struggle That Must Be*, Edwards found it difficult to understand why a substantial number of black athletes still bought into the notion that sports provided them more opportunities than any other facet of American society. He primarily dismissed black athletes who thought this way as "Uncle Toms." What Edwards, and others like him, failed to recognize was that accommodating to racial prejudices, performing to the best of one's ability on the field, and conducting oneself as a productive citizen of American society, was, essentially, the black athlete's experience in America. As Donald Spivey argues convincingly, the very nature of organized sports, with its militaristic player-coach relationships, discourages political activism. It was also compatible with accommodationism. Black athletes were less concerned with making fundamental changes in American society in general and the sport industry specifically. Rather, through collective action, they sought to win greater participation in the existing sport industry.[64]

By the middle of 1968, the movement to boycott the Mexico City games continued to erode, despite demonstrations at track meets, lectures across the country, and the fiery rhetoric that kept the OPHR before the public. Edwards was broke financially and physically exhausted. His weight dropped from 260 pounds to 205 pounds in less than eight months, and he had received several death threats during that same time period. On August 31 at the third National Conference on Black Power, the OCHR announced that they had called off the boycott and reshaped the form of protest black athletes would partake in. The form of protest was left up to the individual athletes, which might include not participating in victory stand ceremonies or victory marches. Thus the OPHR had been reduced to a few symbolic protests that only a handful of black athletes participated in. When Tommie Smith and John Carlos made their infamous Black Power salute after the 200 meters, Edwards remarked that both men "dared to become visible, to stand up for the dignity of Black people, to protest from an international platform the racist inhumanity of American society." He added: "A total Black boycott of the United States Olympic effort was an idea whose time had *almost* come. But this time almost was not only good enough, it was inspiring and it was historic!"[65]

Conclusion

At the conclusion of the 1968 Olympic Games, Harry Edwards spent considerable time reflecting on the previous eighteen months. He pondered the assassinations of Martin Luther King and Senator Robert Kennedy, the rebellions in Detroit and Newark, the Vietnam War, and the Olympic protest movement. Reflecting on these events led Edwards to take on the responsibility of contextualizing the history of the OPHR and the black athlete revolt within the broader theoretical, historical, and political context of the black freedom struggle. He spent a great deal of time documenting his experiences in the black student and black athlete revolt that led to the publication of two books—*Black Students* and *The Revolt of the Black Athlete.*

Edwards spent a lot of time reading about the struggles and triumphs of past generations of black athletes. He read about the career of Jack Johnson, reviewed newspaper stories on the careers of Joe Louis and Jesse

Owens, and examined the exploits of Jackie Robinson and Bill Russell. Paul Robeson became a model and hero to Edwards, a "source of spiritual sustenance in the difficult time of deceleration and disengagement from a political struggle into which [he] had poured everything [he] had." Robeson became a "refuge, an inspiration, and the very embodiment of the Black athlete's long heritage of struggle and sacrifice in pursuit of freedom and dignity." As a social activist, Robeson was a forerunner long before the boycotts by black collegiate athletes and the courageous stands of Tommie Smith and John Carlos, Muhammad Ali, and Curt Flood. Moreover, Paul Robeson influenced Edwards's vision of the black athletes' role and responsibility in American society.[66]

Our vision of the black athlete revolt between 1968 and 1975 as characterized solely and inevitably by black athletes speaking out against racial injustices downplays the efforts of black athletes to improve their condition in an integrated setting. Integration alone did not address issues that affected blacks in the white sports world: the player-coach relationship, student housing, and the social environment. Further, our cinematic vision of the black athlete revolt blurs the racial dilemmas that follow us into the twenty-first century, particularly in light of the phenomenal commercial successes of Michael Jordan and Tiger Woods.

Harry Edwards's role in the black athlete revolt underlies many aspects of the ongoing black freedom struggle—mobilizing blacks toward a position of community and group strength, building a significant power bloc, and developing a group consciousness and pride that would serve them well in their struggle for power. But foremost it testifies to the extent to which, throughout the postwar years, there existed among the black athletes a current of militancy—a current that included the willingness to break down all racial barriers to equality by any means necessary. This facet of African American life lived in tension and tandem with the compelling moral example of nonviolent direct action.

Notes

1. Amy Bass, *Not the Triumph but the Struggle: The 1968 Olympics and the Making of the Black Athlete* (Minneapolis: University of Minnesota Press, 2002). Harry Edwards, *The Revolt of the Black Athlete* (New York: Free Press, 1969). Edwards also deals with the black athlete revolt in "The Olympic Project for Human Rights: An Assessment Ten Years Later," *Black Scholar* 6 (March-April 1979): 2–8; idem., "Reflections on Olympic Sportpolitics: History and Prospects, 1968–1984," *The Crisis* 90 (May 1983): 20–24; idem., *The Struggle That Must Be: An*

Autobiography (New York: Macmillan, 1980); idem., "The Black Athletes: 20th-Century Gladiators for White America," in Andrew Yiannakis, Thomas D. McIntyre, Merrill J. Melnick, and Dale P. Hart, eds., *Sport Sociology: Contemporary Themes* (Iowa: Kendall/Hart, 1976), 167–72; idem., *Sport Sociology* (New York: Macmillan, 1972). Edwards also dealt with black student uprisings on college campuses in *Black Students* (New York: Free Press, 1970). Scholars who have dealt with the revolt of the black athlete include: Douglas Hartmann, *Race, Culture, and the Revolt of the Black Athlete* (Chicago: University of Chicago Press, 2003); David K. Wiggins, *Glory Bound: Black Athletes in a White America* (Syracuse, NY: Syracuse University Press, 1997); idem., "'The Year of Awakening': Black Athletes, Racial Unrest and the Civil Rights Movement of 1968," *International Journal of the History of Sport* 9 (August 1992): 188–208; Randy Roberts and James S. Olson, *Winning Is the Only Thing: Sports in America since 1945* (Baltimore: Johns Hopkins University Press, 1989); William J. Baker, *Jesse Owens: An American Life* (New York: Free Press, 1986); idem., *Sports in the Western World* (Totowa, NJ: Rowman and Littlefield, 1982); Donald Spivey, "Black Consciousness and the Olympic Protest Movement, 1964–1980," in idem., *Sport in America: New Historical Perspectives* (Westport, CT: Greenwood, 1985), 239–62; idem., "The Black Athlete in Big-Time Intercollegiate Sports, 1941–1968," *Phylon* 44 (1983): 116–25. Although it has several drawbacks, Jack Scott deals with the black athlete revolt in *The Athletic Revolution* (New York: Free Press, 1971). Recent autobiographies and biographies that address the black athlete revolt include: Bob Beamon and Milana Walter Beamon, *The Man Who Could Fly: The Bob Beamon Story* (Columbus, Miss.: Genesis, 1999); C. D. Jackson, *Why? The Biography of John Carlos* (Los Angeles: Milligan, 2001).

2. Rustin's assessment of the Black Power movement in Robert Self, "'TO PLAN OUR LIBERATION': Black Power and the Politics of Place in Oakland, California, 1965–1977," *Journal of Urban History* 26 (September 2000): 759. Hugh Pearson, *The Shadow of the Panther: Huey Newton and the Price of Black Power in America* (Reading, Mass.: Addison-Wesley, 1994). William L. Van Deburg, *New Day in Babylon: The Black Power Movement and American Culture, 1965–1975* (Chicago: University of Chicago Press, 1992). Timothy Tyson makes a similar argument regarding this parallel evolution of the Civil Rights and Black Power movements in "Robert F. Williams, 'Black Power,' and the Roots of the African American Freedom Struggle," *Journal of American History* 85 (September 1998): 540–70.

3. I am drawing heavily from Edwards's autobiography to reconstruct both his early childhood experiences in sport and his college career. *Struggle*, 27–28.

4. Ibid., 3.

5. Ibid., 70–71.

6. Edwards, *Struggle*, 97–99.

7. Ibid.

8. Ibid., 108. See also James Brann, "San Jose: The Bullhorn Message," *Nation* 205 (November 6, 1967): 465 for San Jose State's reputation as a "party school."

9. Edwards's conversation with his coach in *Struggle*, 113–14.

10. It is of interest that Tommie Smith characterized Winter as a "humanitarian" to this day. Hartmann, *Race, Culture, and the Revolt*, 226.

11. Mitchell's quote in Manning Marable, *Race, Reform and Rebellion: The Second Reconstruction in Black America, 1945–1982* (Jackson: University Press of Mississippi, 1984), 89.

12. Ibid., 89–90. For an account on the Younge murder, see James Forman, *Sammy Younge, Jr.: The First Black College Student to Die in the Black Liberation Movement* (New York: Grove, 1968); Robert J. Norrell, *Reaping the Whirlwind: The Civil Rights Movement in Tuskegee* (New York: Knopf, 1985), 179–84. For an account on the impact the Vietnam War had on the funding of civil rights enforcement, see Robert Weisbrot, *Freedom Bound: A History of America's Civil Rights Movement* (New York: W. W. Norton, 1990), 189–93; William H. Chaffe, *The Unfinished*

Journey: American Since World War II, 2nd ed., (New York: Oxford University Press, 1991), 280–88.

13. Van Deburg, *New Day*, 42–43.

14. For Major League Baseball's spring training ritual, see Jack E. Davis, "Baseball's Reluctant Challenge: Desegregating Major League Spring Training Sites, 1961–1964," *Journal of Sport History* 19 (1992): 144–62; Jules Tygiel, *Baseball's Great Experiment: Jackie Robinson and His Legacy* (New York: Oxford University Press, 1983), 265–84; Hank Aaron and Lonnie Wheeler, *I Had a Hammer: The Hank Aaron Story* (New York: HarperCollins, 1991), 209–13. Jim Brown's comments in Alex Poinsett, "The Controversial Jim Brown," *Ebony* (December 1964): 66.

15. Dick Gregory, *Nigger: An Autobiography* (London: George Allen and Unwin, 1965), 207–8; Mal Whitfield, "Let's Boycott The Olympics," *Ebony* (March 1964): 95–96, 98–100. See chapter one regarding the AFL boycott.

16. Edwards, *Struggle*, 139; Vincent Harding, *The Other American Revolution* (Los Angeles: Center for African American Studies University of California, Los Angeles, 1980), 180–81.

17. Van Deburg, *New Day in Babylon*, 2.

18. Malcolm X interview in Weisbrot, *Freedom Bound*, 234. Stokely Carmichael, "Pan-Africanism—Land Power," *Black Scholar* 1 (November 1969): 40.

19. Edwards, *Struggle*, 145.

20. Ibid., 158–59; Brann, "San Jose," 465; Bass, *Not the Triumph*, 85.

21. Ibid., Edwards, *Revolt*, 43.

22. Edwards, *Revolt*, 44–46.

23. *San Jose Mercury*, September 18, 1967.

24. Edwards's strategy in Brann, "San Jose," 466; *San Jose Mercury*, September 19, 1967.

25. *San Jose Mercury*, September 19, 1967. For an account on Dr. Robert Clark's tenure at San Jose State, see Benjamin F. Gilbert and Charles Burdick, *Washington Square 1857–1979: The History of San Jose State University* (San Jose: San Jose State University, 1980), 169–82.

26. *San Jose Mercury*, 20, 1967.

27. *San Jose Mercury*, September 21, 1967. See also *Los Angeles Times*, September 21, 1967.

28. Gilbert et. al., *Washington Square*, 179–80; Arnold Hano, "The Black Rebel Who 'Whitelists' the Olympics," *New York Times Magazine* (May 12, 1968): 41. *San Jose Mercury*, September 22, 1967; *Los Angeles Times*, October 3, 1967.

29. *San Jose Mercury*, September 22, 1967.

30. *San Jose Mercury*, 27, 28, 1967; Hano, "The Black Rebel," 41; *New Jersey African American*, October 7, 1967.

31. Bronzan's estimate in *San Jose Mercury*, September 22, 1967.

32. *New York Times*, July 24, 1967.

33. Edwards, *Revolt*, 42–43; Johnathan Rodgers, "A Step to an Olympic Boycott," *Sports Illustrated* 27 (December 4, 1967): 31. Bass points out that Smith's statement was built upon earlier indications of his political leanings. He gave, for example, an arguably controversial answer in a questionnaire for *Track and Field News* magazine's "Profiles of Champions" series. Bass points out whereas most of his responses illustrated his desires to excel on the track, maintain good academic standing, and "become an elementary school teacher," when asked what he disliked, he supposedly replied, "to be exploited." See *Not the Triumph*, 88.

34. Edwards, *Revolt*, 51–54; Rodgers, "Olympic Boycott," 30.

35. *Los Angeles Times*, November 24, 1967.

36. *Los Angeles Times*, November 23, 1967; Rodgers, "Olympic Boycott," 31; Hano, "The Black Rebel," 42.

37. Alcindor quote in Edwards, *Revolt*, 53.

38. Rodgers, "Olympic Boycott," 31. The disturbance outside the church and the decision to alter the plans for an individual vote in Edwards, *Revolt*, 54.

39. *Washington Post*, November 25, 1967; *St. Louis Post-Dispatch*, November 24, 1967. Art Walker's decision not to attend the workshop and Charlie Greene's quote in *Los Angeles Times*, November 25, 1967; *Los Angeles Herald-Examiner*, November 25, 1967.

40. Lee's quote and Owens's criticism of the Olympic boycott in *Washington Post*, November 25, 1967; *Los Angeles Herald-Examiner*, November 25, 1967. Johnson's quote in *San Jose Mercury*, November 25, 1967; *St. Louis Post-Dispatch*, November 26, 1967

41. Smith's comments in *San Jose Mercury*, November 23, 24, 1967; *Los Angeles Times*, November 24, 1967; *Los Angeles Herald-Examiner*, November 26, 1967. Alcindor's indecision whether to boycott the Olympic Games or not in *Los Angeles Times*, November 25, 1967.

42. For accounts that deal with African American thought and ideology, see Kevin K. Gaines, *Uplifting the Race: Black Leadership, Politics, and Culture in the Twentieth Century* (Chapel Hill: University of North Carolina Press, 1996); Bart Landry, *The New Black Middle Class* (Berkeley: University of California Press, 1987); J. H. Harmon, Arnett G. Lindsey and Carter G. Woodson, *The Negro as a Business Man* (College Park, MD: McGrath, 1929), 6–29; Abram L. Harris, *The Negro as Capitalist: A Study of Banking and Business among American Negroes* (Philadelphia: The American Academy OF Political And Social Science, 1936), 49–54; Seth Scheiner, *Negro Mecca: A History of the Negro in New York City, 1865–1920* (New York University Press, 1965), 70–81; August Meier and Elliott Rudwick, *From Plantation to Ghetto*, 3rd ed., (New York: Hill and Wang, 1976), 212–18; August Meier, *Negro Thought in America, 1880–1915* (Ann Arbor: University of Michigan Press, 1964); Michael E. Lomax, "Black Baseball, Black Entrepreneurs, Black Community: The History of the Negro National and Eastern Colored Leagues, 1880–1930 (Ph.D. diss.: Ohio State University, 1996), 178–88. For accounts on how Joe Louis's handlers attempted to craft his image, see Art Evans, "Joe Louis as a Key Functionary: White Reactions toward a Black Champion," *Journal of Black Studies* 16 (1985): 95–111; Lauren Rebecca Sklaroff, "Constructing G.I. Joe Louis: Cultural Solutions to the 'Negro Problem' during World War II," *Journal of American History* 89 (December 2002): 958–83. For accounts on the legacy of Jack Johnson, see Geoffrey Ward, *Unforgivable Blackness: The Rise and Fall of Jack Johnson* (New York: Knopf, 2004); Al-Tony Gilmore, "Jack Johnson and White Women: The National Impact," *Journal of Negro History* 57 (January 1973): 18–38.

43. For Foster's economic philosophy and Hueston's assertion of baseball serving as a leveler of race prejudice, see Lomax, "Black Baseball," 338–39, 462–63. For Bolden promoting his club around the notion of "clean baseball," see Neil Lanctot, *Fair Dealing and Clean Playing: The Hilldale Club and the Development of Black Professional Baseball, 1910–1932* (Jefferson, NC: McFarland, 1994), 47–48.

44. Weisbrot, *Freedom Bound*, 10–11; John Hope Franklin, *From Slavery to Freedom: A History of Negro Americans*, 5th ed., (New York: Knopf, 1980), 450–59. I construct a similar argument regarding the African American experience in professional football in "Review Essay: The African American Experience of Professional Football," *Journal of Social History* 33 (Fall 1999), 163–78.

45. "The Indispensable Man," *Time* 78 (October 1961): 74. For Bob Gibson failing to receive endorsement opportunities after the 1964 World Series, see Bob Gibson with Lonnie Wheeler, *Stranger to the Game: The Autobiography of Bob Gibson* (New York: Penguin, 1994), 104–6.

46. Hano, "The Black Rebel," 39, 48.

47. *New York Times*, December 15, 1967.

48. Edwards, *Revolt*, 65–66; *New York Times*, February 16, 1968.

49. *New York Times*, January 30, February 13, 1968; (Chicago) *Defender*, February 3, 1968; *New York Post*, February 14, 16, 1968; *Los Angeles Sentinel*, February 15, 1968. Larry Merchant quote in *New York Post*, February 15, 1968.

50. Edwards, *Revolt*, 66; Pete Axthelm, "Boycott Now—Boycott Later?" *Sports Illustrated* 28 (February 26, 1968): 25; *Los Angeles Times*, February 16, 1968.

51. *New York Times,* February 14, 16, 1968; *Pittsburgh Courier,* February 17, 1968.

52. *New York Times,* February 17, 1968; *New York Post,* February 17, 1968; Jack Olsen, "Part 3: The Black Athlete: In an Alien World," *Sports Illustrated* 28 (July 15, 1968): 37. Edwards declared that attendance at the NYAC meet was down by more than 50 percent. This appears to be an exaggeration. The new Madison Square Gardens' seating capacity was 20,800. Both the *New York Times* and *New York Post* estimated the crowd to be 14,000. While this estimated figure is over 50 percent, it still appears that the boycott affected the overall attendance of the meet. See Edwards, *Struggle,* 184. For Madison Square Gardens' seating capacity, see Carl Lundquist, "New Madison Square Garden—Place for Sports Heroes," *Sporting News* 144 (January 20, 1968): 20. Beamon, *The Man Who Could Fly,* 93.

53. *New York Times,* February 16, 1968; Edwards, *Revolt,* 92–94.

54. Wiggins, "Year of Awakening," 193.

55. Ibid., 194; Roberts et. al., *Winning,* 175–76; Spivey, "Black Consciousness," 243–45.

56. Hano, "The Black Rebel," 32, 41.

57. Edwards, *Struggle,* 190–92. See, for example, *New York Times,* August 1, 1968.

58. *New York Times,* April 3, 24, June 23, 1968.

59. William J. Baker, *Jesse Owens: An American Life* (New York: Free Press, 1986), 208–9.

60. Ibid.

61. More research is needed regarding the expansion of the team sports industry in the 1960s. For an account on expansion, see Roberts et. al. *Winning,* 133–62; James Edward Miller, *The Baseball Business: Pursuing Pennants and Profits in Baltimore* (Chapel Hill: University of North Carolina Press, 1990), 136–55.

62. Edwards, *Struggle,* 190; Jackson, *Why?,* 168.

63. Scott's quote in Spivey, "Black Consciousness," 249. See also Bass, *Not the Triumph,* 214–26.

64. Edwards, *Struggle,* 180–81.

65. Ibid., 204.

66. Ibid., 206.

4

The Black Panther Party and the Revolt of the Black Athlete

Sport and Revolutionary Consciousness

—Ron Briley

I n the wake of 9-11, American sport, whether at the amateur or professional level, wrapped itself in the flag, using the arena of sport to support American military intervention in Afghanistan and Iraq. This use of sport in the service of empire reflects increasing corporate control over the arena of spectator athletics, encouraging consumption and employing sport in service of the conservative ideology of the American consensus. This ideological construct suggests the athletic playing field is a metaphor for an American meritocracy in which issues of race, gender, and class play no role. Well-paid professional athletes, with some notable exceptions such as Carlos Delgado of the New York Mets, are loath to challenge this corporate and nationalistic hegemony of sport.

Contemporary African American athletes often display the swagger as well as the business acumen which journalist Larry Platt labels "New Jack Jocks."[1] These athletes, living in an age where so much money is at stake, are often reluctant to challenge a system which has provided them with commercial possibilities unattainable by earlier generations. But this was not always the case. Sport historian David Zang argues that the Civil Rights Movement of the 1960s and the divisive Vietnam War produced cultural sport wars in which the athletic clichés of sport as building character and providing a level playing field were challenged by socially active and aware athletes. Accordingly, in a recent piece for the *International Socialist Review*, David Zirin reminds us that the Muhammad Ali who has become an icon of the American establishment was once "reviled by the mainstream press, persecuted by the U.S. government, and defiantly loved throughout the world."[2] Ali was part of the 1960s revolt of the black athlete, whose case was so articulately presented by Harry Edwards, a college track star and sociologist who taught at Cornell University and San Jose State College.

In his manifesto *The Revolt of the Black Athlete*, Edwards asserts,

> The revolt of the black athlete in America as a phase of the overall black liberation movement is as legitimate as the sit-in, the freedom rides, or any other manifestation of Afro-American efforts to gain freedom. The goals of the revolt likewise are the same as those of any other legitimate phase of the movement—equality, justice, the regaining of black dignity lost during those three hundred years of abject slavery, and the attainment of the basic human and civil rights guaranteed by the United States Constitution and the concept of American democracy.[3]

The scholar activist established the Olympic Project for Human Rights (OPHR), which sought to organize black athletes in protest against racial discrimination and oppression in sport which mirrored racism in America and the international community. While the OPHR was unsuccessful in mounting a boycott of the 1968 Olympic Games, the organization convinced black athletes to not participate in events sponsored by the New York Athletic Club, which excluded blacks and Jews from membership. In addition, a threatened boycott by the OPHR encouraged the International Olympic Committee to maintain its ban on the participation of South Africa and Rhodesia due to the racial exclusion policies of the two nations. Thus, historian Michael Lomax argues, "The OPHR epitomized Malcolm X's assertion for the need for black unity and self-determination of the black struggle that became more fully developed and institutionalized in the Black Power era."[4]

Black Power was a term which threatened many whites with visions of urban unrest and reverse discrimination. Black economic power, liberation, and cultural identity failed to call for the absorption into the melting pot mainstream envisioned by many whites. To understand the concept of Black Power in all its manifestations, Jeffrey O. G. Ogbar insists that "one must come to grips" with the Black Panther Party (BPP), an organization which fomented "the cultural shifts that reconfigured politics and identity in America."[5]

The BPP was formed by Huey Newton and Bobby Seale in Oakland, California, during the fall of 1966. To many, the image of the BPP remains one of violence associated with young gun-wielding black males adorned with black berets and leather jackets. However, the ten point program outlined by Newton and Seale included a broader agenda, focusing on such issues as housing, education, employment, police brutality, and reformation of the legal system. The BPP asserted the right for blacks to defend themselves against the police and called for a socialist revolution in America. Yet, this revolutionary rhetoric was coupled with community programs to address sickle cell anemia and provide breakfasts for the elderly and impoverished children.

In the *Shadow of the Panther*, journalist Hugh Pearson challenges the legacy of the BPP, asserting that the violence and drug use of Newton cast a dark shadow over the cause of black liberation and played into the hands of white racists.[6] On the other hand, many scholars of the BPP maintain that the organization enjoyed wide support among the black community until the assassination of leaders such as Fred Hampton and internal divisions exacerbated by government harassment culminated in the disintegration of the Panthers by the mid-1970s.[7]

The appeal of the BPP during its heyday of the late 1960s and early 1970s is evident in the popularity of the party newspaper, *The Black Panther*, whose circulation was estimated between 100,000 and 200,000 with a broad readership abroad due to the BPP's endorsement of global liberation struggles. Journalism historians maintain that *The Black Panther*, between 1967 and 1971, enjoyed the largest circulation of any black newspaper. In addition, the grassroots nature of how the paper was printed and circulated, with newspaper sales helping to finance BPP programs, provided a vehicle through "which members of an oppressed minority group spoke with a strong and vibrant voice."[8] In a January 17, 1970, piece for the paper, The Black Panther Black Community News Service asserted that it was: "the flesh and blood, the sweat and tears of our people. It is a continuation of the story of the middle passage, of Denmark Vesey, of Nat Turner, of Harriet Tubman, of Malcolm X, and countless other oppressed people who put freedom and dignity beyond personal gain. The Black Panther Black Community News Service is truly a mirror of the spirit of the people."[9]

The Black Panther in its heyday did not include a regular sports page, and the image of the BPP is hardly associated with the world of sport. Yet the paper and party ideology of internationalism did make for common cause with the heroic individualism of a Muhammad Ali resisting the American war machine and Harry Edwards's OPHR cooperative approach to combating racism in sport on the international level. Yohuru Williams argues that the BPP exported black nationalism and "tied Black liberation to an international struggle for freedom and independence and pledged leadership and unity with oppressed peoples of the world."[10] Police brutality, economic colonialism, and struggles for national liberation were the major issues addressed by the revolutionary BPP, but the sporting world as a venue for struggle was not ignored by the party. Also, the early 1970s effort by the Panthers to gain political control of Oakland city government through the ballot box induced *The Black Panther* to focus more on sport in the Bay Area. Nevertheless, the inclusion of a full sports page by the mid-1970s seemed to represent a departure from the party's revolutionary rigor and signaled the organization's eventual demise.

In 1968, however, *The Black Panther* pursued the BPP message of organizing for self-defense with the publication of numerous articles depicting the murder of blacks at the hands of white people or the police. The police were usually referred to as "pigs," a term whose origin is usually attributed to Huey Newton. Echoing the argument made by Edwards that sport and social mobility for blacks was a mirage, the newspaper suggested that being a professional athlete would not allow a black man to escape the clutches of white violence and racism. According to *The Black Panther*, Ted Wilkins, who played for the Hamilton Tigercats of the Canadian Football League, and his brother were in an altercation with a San Jose, California, grocery clerk who refused to cash the athlete's check and ordered him to "move his ass out of the store." When Wilkins refused to vacate the shop, he was shot by the clerk and allowed to bleed to death by the police, who asserted the shooting was justifiable homicide because the Wilkins brothers were attempting to rob the store. The moral of this story appeared to be that being a privileged black athlete, earning more than $20,000 a year, would not protect a black man from a legalized lynching by whites and their police allies. Or to put it in the words of Harry Edwards, "The only difference between the black man shining shoes in the ghetto and the champion black sprinter is that the shoe shine man is a nigger, while the sprinter is a fast nigger."[11]

Thus, the best hope for black athletes would be in self-defense, collective action, and liberation, especially in conjunction with the struggle of other colonized peoples around the world. *The Black Panther* devoted considerable space to the 1968 Summer Olympic Games in Mexico City and international efforts to address exploitation and racism reflected through the lens of sport. In the spring of 1968, the newspaper reported that the International Olympic Committee (IOC) had voted to rescind its ban on the apartheid state of South Africa. Accusing IOC chief Avery Bundage of racism, the article concluded that American black athletes would join with African nations, such as Algeria, Uganda, and Ghana, and the Soviet Union and socialist bloc to protest the inclusion of South Africa in the games. *The Black Panther* editorialized, "The boycott is expected to strengthen the hand of militant Black athletes who have planned to decline to represent the United States because of racism at home."[12]

The threatened boycott induced the IOC to withdraw its invitation to South Africa, but black American athletes were less united about how to protest racism on the home front. Tremendous pressure to participate was placed upon black members of the American Olympic squad. Bill Russell of the Boston Celtics informed *The Black Panther* that OPHR organizer Harry Edwards was offered $100,000 to abandon the boycott, but the activist "vehemently" refused to be bribed and silenced.[13] Nevertheless, the Mexico City games did commence with the participation of black athletes from the United States, but the games were not without protest.

On October 16, 1968, sprinters Tommie Smith and John Carlos shocked the Olympic crowd and a national television audience during their medal ceremony. While the Star Spangled Banner played and the American flag was unfurled, Smith and Carlos lowered their heads and raised their fists in a Black Power salute. In the uproar over their protest against racial oppression in the United States, it was almost forgotten that Smith had just established a new world mark of 19.83 seconds in the 200 meters. Former Olympic great Jesse Owens, apparently forgetting about the racism he encountered in America after shattering the myth of Aryan superiority during the 1936 Berlin Olympic Games, expressed his disdain for Smith and Carlos, remarking, "We don't need this kind of stuff. We should just let the boys go out and compete."[14]

The reaction among their teammates was less critical and more understanding. Of the twenty American athletes, both black and white, surveyed after the Black Power salute, fifteen expressed support for Smith and Carlos. Female sprinter Wyomia Tyus also proclaimed her approval of the symbolic protest. However, as Amy Bass demonstrated in her study of the 1968 summer games, the OPHR failed to include and organize black female athletes in their boycott activities—ignoring gender issues and limiting possible areas of support. The United States Olympic Committee

(USOC) responded in a less favorable manner. Seeking to prevent further protest by making examples of Smith and Carlos, the USOC revoked the credentials of the two sprinters and expelled them from the Olympic Village. Deprived of their credentials, the two left Mexico within forty-eight hours and returned to the United States, where they were denied the recognition and financial endorsements usually reserved for world-class athletes.[15]

The BPP, however, was eager to embrace Smith and Carlos, recognizing that the symbolic protest of the sprinters signified solidarity with the Black Power and liberation struggles championed by the Panthers. After applauding the sprinters for their courage, a BPP statement concluded, "We hereby serve notice to all pigs that these two brothers—Tommie Smith and John Carlos—have earned the respect and protection of the Panther. In other words, DON'T EFF WITH THEM! If you do, you must surely face the wrath of the armed Black people." Another interesting piece in *The Black Panther* ridiculed the notion by the USOC that "political gestures" had no place in the "non-political" Olympics. Yet in the 1936 Berlin Olympics when athletes from Germany raised their hands in the Nazi salute during medal ceremonies, no words of censure were forthcoming from Avery Bundage and the IOC. Finally, *The Black Panther* printed a letter of support from Shirley Graham DuBois, the widow of W. E. B. Du Bois who was living in Egypt. Expressing her solidarity with Smith and Carlos, Graham DuBois asserted, "Their Black Power demonstration roared to the skies far above all the Olympic banners, and flags—it was heard around the world far beyond the loudest trumpets. I greet these young Black men with joy for myself and my husband. I can hear His voice hailing them and saying proudly: 'Souls of Black Folk, march on, march on towards the Dawn of Our New World!'"[16]

Neither was the historical context of student protest on the eve of the Mexico City games lost on the BPP. Party Minister of Information Eldridge Cleaver interpreted the uprising of Mexico City students and their violent suppression by Mexican authorities days before the opening ceremonies of the Olympic Games as part of a revolutionary struggle in which students were confronting "pigs around the world." BPP Chairman Bobby Seale issued a statement of solidarity with Mexican students, proclaiming:

> We support their demands for the removal of racist, decadent school administrators and their policies, and for the immediate removal of the

fascist, tactical pig forces in Mexico which storm their communities and college campuses with their show of force and reign of terror. We strongly support the demands for the release of their comrades who were made political prisoners as a result of their work to liberate themselves and their people from the clutches of their oppressors.

Thus, the BPP incorporated Olympic Black Power salutes into the revolutionary ideology of liberation for oppressed colonial peoples around the world.[17]

The BPP identified with Muhammad Ali in a similar fashion. As Cassius Clay, he earned a Gold Medal at the 1960 Rome Olympics, only to be refused service at a Louisville hamburger joint. The disillusioned fighter threw his Olympic medal in the Ohio River and searching for a source of refuge in a racist America joined the Nation of Islam. After defeating Sonny Liston and attaining the Heavyweight Championship of the World, Clay made his conversion to the Nation of Islam public and changed his name to Muhammad Ali. In 1966, Ali was declared eligible for the military draft, but he made his aversion to the Vietnam War apparent, insisting, "Man, I ain't got no quarrel with them Vietcong." On June 19, 1967, Ali was found guilty of draft evasion by an all-white Houston, Texas, jury and was sentenced to five years in prison and forced to relinquish his passport while the case was appealed. In addition, the undefeated champion was stripped of his heavyweight title and barred from the ring. But Ali was not silenced, proclaiming in a 1968 speech, "I'm expected to go overseas to help free people in South Vietnam and at the same time my people here are being brutalized, hell no! I would like to say to those of you who think I have lost so much, I have gained everything. I have peace of heart; I have a clear, free conscience. And I'm proud."[18]

The Supreme Court of the United States in 1970 overturned Ali's conviction, and the next year he returned to the ring after a three-year absence, losing a decision to Joe Frazier in an exceedingly brutal fight. *The Black Panther* declared that Ali was "still our champ," and BPP Minister of Defense Huey Newton prepared an open letter to Ali, asserting that the bout with Frazier was "only an incident when we consider the fight you have waged against U.S. imperialism. You dared say 'no' to fascism, they took your crown and tried to destroy you, but still you did not compromise. They immobilized you (as a boxer) for three years, but they did not immobilize your spirit. We can only salute this kind of courage." The paper also recorded Wisconsin State Assemblyman Lloyd A. Barbee's efforts to pass a measure honoring Ali. Barbee's motion referred to the overturning of Ali's conviction and urged the Assembly to "commend Muhammad Ali for continuing to fight for his religious beliefs, for behaving like a champion of life and his race, as well as his sport and wishing him well." The motion, however, was tabled by a vote of 67 to 32. Instead, the Wisconsin Assembly commended traditional cowboy riders and rodeos, which appeared less threatening to the establishment.[19]

The ideological respect with which the BPP leadership viewed Ali was perhaps best presented in a passage from Eldridge Cleaver's *Soul on Ice*, explaining the differences between Ali and Floyd Patterson, a former black heavyweight who was preferred by white audiences if no "White hope" were available. Cleaver maintained that until Ali, black champions were manipulated in their private lives by the white power establishment to control their public images. According to Cleaver, Ali was the first "free" black champion and could be considered "the black Fidel Castro of boxing," who was a genuine revolutionary. Ali's victory over Floyd Patterson in Las Vegas "inflicted a psychological chastisement on white America similar in shock value to Fidel Castro's victory at the Bay of Pigs. If the Bay of Pigs can be seen as a straight right hand to the psychological jaw of white America, then Las Vegas was a perfect left hook to the gut."[20]

While Cleaver always insisted upon placing sport within an international revolutionary context, by the early 1970s others within the BPP were beginning to argue that the revolt of the black athlete be placed within a more national and local framework. In fact, this split in party ideology led Newton to expel Cleaver and the entire International Section of the party in 1971. Others on the American left, however, such as William Patterson, head of the American Communist Party, continued to maintain that the struggle of the black athlete in the United States could not be isolated from its class and social roots. In a piece published in *The Black Panther*, Patterson asserted the fight of the black athlete in America was "part and parcel of the Black Liberation struggle and part of the fight against imperialism."[21]

By early 1971, however, Newton, in an effort to maintain control of the BPP, was moving away from the international struggle against imperialism and was, instead, emphasizing what Newton referred to as the "survival pending revolution" program.[22] Under Newton's new direction, the BPP was increasingly engaged in more conventional economic and political activities, such as electing Panther leaders Elaine Brown to the

Oakland City Council and Bobby Seale to the position of mayor. This more community-oriented approach also resulted in the BPP paying more attention to the role of sport in Oakland. During the early 1970s the Oakland A's established a baseball dynasty, winning five American League Western Division titles from 1971 to 1975 and world championships in 1972, 1973, and 1974. One of the stars of the A's was left-handed starting pitcher Vida Blue, who won twenty-four games in 1971 and was honored by being selected to receive the American League's Most Valuable Player and Cy Young Awards. Blue was paid only $14,750 for the 1971 season, and the pitcher sought a significant raise for the 1972 season, initially asking for $115,000. Insurance executive Charles O. Finley who owned the A's countered with an offer of $50,000. An outraged Blue threatened to retire from the game, until an intervention by Baseball Commissioner Bowie Kuhn resulted in the pitcher signing his 1972 contract for a compromise package of $63,000. The final pact was essentially a triumph for Finley and management, although it contained a face-saving $13,000 for Blue.[23]

The Black Panther viewed Blue as another victim of the reserve clause which prevented players from attaining free agency. The paper supported the antitrust lawsuit of St. Louis Cardinals outfielder Curt Flood, who protested his trade to the Philadelphia Phillies as a violation of antitrust law and the thirteenth amendment outlawing involuntary servitude or slavery. In agreement with the case made by Harry Edwards, the paper editorialized that the major sports, such as baseball, were capitalistic exploiters of black labor rather than a path for social mobility. Following the Oakland A's 1972 World Series victory, the BPP offered its congratulations to the home team, but expressed regret over the failure of Oakland management to make proper use of Blue. *The Black Panther* labeled Finley a racist who "acted like the plantation owner with Brother Vida Blue." The Panthers called upon the people to "not allow the dignity of a Black athlete to be slighted in so callous a manner."[24]

The BPP assault on Finley was not merely rhetorical. In their endeavors to take electoral control of the Oakland city government, the Bobby Seale-Elaine Brown Campaign to Rebuild Oakland called for an immediate raise in rental payments by the A's and other organizations using the Oakland Coliseum. The goal was to increase city revenues and offset the $750,000 annually which was spent on the stadium. The Panthers believed the city government and Oakland taxpayers were subsidizing big business with the Coliseum which had never been approved by the voters. The city of Oakland and Alameda County were each paying $750,000 annually to pay off the bond issues which construction of the sports venue required. Meanwhile, the A's paid only $1,236.02 in taxes on a team assessed at only $37,000: approximately one-half of Vida Blue's 1972 salary. The BPP insisted that Finley would pay his fair share and the city of Oakland, under Panther leadership, would "gain control over public facilities and use them to benefit, rather than impoverish" the financially strapped city.[25]

The BPP also championed people's control of community recreation centers administered by the Department of Parks and Recreation. The Panthers challenged the firing of Bobbie Dell Watson as Director of the Campbell Village (a government-owned housing project) Recreation Center in West Oakland. According to *The Black Panther*, Watson was relieved of her duties for allowing the center's facilities to be used each morning by the BPP-sponsored Free Breakfasts for School Children Program. In addition, Watson would not inform police about youth frequenting the center, which she insisted was to serve the community and not the probation department. The BPP argued for "Sister Bobbie Watson to be reinstated and the Campbell Village Recreation Center remain open. The community is beginning to come together as one in the common fight for our survival and self-determination."[26]

Control over community assets was a powerful issue for the Panther candidates. However, they were unsuccessful in their efforts to wrest control of the city from the entrenched Oakland establishment—although Seale did at least force a run-off election in the mayor's contest. Seale, however, refused to become discouraged, and a July 14, 1973, article in *The Black Panther* featured a photograph of Seale pitching a softball game for The Lamp Post, a popular bar and restaurant in downtown Oakland. Seale and several teammates were members of the New Oakland Democratic Organizing Committee. The former mayoral candidate explained that in joining the softball team he wished to "become involved with the various activities that people engage in, and make these activities more relevant to the community, organizing around them."[27] Seale was increasingly moving from the role of international revolutionary to that of community organizer as the face of the party changed.

As the BPP evolved in a more reformist direction, *The Black Panther* expanded its sports coverage, featuring numerous articles on baseball. For example, the BPP issued statements on the deaths of Jackie Robinson and Roberto Clemente. Although Robinson was critical of black militants and joined the Republican Party, the Panthers had only positive things to say about the athlete who shattered baseball's color line in 1947. The BPP statement described Robinson as "a man who refused to see Black people denied or exploited in the field of sports. A man who loved baseball and found great dignity in winning for the people; he fought hard to have Black men included in major league teams. He struggled past the racist coaches and booing crowds to excel in his field."[28]

The Black Panther was more effusive in its praise of Pittsburgh Pirates star Roberto Clemente, who perished in a plane crash while attempting to get supplies to the victims of an earthquake in Nicaragua. Clemente was described as a man who served the poor black and Latin communities, while racist sportswriters attacked him for being a malingerer even though he played with a chronic backache. He was credited with financially supporting the community service projects of the Philadelphia Chapter of the BPP, and along with other Pittsburgh players such as Willie Stargell, Clemente contributed to the fight against sickle cell anemia. The BPP statement concluded, "Roberto Clemente was simply a man, a man who strove to achieve his dream of peace and justice for oppressed people throughout the world."[29]

The Black Panther also acknowledged the racist hatred directed against Hank Aaron of the Atlanta Braves as he challenged and surpassed Babe Ruth's all-time Major League home run mark. Institutional racism within baseball was condemned in the failure of Baseball Commissioner Bowie Kuhn to send Aaron a congratulatory telegram for hitting home run number 700, as well as for the sport's abysmal record in hiring blacks and Latinos for management positions. Aaron, however, deserved praise "for his determination to struggle against the realities of racism and ignorance, and still come up swinging hard."[30]

Such sporting clichés were appearing more frequently in *The Black Panther* by the mid-1970s as the paper added a sports and entertainment page. Some of the articles seemed like pieces from more mainstream black periodicals such as *Jet* or *Ebony*. For example, the BPP congratulated golfer Lee Elder for winning the Monsanto Golf Tournament and becoming the first black to qualify for the Master's Tournament in Augusta, Georgia. On the other hand, a little venom could still rise to the surface as exemplified by the Oakland A's hiring Alvin Dark to manage the team in 1974. Dark had a reputation for racist remarks and attitudes, including a comment a decade earlier, when he was managing the San Francisco Giants, that black and Latino players did not have the team pride displayed by white athletes. While Dark insisted that he was now a more enlightened man on matters of race, *The Black Panther* asserted that owner Finley was looking for a manager "to try to control his niggers and just make them play ball—both on the field and at the bargaining table."[31] Nevertheless, the paper expressed confidence that such A's black players as Vida Blue, Bill North, and Reggie Jackson would resist and forestall Finley's plan.

As membership in the BPP declined and circulation figures for *The Black Panther* dropped, the paper ran a series of articles documenting that racism was prevalent in American sport, which neither provided a level playing field nor a path to social mobility for black Americans. In March 1974, *The Black Panther* began a series entitled, "The Battle over Racism in Sports," by Paul Hoch, a professor in the sociology of sports at Dawson College in Canada. Hoch argued that the way college sports exploited black athletes was similar to the slave trade. The series by Hoch was followed by articles from Mark Naison, instructor for the Afro-American Institute at Fordham University, asserting that sport was being employed to promulgate an American empire.[32] Many of the ideas presented by Hoch and Naison are today embraced by scholars of American sport.

For example, Richard Lapchick, who headed the Northeastern University Center for the Study of Sport, concluded that it is a myth that sports break down racial and international barriers. "Sports," writes Lapchick, "were supposed to be the way out of poverty for millions of American blacks, when in fact they have helped perpetuate that poverty as the masses have pursued the 12,000 to 1 odds a high school athlete faces to become a pro." On the other hand, John Hoberman is concerned that the success of blacks on the athletic field will perpetuate racial stereotypes of blacks as physically superior but mentally inferior to whites.[33]

Damned if they do and damned if they don't, sport has proven to be a treacherous minefield for black athletes to navigate. Many of the pitfalls pointed out by contemporary scholars are similar to those identified by Harry Edwards in the late 1960s. Yet as Edwards observes in his autobiography, we must not despair if these problems persist, for much of the glory and purpose resides in the struggle. Edwards writes: "But I also believe that in knowledge there is hope, that understanding is self-redemptive, that there is something to be said for the struggle to live more fully rather than settling for mere existence at the whim of circumstance, and that the more desperate the circumstances, the more justified and imperative the struggle for a fuller life."[34] Edwards's words encompass the struggle of the black athlete as well as the Black Panthers, who employed sport in their revolutionary rhetoric and efforts to forge Black Power and liberation both on the national and global levels. The flying fists and dancing feet of Muhammad Ali, the clinched fists of Tommie Smith and John Carlos, the home runs of Hank Aaron despite threats on his life, the courage of Jackie Robinson, and the humanitarianism of Roberto Clemente provide inspiration and remind us of the struggles of common people in the United States and the world to acquire a sense of self-determination and dignity beyond the contemporary emphasis of American sport upon nationalism and empire. The revolutionary context of the 1960s which forged the BPP is missing today, but the desire to combat inequality and forge racial justice remains a powerful force both on and off the fields of play.

Notes

1. Larry Platt, *New Jack Jocks: Rebels, Race and the American Athlete* (Philadelphia: Temple University Press, 2002).

2. David W. Zang, *Sports Wars: Athletes in the Age of Aquarius* (Fayetteville: University of Arkansas Press, 2001); David Zirin, "Muhammad Ali and the Revolt of the Black Athlete," *International Socialist Review*, 33 (January–February 2004), 60.

3. To better reflect the vocabulary used for racial identity in the 1960s, this paper will employ the term black rather than African American. Harry Edwards, *The Revolt of the Black Athlete* (New York: Free Press, 1969), 38; Jack Scott, *The Athletic Revolution* (New York: Free Press, 1971).

4. Michael E. Lomax, "Revisiting *The Revolt of the Black Athlete*: Harry Edwards and the Making of the New African-American Sport Studies," *Journal of Sport History*, 29 (Fall 2002), 474.

5. Jeffrey O. G. Ogbar, *Black Power: Radical Politics and African American Identity* (Baltimore: John Hopkins University Press, 2004); Stokely Carmichael with Ekwueme Michail Thelwell, *Ready for Revolution: The Life and Struggles of Stokely Carmichael (Kwame Ture)* (New York: Scribner, 2003); Stokely Carmichael and Charles V. Hamilton, *Black Power: The Politics of Liberation* (New York: Vintage Books, 1967).

6. Hugh Pearson, *The Shadow of the Panther: Huey Newton and the Price of Black Power in America* (Reading, Massachusetts: Addison-Wesley, 1994).

7. Judson L. Jeffries, *Huey P. Newton: The Radical Theorist* (Jackson: University Press of Mississippi, 2002); Charles E. Jones, ed., *The Black Panther Party Reconsidered* (Baltimore: Black Classic Press, 1998); Kathleen Cleaver and George Katsiaficas, eds., *Liberation, Imagination, and the Black Panther Party: A New Look at the Panthers and Their Legacy* (New York: Routledge, 2001); Philip S. Foner, *The Black Panthers Speak* (New York: Da Capo, 1995).

8. Rodger Streitmatter, "*Black Panther Newspaper*: A Militant Voice, a Salient Vision," in Todd Vogel, ed., *The Black Press: New Literacy and Historical Essays* (New Brunswick, New Jersey: Rutgers University Press, 2001), 228–41.

9. "*The Black Panther*: Mirror of the People," *The Black Panther*, January 17, 1970, 8.

10. Yohuru Williams, "American Exported Black Nationalism: The Student Coordinating Committee, the Black Panther Party, and the Worldwide Freedom Struggle, 1967–1972," *Negro History Bulletin*, 60 (July–September 1997), 13–20.

11. "Black Pro Athlete Killed by 2 White Clerks," *The Black Panther*, June 10–17, 1968, 3; Edwards, *Revolt of the Black Athlete*, 20.

12. "African Nations to Boycott Olympics," *The Black Panther*, March 16, 1968, 3; Jack Scott, "The White Olympics," *Ramparts*, 6 (May 1968), 54–61.

13. "$100,000 Offered Olympic Boycott Organizers," *The Black Panther*, November 2, 1968, 4.

14. *New York Times*, October 17, 1968; Donald McRae, *In Black & White: The Untold Story of Joe Louis and Jesse Owens* (New York: Scribner, 2002).

15. Amy Bass, *Not the Triumph but the Struggle: The 1968 Olympics and the Making of the Black Athlete* (Minneapolis: University of Minnesota Press, 2002); Douglas Hartman, *Race, Culture, and the Revolt of the Black Athlete: The 1968 Olympic Protests and Their Aftermath* (Chicago: University of Chicago Press, 2003).

16. "BPP Statement," *The Black Panther*, October 26, 1968, 1; and "Berlin, 1936: Political Gestures?" *The Black Panther*, January 25, 1969, 5; "Letter from the Wife of W. E. B. Du Bois," *The Black Panther*, December 21, 1968, 2.

17. "Pig Power Structure Uptight," *The Black Panther*, October 26, 1968, 1; "Solidarity with Mexican Students," *The Black Panther*, July 26, 1969, 18; "Children of Zapata," *The Black Panther*, March 9, 1969, 10.

18. Zirin, "Ali and the Revolt of the Black Athlete," 60–66; Thomas Hauser, *Muhammad Ali in Perspective* (New York: HarperCollins, 1996), 20; Mike Marqusee, *Redemption Song: Muhammad Ali and the Spirit of the Sixties* (New York: Verso, 1999), 232.

19. "Muhammad Ali You're Still Our Champ," *The Black Panther*, March 17, 1971, 15; "Open Letter to Muhammad Ali," *The Black Panther*, April 17, 1971, 5; "Barbee Praises the People's Champ," *The Black Panther*, August 2, 1971, 7.

20. Eldridge Cleaver, *Soul on Ice* (New York: McGraw-Hill, 1968), 91–94, as cited in David K. Wiggins and Patrick B. Miller, *The Unlevel Playing Field: A Documentary History of the African American Experience in Sport* (Urbana: University of Illinois Press, 2005), 303–6.

21. William Patterson, "The Black Athlete and Democracy U.S.A.," *The Black Panther*, December 13, 1969, 13.

22. Jeffries, *Newton: The Radical Theorist*, 100–105.

23. For Charles Finley, Vida Blue, and the Oakland A's see Bruce Markusen, *Baseball's Last Dynasty: Charlie Finley's Oakland A's* (Indianapolis: Masters, 1998); Bill Libby, *Charlie O. and the Angry A's* (New York: Doubleday, 1975); Vida Blue with Bill Libby, *Vida: His Own Story* (Englewood Cliffs, New Jersey: Prentice-Hall, 1971); Ron Reid, "Vida Blue Stars in the Great Bathroom Farce," *Sports Illustrated*, 36 (March 20, 1972), 19–20; Vida Blue, "Next Year Is Going to be Different," *Ebony*, 27 (October 1972), 133.

24. "Black and Blue," *The Black Panther*, May 6, 1972, 7–8; "Congratulations—Oakland A's," *The Black Panther*, October 28, 1972, 8.

25. "The Oakland Coliseum: Fame but No Fortune," *The Black Panther*, March 31, 1973, Supplement XXXVI; James Quirk and Rodney Fort, *Hard Ball: The Abuse of Power in Pro Team Sports* (Princeton, NJ: Princeton University Press, 1999); Paul D. Staudohar and James A. Mangan, eds., *The Business of Professional Sports* (Urbana: University of Illinois Press, 1991); Andrew Zimbalist, *Baseball and Billions: A Probing Look Inside the Big Business of Our National Pastime* (New York: Basic Books, 1994).

26. "Sister Bobbie Watson Won't Play the City's Games," *The Black Panther*, February 12, 1972, 9 and 15–16.

27. "Lamp Post Team Leads Softball League," *The Black Panther*, July 14, 1973, 15; Bobby Seale, *A Lonely Rage: The Autobiography of Bobby Seale* (New York: Times Books, 1978).

28. "We Remember Jackie Robinson," *The Black Panther*, November 4, 1972, 8; Arnold Rampersad, *Jackie Robinson: A Biography* (New York: Knopf, 1997).

29. "Roberto Clemente," *The Black Panther*, January 13, 1973, 5; Kal Wagenheim, *Clemente* (New York: Praeger, 1973).

30. "Hank Aaron Swings Hard against Baseball Racism," *The Black Panther*, August 4, 1973, 13; Hank Aaron with Lonnie Wheeler, *I Had a Hammer: The Hank Aaron Story* (New York: HarperCollins, 1991).

31. "Lee Elder Wins Big One, Qualifies for Masters," *The Black Panther*, April 27, 1974, 21; "New Oakland A's Manager a Proven Racist," *The Black Panther*, March 16, 1974, 19.

32. Paul Hoch, "The Battle over Racism in Sports," *The Black Panther*, March 9, 1974, 19; Mark Naison, "Sports and the American Empire," *The Black Panther*, August 27, 1974, 21.

33. Richard E. Lapchick, ed., *Fractured Focus: Sport as Reflection of Society* (New York: Lexington Books, 1986), 369; John Hoberman, *Darwin's Athletes: How Sport Has Damaged Black America and Preserved the Myth of Race* (New York: Houghton Mifflin, 1997).

34. Harry Edwards, *The Struggle That Must Be: An Autobiography* (New York: Macmillan, 1980), 3.

5

Dark Spirits

The Emergence of Cultural Nationalism on the Sidelines and on Campus

—*Kurt Edward Kemper*

I n early October 1972, the hapless Oregon Ducks football team visited
the Los Angeles Memorial Coliseum to play the host UCLA Bruins.
The Bruins sported the number-one rushing team in the nation and en
route to setting the NCAA single-season rushing record they demolished
the Ducks 65-20. Strangely enough, however, portions of the student
section stood throughout the game with their backs turned to the field of
play and at other times they booed. What generated such animosity from
the student section was not a display of poor sportsmanship towards the
Ducks or frustration over the lopsided score that night. Rather, students
directed their venom at UCLA's cheerleaders by hurling boos, invectives,
and trash in their direction.[1]

Usually consisting of male yell leaders and female song girls, UCLA's
spirit squad in 1972 also consisted, for the first time, of a group known
as cheerleaders. It was this group which faced such withering hostility
in the Oregon game and throughout the season because it forced the
school administration to acknowledge the exclusive nature of the UCLA's
undergraduate extracurriculum; because it had the temerity to challenge
the decades-old sorority control of UCLA spirit groups; because it challenged existing notions of traditional undergraduate femininity; and because all of its members were black. The cheerleaders shrewdly aligned
themselves with the campus Black Student Union at a time when that
group placed itself at the forefront of the movement that would carve

out a greater role for blacks on campus. Thus, the cheerleaders found their local struggle for justice and equality placed within the larger context of Black Power. In addition to its political significance, the event simultaneously demonstrated the emerging strains of black cultural nationalism and campus feminism. In marking a significant departure from demands for mere inclusion to expectations of cultural autonomy in athletic participation, the episode foreshadowed the current debate in athletics regarding the hair, tattoos, and the "gangsta" persona of many athletes, both black and white. The cheerleaders at UCLA not only successfully demanded access to the already acute shortage of female extracurricular outlet on campus, but did so by insisting on replacing dominant assumptions of white femininity with a new Black aesthetic. Thus, blacks, whether playing on the field or posing on the sideline, would no longer apologize for being black.

When William Van Deburg published his groundbreaking examination of Black Power and American culture, *New Day in Babylon* in 1992, he persuasively argued that the Black Power movement exceeded mere political boundaries and implied a broad and far-reaching movement to assert an empowered, autonomous black presence in every facet of American cultural, social, and intellectual life.[2] Indeed, though Black Power initially emerged as an expression of opposition to political exclusion, its most articulate proponents always envisioned a far more expansive application. In their 1992 reexamination of Black Power, Stokely Carmichael and Charles Hamilton declared that Black Power inherently sought out new forms and rejected externally imposed boundaries by its "bold readiness to be 'out of order.'"[3] As such, it was important for adherents of Black Power to exhibit a willingness to assert themselves across a broad spectrum of institutional authority. For Black Power to succeed and resonate with the people, however, it did not have to limit itself to institutions of power per se, such as government, police, and social agencies. Indeed, notions of Black Power could and did arise wherever exclusion or proscription occurred, whenever an establishment expected deferential behavior. Adherents to Black Power felt it was just as important to challenge these institutions not for what success would bring, but for what failure to challenge them at all represented. Thus, Black Power was less about which institutions were challenged than in the process itself. In this context, the clues to deciphering Black Power as a process are not found in the target or the dividends, but the rhetoric and the circumstances.

Historians generally agree that at its heart, Black Power implied control over institutions that affected black life in America. Frequently, the realization of Black Power required the creation of new institutions, such as community empowerment centers at the local level or black studies curricula at the university level. Just as frequently, the assertion of Black Power required a direct challenge to existing white institutional control, a challenge often resisted by white opponents whose opposition left them open to charges of racism. Carmichael explicitly stated that Black Power was "a call to reject the racist institutions and values of this society."[4] On predominantly white college campuses well past the first half of the twentieth century, few institutions could match the exclusiveness and racism of athletic support groups and the Greek system. Embedded in those two mainstays of white American undergraduate life were generations of exclusion across racial lines, proscription across gender lines, and a white male expectation of deferential behavior that crossed lines of both race and gender.

Historian Mary Ellen Hanson has noted that institutionalized cheer-leading evolved in tandem with the development of college football at the end of the nineteenth and early part of the twentieth century. Just as football originated as a student game which was eventually brought under administrative and/or faculty control when those latter bodies saw the game could serve their own interests, cheerleading followed a similar pattern. Originally an independent expression of student spirit and excitement, school spirit leaders existed outside the regulation of school administrators. As universities consciously allowed football, and those associated with it, to serve as the public face of the university as a whole, however, faculty and administrators soon brought cheerleading under its institutional control. Aiding administrative efforts to direct and control the extracurriculum were alliances, sometimes tacit, sometimes explicit, with the campus Greek system.[5] Created in the nineteenth century as a way to replicate the social stratification of American society, Greek let-ter organizations on predominantly white campuses were exclusive by intention. As such, almost all limited membership to Euro-Americans, while others went so far as to exclude Jews and Catholics as well.[6] According to Paula Fass, white fraternities and sororities, already "conspicuous in cam-pus life by the 1890s," were "at the center of college life" by the decade of the 1920s. On predominantly white college campuses, Greek domination of such extracurricular activities as cheerleading came with the sanction of university administrators who essentially found a partner willing to promote a benign university image acceptable to institutional authority which was "useful in the supervision and control of students."[7] Thus, university administrators tacitly reserved much of the extracurriculum on predominantly white campuses, particularly cheerleading, for white students.

In a phenomena witnessed on campuses across the nation beginning in the years following World War II, fraternities and sororities at UCLA came under increasingly withering criticism over their racially and religiously exclusive membership clauses. Although houses that insisted on maintaining such clauses finally faced dissociation by the university in 1965, they remained the campus's Ancièn Regime when it came to matters of race and liberal progress. Whereas their hold on campus politics diminished with changing social values of the time, the dominance of cheerleading by the sororities remained as steadfast as ever.[8] This sorority dominance also reinforced longstanding social and cultural assumptions of collegiate beauty and femininity. Aided largely by a culture based on consumption, shaped and pushed by the advertising industry, those assumptions created a homogenized collegiate image of white, middle-class girls whose main responsibility on campus was preparing themselves to win a man. In her examination of American youth in the 1920s, Paula Fass noted, "freshmen arrived aping the mannerisms and styles associated with the college image. Conformity to what was believed to be the collegiate style epitomized by [the Greeks] was already self-imposed."[9] By the 1950s, sociologist Wini Breines argues, "being middle-class and white were the indispensable building blocks [to beauty]. . . . It was a white Anglo-Saxon Protestant version of beauty that millions of girls . . . could never hope to emulate."[10] Even students at UCLA who recognized the stifling nature of such conformity felt powerless to confront it, by outwardly accepting it but inwardly rejecting it. This included recognizing, but never questioning, the exclusion of non-whites from the ideal.[11]

Compounding the pervasiveness of traditional white undergraduate femininity at UCLA was the fact that female students largely absented themselves from the stirrings of the feminist movement of the 1960s and early 1970s. Women played only peripheral roles in existing student activist movements on campus and rarely found their voice when sexist inequality appeared.[12] Traditionally the most vocal advocate of liberal reform, even the student newspaper, *The Daily Bruin*, ran two egregiously sexist advertisements during the period. One, advertising a t-shirt which male undergraduates were presumably expected to purchase for their girlfriends, featured a female with large breasts, no bra, and visibly erect nipples in a shirt that read simply, "Cornucopia." The caption for the ad stated, "You may have to explain it to her." The other, for a local music store advertising a trade-in program, also featured a large breasted female, nipples erect, without a bra, wearing a shirt stating, "Tit for tat." Neither ad garnered any protest, published letters to the editor to speak of, nor act of contrition on the part of the editorial staff.[13] Indeed, when Dr. Rosemary Park accepted an administrative position at UCLA in 1967 after working at schools in the East, she was stunned at the socially conservative nature of mainstream campus women. Their lack of feminist perspective ascribed them to "a prior generation" in her opinion.[14] Far from threatening the status quo, sorority women were at the forefront of maintaining a culture that ascribed them a privileged role as esteemed socialites and campus sex symbols. Thus, the Greek/song girl alliance of the period represented not a cross-section of the student body, but a limited, exclusive, conservative minority, replete with traditional assumptions of white undergraduate femininity. For black students to breech this wall would require a challenge not only to the Greek monopoly, but their own perceptions of beauty and the acceptance of a black aesthetic by a larger white audience.

The pervasiveness of Greek domination in the spirit groups and the challenges of minority students to demand and receive equality of opportunity did not suddenly come into focus in the fall of 1972. Indeed, those very issues arose sixteen years earlier, with very different results. Like most large universities at the time, particularly those with big-time athletic programs, UCLA maintained an all-female organization, the Bruin Belles, whose purpose was to serve as hostesses for campus visitors and various functions. Within the context of athletics, they frequently served as dates for the visiting teams. While the Greeks did not completely monopolize Bruin Belle membership, the vast majority of girls belonged to sororities and none of the handful of minority students who participated belonged to Greek houses. When the University of North Carolina football team came west in October 1956 to play USC, the Tar Heel head coach asked the Bruin Belles, rather than USC's group, as would have been customary, to serve as hostesses. Although UNC was integrated, its football team was not and UCLA's director of student activities asked black Belles to forgo their hostess responsibilities on this occasion. Although the incident garnered two signed editorials in the *Bruin* and three letters to the editor the day after the story broke, it received no coverage whatsoever in the two major Los Angeles dailies at the time and the incident soon passed.[15] Indeed, as further evidence of popular assumptions of acceptable activities for undergraduate women, while the *Los Angeles Times* ignored the potential racial controversy at UCLA, it ran an above-the-fold article, complete with pictures, of the finalists, all white and Greek, for homecoming queen at USC.[16] The absence of any sustained protest on the part of a black student group or an administrative policy prohibiting future "debacles" of this sort can only be explained by looking through the prism of the Cold War and examining the sacrosanct campus role played by the Greeks and the perceived threat of minority student activism.

In the years following World War II, mostly white student activists attempted to use the existing student government machinery to challenge campus discrimination. The fact that much of that discrimination emanated from the Greeks made them a constant target throughout the 1950s. However, the entrenchment of the Greek system both at UCLA and in the American university system as a whole made them a tough opponent to dislodge. The entrenchment that Fass found before World War II grew even stronger in the 1950s. From UCLA's founding in 1919 until 1965, only three non-Greeks captured the student body presidency.[17] The widely held assumption that fraternities and sororities represented everything wholesome, fun, decent, and memorable about American campus life gained added credence during the Cold War when anything which was held in such esteem took on the added symbolism of providing a bulwark against Communism. Addressing the National Interfraternity Council in 1960, Senator Barry Goldwater of Arizona declared that "where fraternities are not allowed, communism flourishes," referring to the Greek system as "a bastion of American strength."[18]

Defenders of the Greek system made this connection even more direct when it labeled the activists challenging discrimination as Communist or Communist-inspired. When the California State Legislature considered a 1957 bill which would have prohibited discrimination in any organization publicly affiliated, including those on state university campuses, one critic claimed the legislative effort was the fault of "minority groups seeking to legislate social privilege and create a 'classless society . . .' The target is really what we know as the 'American Way of Life.' "[19] UCLA's Dean of Students during the period, Milton Hahn, saw every attempt to move against the Greek system within the context of the Cold War. In a 1954 letter to UCLA's chancellor about an attempt to end discrimination in off-campus housing, Hahn alleged a vast communist conspiracy against not just the Greeks, but UCLA as a whole, claiming such groups had provided "constant pressure for years to get questionable organizations into the University family so they can damage UCLA from the inside."[20] The extent to which the administration at the time favored the Greeks seemingly knew no bounds. One of the staunchest opponents of the legislature's 1957 anti-discrimination bill, the Interfraternity Alumni Association of Southern California, retained the lobbying and advisory services of Dr. Clyde Johnson, who was then *currently on the state payroll* (emphasis added) as Assistant Dean of Undergraduates, an arrangement well known by both his immediate supervisor, the Associate Dean, as well as the university chancellor.[21]

One of the groups Hahn found so "questionable" was a student chapter of the NAACP. On several occasions, Hahn rejected the group's application for status as an on-campus organization, stating that its control by a national organization did "not fit well into the . . . operational structure of the University."[22] Hahn argued that he was merely following regental directive by stating "the Regents would have to change policy" for the NAACP to gain recognition.[23] The fact that the Berkeley campus, home of the Regents, had granted recognition to the NAACP as far back as 1953 highlighted Hahn's duplicity, as did his reliance on the "national organization" argument, which should have ruled out the fraternities and sororities as well. The NAACP attacked Hahn for this hypocrisy when it asked, "why your administration has shown such favoritism for the Greek letter organizations, who have publicly declared that they are both required and willing to [continue their discriminatory clauses]?"[24] The answer of course, lay in Milton Hahn's perceptions of the Greek system as upholding everything "American" while viewing groups such as the NAACP as "subversive" and destructive to UCLA and, hence, the very fabric of the Republic. Willard Johnson, president of the student NAACP at the time and UCLA's second black student body president in 1956–57 summed up the administration's thinking as being "overly suspicious of students concerned about race relations, restrictive clauses, the independent authority of student government, and student concern with broader social and political issues."[25]

Amidst this atmosphere, it was little wonder the Bruin Belle controversy of 1958 engendered so little discussion or protest. Criticizing the makeup or policies of the Bruin Belles meant challenging the Greeks; criticizing the administration's role in the affair meant running afoul of Milton Hahn, either of which exposed such critics to the likelihood of redbaiting. Most importantly, the episode illustrated the importance of institutions in the process of affecting social change. Without control of student government, unable to fend off administrative interference, and lacking their own advocacy groups, student activists found themselves vulnerable. So long as the administration withheld recognition of the campus NAACP, and its attendant benefits of student funds, campus resources, and equal-space provision in the *Bruin*, minority students and their allies stood on the outside looking in, leaving participants in things like athletics and the Bruin Belles at the mercy of others or excluded altogether.

The tremendous social upheaval of the 1960s provided a concerted challenge to such a status quo, however. Larger numbers of black students on predominantly white campuses such as UCLA soon challenged existing exclusions and proscriptions by demanding equal access to the campus extracurriculum. White Greek domination of UCLA's athletic support groups began eroding in the mid-1960s with the male Yell King position. In 1966, the student body elected Eddie Anderson as the school's first black Yell King. Anderson, according to Hanson, is generally "credited with introducing soul yells and soul cheers to collegiate cheering in California," though Anderson still made frequent use of more traditional cheers and techniques.[26] The students again elected a black Yell King in 1969 in Vernoy Hite who, unlike Anderson, then subsequently selected five other black males along with one white student to serve as yell leaders. Hite immediately intimated that cheering in 1969 would take on a far more culturally racialized meaning than Anderson's tenure by naming his cheer theme "The Soul Plane." Asked what that meant, he replied, "We gonna funk!" Hite's Soul Plane placed an emphasis on what he called rhythm cheers, a maximum of body movement and a call-and-response interaction with the crowd, as opposed to the static and passive engagement of the student section in the past.[27] The Soul Plane theme did not sit well with some students, perhaps because they felt uncomfortable with the increased importance and prominence of muscular black male bodies or merely because they felt they took attention away from the football team. The criticism, however, took on an overtly racialized tone. One anonymous note in the *Daily Bruin* derisively referred to Hite's theme as "Soul Train," telling him to "go back to Compton."[28]

While this sort of criticism may have been aimed only at Vernoy Hite, it is crucial to remember that blacks made several noteworthy gains on campus at the same time. Two years before Hite's election as Yell King, black students founded a Black Student Union (BSU) and pushed shortly thereafter for the creation of *Nommo*, the campus's black student media outlet. Largely as a result of the efforts and energies of the BSU, the school's administration agreed to create a campus Black Studies Center in 1969.[29] The authority and presence the BSU enjoyed did not result from forceful threats or ghetto bluster as it did on many campuses, but from an articulate and intellectual vision for both the social and academic role of blacks on campus. The Chancellor at the time, Dr. Charles E. Young, would later refer to the group, which included a future Rhodes Scholar, as "the finest group of students UCLA ever had."[30] Armed with the support of the Chancellor and some of the faculty, the BSU quickly established itself as a vocal component in the evolving dialogue that elevated students to fully vested shareholders in the university enterprise. The BSU quickly set about criticizing and exposing campus groups which persisted in maintaining exclusive and potentially racist practices. Due to its sheer visibility both on and off campus, no group loomed as large as the song girls.

Not surprisingly, when the student association announced the 1968 song girl squad, no black students made the squad and all seven hailed from campus sororities. Unlike the male Yell King position determined by a campus-wide election, a tryout process selected the song girls, determined by a handful of student personalities, with the returning song girls holding the preponderant voting majority. Thus, for years the song girls had been virtually self-selecting and the group's exclusivity self-perpetuating. This situation was so well known that one student critic later referred to the process as "tradition" to have "seven white song girls every year from the sororities."[31] In 1968, however, two black students made it to the finals before being eliminated. After allegations surfaced that only sorority sisters of returning song girls were given help learning the tryout routine, the BSU cried foul. The group circulated a petition demanding a reexamination of the process, to which the administration responded by adding the highest black vote getter to the squad.[32] The decision to add the black student to the squad also came with a stern warning that the entire process needed to be revamped. "It is entirely incumbent on us right now," intoned one official, "to come up with a selection process for next year which will avoid these problems."[33] The comment would prove prophetic.

The administration's resolution of the issue, however, did not sit well with the BSU. In a letter to the *Daily Bruin*, one member criticized the administration's unwillingness to reform the entire selection process immediately and labeled the inclusion of a single black student as tokenism.[34] The specter of tokenism had always threatened to derail the Black Power movement with what Stokely Carmichael called "apparent power as opposed to real power."[35] By the very use of the term tokenism, its employers perceived the episode within the context of Black Power. The context grew even more explicit in light of events the previous spring when *Nommo* gave such tokenism a localized label: "Black Queenism." The fall of 1968 witnessed no less than four black homecoming queens at southern California universities, including UCLA, USC, UC Riverside, and California State at Los Angeles.[36] A *Nommo* editorial declared Black Queenism a "political phenomena," decrying such "circus coronations" as a prime example of Carmichael's warnings of apparent power. Declaring the public university "a microcosm of [how] society-at-large operates," Black Queenism was "only a political tactic to create the illusion of power." The editorial finished with a blunt statement of Black Power: "We do not seek to participate in our destiny, we seek to control it."[37]

Nommo and the BSU were not the only ones on campus who saw the events of 1968 in racialized political terms. White student opposition to the song girl controversy criticized neither the girls involved nor the administration for their attempted resolution of it, but the BSU for involving itself at all. One student decried the BSU's attempt "to force a Negro girl on the songleading squad," and alleged that the BSU pressured the administration "into accepting less qualified girls."[38] Though no force, real or implied, had been used or even alleged up to that point illustrates that at least some white students were growing uneasy with the increasing attention on campus paid to matters of race, seeing only a demand for "special privileges."

The advocacy role played by campus BSUs throughout the country intensified in the late 1960s and early 1970s, and they frequently targeted the exclusion of blacks from athletic support groups. Mary Ellen Hanson has uncovered several incidents where black student activism forced a change in the makeup and selection process of these groups. At Purdue in 1967, a black campus group demanded black representation on the all-white spirit squad when all ten members came from the school's Greek system. Campus protests over similar exclusions at high schools in Illinois, New York, and North Carolina, resulted in boycotts, walkouts, rioting, and at least one death. None of these cases however, equaled the sequence of events that unfolded at UCLA in 1972.[39]

In both 1969 and 1970, the student selection process named a single black student to the song girls, but 1971 again found an all-white group.

Spring song girl tryouts in 1972 similarly produced a squad lacking any black faces, with six of the seven students selected coming from campus sororities and four from the same house as the captain. Before conclusion of the spring term, five black students who had tried out, but were cut because they "couldn't dance as well as the white girls," challenged the selection procedure and its results with the Stadium Executive Committee (SEC), an administrative agency within the athletic department responsible for the student spirit groups. The committee refused to reconsider the process or the judging criteria, resulting in one of the five students bringing the matter before the Student Legislative Council (SLC) in a forty-three-page report. While the SLC promptly referred the matter to an ad hoc investigatory committee, the SEC offered no comment on the matter whatsoever. The student investigation criticized not only the self-perpetuating selection process and the preponderant role of sororities, but the SEC's actions as well. The student report called on the committee to declare the tryouts null and void and initiate a new selection process immediately. The committee refused but agreed instead to the startling compromise of allowing the five girls who felt discriminated against to form a second spirit group, known as the cheerleaders.[40] Thus, UCLA, the school which so loudly touted its integrationist tradition that included former students and alumni like Jackie Robinson, Rafer Johnson, and Arthur Ashe, found itself in the fall of 1972 with two separate spirit squads, one white and one black.

By most accounts, the experience was a disaster. By the cheerleaders' own admission, they came unprepared to the season opener against defending national champion Nebraska for the logistics and intimidation of the 100,000 seat LA Coliseum. By the second home game, however, spectators and other spirit groups had already turned against the cheerleaders.[41] On two different occasions, the *Bruin* editorialized on how badly the atmosphere at football games had deteriorated. The male yell leaders, the white song girls, and the black cheerleaders not only lacked coordination and cooperation, but the student cheering section grew hostile on occasion. One editorial referred to the efforts as "possibly the worst showing of UCLA spirit groups in recent years," claiming the only spirit evident was "divisiveness."[42] A month later, the paper described the spirit groups' efforts as "unorganized, annoying, and chaotic," calling for the abolition of all three if the situation did not improve.[43] Many students also made their displeasure known, though they seemingly aimed all of their animosity at the cheerleaders. Sigma Chi fraternity members stood en masse and turned their backs at the Oregon game whenever the cheerleaders performed, only to retake their seats upon the squad's completion and boo while other students threw garbage at the cheerleaders.[44] Worse than the public humiliation was the private intimidation and harassment they received. Anonymous letters and phone calls from both on and off campus threatened violence or suggested the women's actions resulted from a lack of sexual attention. Letters and phone calls suggested that an absence of romantic male attention spurred the women's behavior by asking rhetorically, "Where are the black men at UCLA?" With even less subtlety, several midnight callers crudely exclaimed, "We know you're just doing this because you like to fuck." The intensity and viciousness of the calls forced the group leader, Marilyn Joshua, to have an unlisted phone number, even though she also served as a dorm counselor, a mentoring-type position that required maximum accessibility.[45]

Criticism from more mainstream sources also came in racialized terms, albeit more discreetly. Marilyn Burkett of the affluent Rolling Hills area of Los Angeles wrote a letter to the *Times* to register her "disgust" at the cheerleaders, whom she labeled "uncouth, unclever, and uncute . . . the cheers and accompanying hand gestures are pathetically juvenile."[46] Burkett held up for special condemnation what she called the group's "soul cheers" as indicative of their lack of originality. Her criticisms of the group, particularly labeling them "uncouth" suggested that in the eyes of Burkett and many others, any attempts by black students to encroach on previously all-white domains of the extracurriculum placed them outside the bounds of deferential propriety. Which is to say, they ceased to be "good Negroes?" Additionally, Burkett's attack on the girls' physical attractiveness revealed that any challenge to traditional representations of undergraduate femininity involved hostile assumptions about black physical features.

On campus, criticism stayed away from Burkett's nakedly racialist assumptions, but still linked the cheerleaders episode with the ongoing social upheaval surrounding the issue of race. A letter to the *Bruin* suggested the administration only permitted the second squad "in order to avoid a major conflict with the black students."[47] Indeed, as the controversy continued throughout the fall, one white student politico opposed disbanding the cheerleaders because "we don't want to start another Cornell," referring to the armed takeover of that campus by the local BSU during parents day weekend in 1968.[48]

The hostility directed at the cheerleaders did not, however, deter them. Though the administration, through the SEC, allowed the cheerleaders official status, they did not provide them any money. Thus the group threw parties over the summer and early fall to pay for their uniforms. When the SEC discussed the issue in meetings, male members of the BSU attended to show support, an effort that elicited racist criticism when white attendees declared that by their mere presence, BSU members attempted to intimidate the committee. Interpretations of black students' assertion of participation as threats of force or attempted intimidation, which had surfaced in the 1968 episode as well as more recent references to the situation at Cornell and the SEC meetings, revealed much about the presumptions of such critics and their ready acceptance of the threatening, militant, black male stereotype. After the Oregon game and the booing and trash throwing, the BSU also marshaled the black student body to attend games and sit as a block directly in front of the cheerleaders to deter continued hostility, a move that largely succeeded. Through it all, the cheerleaders maintained their sense of humor, privately referring to themselves as the Dark Spirits, suggesting not just their skin color, but their own facetious acknowledgment of how others, particularly the administration, viewed them.[49]

Indeed, the discomfort felt by the UCLA administration and the potential challenge to the school's finely crafted image as an interracial paradise dating back to Jackie Robinson's day created no small amount of angst. Chancellor Young said of the group, "if it had been my decision, their group would not have been created. Whoever made the decision to create the group got us into a peck of trouble."[50] Athletic Director J. D. Morgan termed the entire controversy "ridiculous," while another campus official dismissed the episode as "a teapot tempest."[51] In an attempt to minimize the appearance of conflict between the spirit groups, the SEC ordered the two female groups to compose a dance routine that included both of them. Additionally, when the groups posed for their yearbook photograph, while the Yell Leaders stood together in the center row, the song girls and cheerleaders were perfectly spaced so that nobody from one group stood next to another member of their squad and that an equal number from each group occupied each of the three rows in the photograph, providing the illusion of seamless cooperation, suggesting the three groups created a single, harmonious whole.[52] The obvious impression that the photograph had been posed was unmistakable. One participant declared that the "picture was done to send a message that the problem had been resolved."[53]

That many white students might oppose the creation of a second all-black squad in 1972 should come as no surprise. The issue offended their basic and long-held beliefs in integration and their assumptions about equality of opportunity. Additionally, previous criticism of blacks as cheerleaders, both male and female, came in racialized terms. For black students however, the incident indicated an increasing lack of patience for white liberals to slowly discover every form of discrimination and the process required to root it out. Had the BSU chosen to make sorority domination the issue and demand change from that perspective, they could foresee a very predictable process. Existing student institutions such as the *Daily Bruin* and the SLC would discuss the issue over a length of time, with the SLC possibly sending the issue to a committee, further drawing out the process, while the discussions of the SEC, an administrative body, occurred outside the purview of the students entirely. At the earliest, these groups might reach a resolution in time for the following year's selection process, with no guarantees that resolution would be satisfactory to the BSU. In addition, the very reliance on institutions such as the *Bruin* and the SLC ran counter to the notion of Black Power. Quite simply, black students felt they had waited long enough.

The coexistent themes of race and gender ran throughout the entire episode. When white students challenged the very creation of the cheerleaders, they used the same rhetoric they had used when challenging things like minority special admissions programs or the creation of the Black Studies Center. Additionally, the use of crude carnal language reduced the cheerleaders to the timeworn libidinous Jezebel myth of plantation slavery. Beginning in the antebellum period, whites mythologized the African female as "governed almost entirely by her libido," someone who lacked the Victorian notions of self-restraint, social respectability, and sexual dignity. Whites described African women and their female descendants as someone who sought constant sexual gratification, particularly from whites, and who were even "gratified by the criminal advances of Saxons."[54] As such, critics racialized the episode and made the issue gender-specific by sexualizing the debate. Thus, while Vernoy Hite faced derisive, racialist references in 1969, the added criticisms of gender in 1972 revealed that critics found the cheerleaders' challenge to traditional undergraduate femininity every bit as troubling as their race.

The episode garnered so much attention and achieved such significance in 1972 for the fundamental reason that athletic support groups remained one of the only avenues of participation for undergraduate women on American college campuses at this time. Scholars have demonstrated that college sports emerged as the dominant form of the undergraduate extracurriculum throughout the twentieth century, providing those who participated in it with exalted status.[55] Prior to the passage of Title IX legislation, however, all undergraduate women faced the marginalization ensured by their exclusion from one of the central components of American undergraduate life. Indeed, even the band at UCLA, and many other schools, remained closed to women at this time.[56] When black women demanded equal access to the few extracurricular institutions available to women, it exaggerated the already acute shortage of acceptable female outlets on campus. By comparison, when black males began participating as Yell Kings, even to the exclusion of whites as in 1969, the opposition never reached the fever pitch of 1972 because male students enjoyed so many more options within the extracuriculum. In contrast, faced with the loss of a monopoly on athletic support groups, white undergraduate women had nowhere to go and the campus had nowhere to put them.

The fact that cheerleading provided women their only role within the athletic venue also illustrated the limitations of women attempting to use sport as a platform for social change. The absence of mainstream news coverage of the event marked only one example of that. Because it involved women and cheerleading, and thus "not really sport," sports editors largely ignored the story; though because it was controversial, particularly involving race, women's and social page editors stayed away from the story as well, leaving it to languish largely forgotten. Even when the *Times* finally covered the controversy, it paternalistically noted the renown of UCLA's "pretty young things who bounce around in front of the stands."[57] The coalescence of sport and racial protest by the early 1970s, however, was well established and earlier instances had received tremendous coverage. The threat of a potential boycott of the 1968 Olympics by America's black athletes garnered national attention. While the scope of the story was much greater, occurring on a national, indeed an international, scale, it too, illustrated the marginalization of women within the athletic venue. Although American black women, mostly in track and field, enjoyed tremendous success, including gold medals and world records, the boycott's organizing group, the Olympic Committee for Human Rights (OCHR), completely excluded them, largely under the assumption that race trumped gender in the hierarchy of social injustice. According to Amy Bass, "it was assumed that black female athletes did not mind their exclusion from the [boycott], because in the face of [white elitism and racism], it was understood that they would, quite literally, stand by their men."[58] The national media also ignored whether female athletes would take part or even their opinions on the subject. While both *Life* and *Sports Illustrated* provided extensive discussion of the role of the black athlete that year, neither discussed women in any capacity other than as objects.[59] Black female athletes, according to Bass, were "treated as virtually a nonfactor . . . by both the [OCHR] and the media, reflecting . . . the subordinate position of women within athletics."[60] Thus, so long as women continued to be excluded, ignored, or limited to the sidelines within the realm of sport, their ability to use sport as a vehicle to effect social change remained severely proscribed.

Within the context of the Black Power movement, the episode is even more instructive. At one level lies the direct challenge to traditional undergraduate femininity as it had been defined by generations of college students on predominantly white campuses. White skin, sorority membership, and passive behavior served as the standard up to this period. As such, successful participation in campus activities such as beauty contests and cheerleading required complete conformity to the existing ideal of traditional undergraduate femininity. By their mere insistence on equal access to the activities of undergraduate campus life, the cheerleaders effectively shunned generations of such expectations. More than that, it also required them to embrace what had traditionally been held in contempt, the physical features of blacks, particularly women. For many individuals coming to grips with a new black, as distinctly separate from Negro, consciousness, the disposition of their hairstyle said much about their politics. As Kobena Mercer has written, "within racism's bipolar codification of human worth, black people's hair has been historically devalued as the most visible stigmata of blackness, second only to skin."[61] The willingness, indeed the insistence, of students of the Black Power era to wear their hair in the natural or "Afro" fashion, to lead "soul cheers," to dance demonstratively in the black style in front of tens of thousands of white spectators not only rejected the existing norms but embraced a new Black Power aesthetic, or what Van Deburg calls the "soul style." "If [blacks] were to succeed," he argued, "they must define and establish their own values while rejecting the cultural prescriptions of their oppressors."[62] Noted activist and scholar Angela Davis has written that part of both her gender and racial consciousness came when she realized she "needed to say 'Black is beautiful' . . . I needed to explore my African ancestry, to don African garb, to wear my hair natural."[63] Thus, while Black Power implied a larger shift of control at the institutional level, it also meant a fundamental revolution in self-worth at the individual level. Head cheerleader Marilyn

Joshua explicitly stated, "It was a self-esteem issue. We were not ready to accept [second-class status]," a sentiment similarly echoed by other shapers of the Black Power era.[64] Noted black feminist author Alice Walker wrote of one of her characters, "A necessary act of liberation within myself was to acknowledge the beauty of *black* black women."[65] Stokely Carmichael was even more direct, "We have to stop being ashamed of being black. A broad nose, a thick lip, nappy hair is us and we are going to call that beautiful whether they like it or not."[66] Finally, the embrace of Black Power also sought to confront existing white stereotypes of blacks, in this instance, the libidinous black female and the militant black male. Thus, the embrace of the Black Power aesthetic, at both the physical and intellectual levels, was nothing less than the tangible manifestation of the emerging concept of "Black is Beautiful!"

It is ironic that while the episode illustrated the limitations of women in sport, it marked an evolution in the struggle for black athletic participation. By the early 1970s, activists resolved the conflict over the inclusion of black athletes. Every major professional team was integrated and in the college ranks, even the die-hard Southeastern Conference accepted integration.[67] The next phase witnessed a rejection by black athletes of the cultural proscriptions whites had imposed since the days of Jackie Robinson. Once it became apparent that blacks had much to offer in terms of talent, whites accepted black athletes, so long as they did not appear "too black." White criticisms of hair length and style, dialogue, and behavior illustrated that they were happy to have black teammates and heroes, provided they did not call attention to their blackness. If Black Power suggested that rhetoric was just as important as results, then the ability to strike the pose equaled the right to play the game.

The cultural conflict in athletics sparked by the Black Power era has continued unabated to the present day. Former professional football player-turned-academic Michael Oriard noted that in the 1970s, while black players in the NFL increasingly tended to engage in the gripped thumbs "soul shake" before the pre-game coin toss, one white veteran angrily refused, extending a hand to a black opponent at mid-field saying, "Regular, damn it, regular!" By the following decade, football players, predominantly black, initiated "elaborately choreographed" end zone dances and on-field celebrations. According to Oriard, "an indisputable black football style had arrived."[68] Even more recently, when the NBA placed Allen Iverson on the cover of its magazine, it airbrushed his upper torso tattoos in an attempt to minimize his "thuggish" image. Additionally, much has been made of the cornrow hairstyle that Iverson and many other pro athletes wear as too evocative of street gangsters.[69] For many, the pose is still troublesome, but for others it has achieved unparalleled importance, thanks to the tremendous increase in the marketing of athletic apparel. Mainstream media publications such as *Sports Illustrated* and sports apparel manufacturers such as Nike now speak openly of a player's ability to bring "street cred" to an endorsement relationship. The increased purchasing power of youth-oriented inner city consumers is undeniable when Iverson responds to critical questions about his lifestyle that includes associations with known felons and ownership of guns by stating, "I'm all about keepin' it real, yo." For these consumers, it is all about the pose.

While the 1972 UCLA cheerleaders were not attempting to attract a marketing demographic, they were, in their own way, about "keepin' it real." As one cheerleader later remarked, "We felt [whites] are kind of culturally deprived if they've never seen cheers that came out of black schools."[70] In that respect, they affected the pose and the rhetoric of Black Power simply by asserting that they would participate on their political terms and embrace their cultural practices and do so, most importantly, by not apologizing for either.

Notes

1. For a discussion of UCLA football, see Hendrik Van Leuven, *Touchdown UCLA: The Complete Account of Bruin Football* (Tomball, TX: Strode, 1982); Steve Springer and Michael Arkush, *60 Years of USC-UCLA Football* (Stamford, CT: Longmeadow, 1991).

2. William Van Deburg, *New Day in Babylon: The Black Power Movement and American Culture, 1965–1975* (Chicago: University of Chicago Press, 1992).

3. Kwame Toure (Stokely Carmichael) and Charles V. Hamilton, *Black Power: The Politics of Liberation in America* (New York: Vintage, 1992).

4. Ibid., p. 44.

5. Mary Ellen Hanson, *Go! Fight! Win!: Cheerleading in American Culture* (Bowling Green, OH: Bowling Green State University Popular Press, 1995), 12–14. On the development of college football by students and its subsequent takeover by university officials, see Ronald A. Smith, *Sports and Freedom: The Rise of Big-Time College Athletics* (New York: Oxford University Press, 1988).

6. Anthony W. James, "The Defenders of Tradition: College Social Fraternities, Race and Gender, 1945–1980," (unpublished PhD diss: University of Mississippi, 1998).

7. Paula Fass, *The Damned and the Beautiful: American Youth in the 1920s* (New York: New York University Press, 1977), 144–45. See also Helen Lefkowitz Horowitz, *Campus Life: Undergraduate Cultures from the End of the Eighteenth Century to the Present* (Chicago: University of Chicago Press, 1987), 39, 50.

8. For a thorough discussion of the dominance and the eventual fall of the Greek system at UCLA, see Kurt Kemper, "Reformers in the Marketplace of Ideas: Student Activism and American Democracy in Cold War America," (unpublished PhD diss: Louisiana State University, 2000).

9. Fass, *The Damned and the Beautiful*, 150–51. Elaine Tyler May has shown how such gendered conformity reached into the 1950s. Women, according to May, found little reward, and great risk, in stepping outside the bounds of existing assumptions of beauty and propriety, Elaine Tyler May, *Homeward Bound: American Families in the Cold War Era* (New York: Basic Books, 1988).

10. Wini Breines, *Young, White, and Miserable: Growing Up Female in the Fifties* (Boston: Beacon, 1992), 95–96.

11. Bonnie Morris, *The High School Scene in the Fifties: Voices from West L.A.* (Westport, Conn.: Bergin & Garvey, 1997). Six of Morris's seven interview subjects for the book, all white, matriculated to UCLA.

12. Kemper, "Reformers," 241–45.

13. The ads ran in the *Daily Bruin* during the spring quarter 1972.

14. Rosemary Park, "Liberal Arts in the Modern University," p. 132, UCLA Oral History Program, Department of Special Collections, Young Research Library, UCLA.

15. *Daily Bruin*, October 7, 1958, and October 8, 1956.

16. *Los Angeles Times*, October 10, 1958.

17. William C. Ackerman, *My Fifty-Year Love-In at UCLA* (Los Angeles: Fashion Press, 1969). Ackerman provides brief biographies, including campus affiliations, of each student body president.

18. *New York Times*, November 27, 1960.

19. James, "Defenders of Tradition," p. 82.

20. Letter from Milton E. Hahn to Chancellor Raymond B. Allen, dated November 3, 1954, obtained and reprinted in *The Observer*, an underground student paper, March 30, 1955, found in folder "1954," Box #6, Student Activism Collection, University Archives, Powell Library, UCLA.

21. Letter from Byron Atkinson to Chancellor Raymond B. Allen, April 24, 1957, folder #247, Box #325, Records of the Chancellor's Office, Administrative Files, 1936–59, University Archives, Powell Library, UCLA. For a contextual discussion of the bill and Johnson's role in its defeat, see James, "Defenders of Tradition."

22. Letter from Milton E. Hahn to Miriam Fisher, undated, reprinted as "An Open Letter," *Daily Bruin*, October 31, 1955.

23. *Daily Bruin*, October 31, 1955.

24. *Daily Bruin*, November 9, 1955.

25. Ackerman, *Love-In*, 87–88.

26. Hanson, *Go! Fight! Win!*, 83.

27. *Nommo*, May 19, 1969.

28. *Nommo*, October 28, 1969.

29. For the evolution of the BSU at UCLA and its role in the creation of the school's ethnic studies component, see Kemper, "Reformers," chapter 5.

30. Oral interview by the author, Dr. Charles E. Young, Los Angeles, CA, August 8, 1999.

31. *Daily Bruin*, September 28, 1972.

32. *Daily Bruin*, May 23, 1968.

33. Ibid.

34. *Daily Bruin*, May 28, 1968.

35. *Nommo*, December 4, 1968.

36. Ibid.

37. Ibid.

38. *Daily Bruin*, May 23, 1968.

39. Hanson, *Go! Fight! Win!*, 33–34.

40. *Daily Bruin*, September 27, October 2, 3, 4, November 28, 1972; *Nommo*, October 30, 1972: *Los Angeles Times*, October 17, 1972, part III, p. 1; the "dance" quote comes from Oral Interview by the author with Dr. Marilyn Joshua-Shearer, August 3, 2003, San Diego, CA.

41. Joshua-Shearer interview.

42. *Daily Bruin*, September 28, 1972.

43. *Daily Bruin*, October 4, 1972.

44. *Daily Bruin*, October 3, 1972.

45. Joshua-Shearer interview.

46. *Los Angeles Times*, October 21, 1972.

47. *Daily Bruin*, September 28, 1972. UCLA was not the only campus to witness resistance to black cheerleaders and the use of "soul" cheers. At San Jose State during the same period, cheerleaders were met "with complete silence" when confronted with soul cheers, see *Los Angeles Times*, October 29, 1972.

48. *Daily Bruin*, October 3, 1972.

49. *Los Angeles Times*, October 17, 1972.

50. *Daily Bruin*, November 22, 1972.

51. *Los Angeles Times*, October 17, 1972.

52. *Southern Campus*, 1973.

53. Joshua-Shearer interview.

54. For a discussion of the Jezebel myth, as well as other stereotypical interpretations of the black female dating to the nineteenth century, see Deborah Gray White, *Aren't I a Woman?: Females Slaves in the Plantation South* (New York: W. W. Norton, 1985), pp. 27–31.

55. Smith, *Sports and Freedom*, Fass, *The Damned and the Beautiful*, Horowitz, *Campus Life*.

56. *Daily Bruin*, May 9, 1972.

57. *Los Angeles Times*, October 17, 1972.

58. Amy Bass, *Not the Triumph but the Struggle: The 1968 Olympics and the Making of the Black Athlete* (Minneapolis: University of Minnesota Press, 2002), 189–90.

59. See "The Olympic Jolt: 'Hell no, don't go!'" *Life*, (March 15, 1968); Jack Olsen, "The Black Athlete—A Shameful Story," *Sports Illustrated*, 28 (July 1, 1968): 12–18. The *SI* article ran as a five-part series throughout the month of July and Olsen ultimately expanded it into a book with the same title. For a discussion of the significance of the article, "the single most important piece in *SI*'s history," see Michael MacCambridge, *The Franchise: A History of Sports Illustrated Magazine* (New York: Hyperion Books, 1997).

60. Bass, *Not the Triumph but the Struggle*, 204.

61. Kobena Mercer, "Black Hair/Style Politics," in Kobena Mercer, ed., *Welcome to the Jungle: New Positions in Black Cultural Studies* (New York: Routledge, 1994), 102.

62. Van Deburg, *New Day in Babylon*, 27.

63. Angela Y. Davis, "Black Nationalism: The Sixties and the Nineties," in Gina Dent, ed., *Black Popular Culture* (Seattle: Bay Press, 1992), 317–24. The significance of hair, particularly the Afro style in connection with Davis cannot be understated. Davis states that decade after her media notoriety, she is still sometimes simply referred to as "the Afro."

64. Joshua-Shearer interview.

65. Quoted in Breines, *Young, White, and Miserable*, 98.

66. Quoted in Van Deburg, *New Day in Babylon*, 201.

67. For a discussion of integration in Major League Baseball, see Jules Tygiel, *Baseball's Great Experiment* (New York: Oxford University Press, 1997); on desegregating the National Football League, see Thomas G. Smith, "Outside the Pale: The Exclusion of Blacks from the

National Football League, 1934–1946," *Journal of Sports History*, 15 (Winter, 1988): 255–81; idem., "Civil Rights and the Gridiron: The Kennedy Administration and the Desegregation of the Washington Redskins," *Journal of Sports History*, 14 (Summer 1987): 189–208; Ron Thomas, *They Cleared the Lane: The NBA's Black Pioneers* (Lincoln: University of Nebraska Press, 2002).

68. Michael Oriard, *King Football: Sport and Spectacle in the Golden Age of Radio and Newsreels, Movies and Magazines, the Weekly and the Daily Press* (Chapel Hill: University of North Carolina Press, 2001), 364–65. While black players received the majority of credit and criticism over the initiation of lavish on-field displays, white players, too, engaged in such behavior, most notably Mark Gastineau of the New York Jets, who invented the "Sack Dance."

69. Iverson remains a controversial figure for his outspoken behavior and frequently misogynistic comments; cloaking his numerous run-ins with the law within the legitimacy of Black Power is a disservice to the latter. However, the criticism Iverson receives over his hair, tattoos, and vocabulary undeniably fits within the Black Power context when similar behavior by white athletes goes unnoticed.

70. Joshua-Shearer interview.

6

Title IX and African American Female Athletes

—Sarah K. Fields

On June 23, 1972, President Richard Nixon signed Title IX, a law stating that "no person in the United States shall, on the basis of sex, be excluded from participation in, be denied the benefits of, or be subjected to discrimination under any education program or activity receiving federal financial assistance."[1] At the time, the law seemed to be about opening opportunities for women and girls in the classroom, and almost no one anticipated the impact that Title IX would have on athletics. Title IX, by force of cultural rather than legal will, did change the gender of school- and college-aged athletes.[2] Sports went from being a purely masculine preserve to one in which American females were tolerated, if not always accepted. What has been less clear, however, is what role Title IX has played in increasing the sporting opportunities for African American women and girls. Although African American women and girls have benefited from Title IX, they have not gained as much as their white counterparts largely because of a combination of sociological, economic, and historical factors. Too frequently African American female athletes have fewer sporting options, and scholars, politicians, and activists ignore these women and girls because they are either classified by their gender or their race, and rarely are they recognized as a distinct group. Perhaps in part because the language of the law focuses solely on gender, black women and girls have been overlooked in athletics and as a result have not received the full benefits Title IX promised all women.

A Brief Sporting History of Black Women and Girls

Although comparatively few white women participated in sports prior to the enactment of Title IX, black women and girls seem to have found more athletic opportunities earlier. These openings expanded dramatically in a variety of different sports between 1920 and 1960 for both collegiate and high school athletes. For example, black women played competitive basketball, frequently full-court rather than the feminized version of six-on-six that white women played, and in 1926 the Georgia-South Carolina Athletic Association representing seven historically black schools offered a conference championship for the women's collegiate teams.[3] As early as the 1930s black girls could compete for a high school state championship in North Carolina even though no parallel tournament existed for white girls. Black women were also welcomed into the American Tennis Association (ATA), which was founded in 1916 as an alternative to the all-white United States Lawn Tennis Association. The very first ATA tournaments included women's singles competitions as well as men's, and a girls' division was added in 1935, two years before the creation of a boys' division. Ultimately the girls' division of the ATA produced the great Althea Gibson.[4]

The history of black women's success in track and field is perhaps more widely recognized because of their achievements both nationally and internationally.[5] In 1937, the Tuskegee Institute women's team won the track and field championships of the Amateur Athletic Union for the first of fourteen times. In the 1950s, the Tennessee State University Tigerbelles joined Tuskegee as one of the nation's most dominant track and field teams, training Olympians like Willye White and Wilma Rudolph. The dominance of black women on the track was such that throughout the 1950s, two thirds of the Olympic track and field teams were African American women, a dominance which continues to the present day.[6]

The opportunities and the success of these early African American female athletes seem to stem both from a different ideal of femininity than that in white America as well as a greater support for physical activity from the African American community as a whole. Sport scholar Cindy Hines Gissendanner argues that physical strength was more valued in black America than in white America and as a result, "beauty, personality, and athleticism were not considered to be mutually exclusive qualities."[7] Historian Susan Cahn notes that although black women athletes were subordinate to their male counterparts, the black press did report regularly on women's sports and "only rarely hinted of condescension." She adds that regular reporting allowed these female athletes to become well-known personalities which in turn increased interest and support of female athletics.[8] Rita Liberti's work, however, is careful to emphasize the effect of class on the female African American athlete, noting that many elite black women's colleges restricted female athletic involvement in the middle of the twentieth century.[9]

Scholars in general, however, have not adequately explored the rich history of black female athletes. Most broad histories of black athletes focus on male African American athletes with only passing reference to the feats of women. For example, David Wiggins's *Glory Bound: Black Athletes in a White America* focuses almost exclusively on the history of men. He mentions that slave girls jumped rope as a form of entertainment in what little free time they had, but then only mentions women and girls' experiences in sport towards the end of the book when he notes that the Harry Edwards-led revolt of the black athlete in the late 1960s ignored women. He concludes that the root cause of black women's oppression is racism and not sexism without inquiring as to why that should result in their exclusion from black sports history.[10] Scholar Gary A. Sailes writes in his reader's preface that he intentionally excludes women from his work, preferring to describe himself as a leader in the field of "African-American Male Studies," but his book is more broadly and inaccurately entitled *African-Americans in Sport.*[11] These examples show how scholars conflate the experiences of black women with those of black men. The problem is not the substance of the books but the titles' assumptions that all African Americans in sport are male. Historian Jennifer Lansbury argues that that the achievements of African American female athletes are forgotten because scholars have focused on their status as members of their racial or gender class rather than upon their individual talents.[12] Amy Bass maintains that in 1968 black women were excluded from the Olympic Project for Human Rights because race was privileged over gender and that it was "understood that [black women] would, quite literally, stand by their men."[13] This historical attitude has carried over to the present in that the history and study of African American female athletes is but a small subset of the study of black athletes in general.

History of Title IX Generally

After Title IX became law in 1972, the Department of Health, Education, and Welfare (HEW) was assigned the task of promulgating its enforcement regulations. HEW took three years to accomplish this task, taking so long in part because no one, including Congress, was quite sure how to deal with the role of athletics and Title IX. The law's intended primary purpose was simply to prevent discrimination in the classroom: for example, Title IX would stop schools from excluding girls from physics classes and ensure that all students, regardless of gender, had the opportunity to acquire financial aid. The implication that the legislation had for athletics was never really discussed during congressional debates. At the time, the only record of any discussion of sport and Title IX was the comment by Senator Birch Bayh, the bill's co-sponsor, that the law would mandate neither the desegregation of football fields nor men's locker rooms.[14]

Soon after enacting Title IX, many in Congress became quite concerned that the legislation would put girls into baseball dugouts, or, more disconcerting to collegiate sports fans, onto the college gridirons. In an attempt to clarify the scope of Title IX, both houses of Congress debated how to direct HEW's attempts to draft enforcement regulations; neither house, however, was certain of just how to do this. In 1974, an amendment stating that Title IX would not apply to revenue-producing intercollegiate sports at all was defeated, but in 1975 Congress passed an amendment instructing HEW to create a provision in the regulations that would "include with respect to intercollegiate athletic activities reasonable provisions considering the nature of the particular sports."[15] Thus Congress seemed to be asking HEW not to take Title IX literally but rather to defend male collegiate sport from women. Nothing in the record suggests any characteristic such as race was discussed: the gender of the athlete was the primary concern.

In the final version of the enforcement regulations, HEW chose to distinguish between contact and non-contact sports.[16] The final version stated "where a recipient [of federal funding] operates or sponsors a team in a particular sport for members of one sex but operates or sponsors no such team for members of the other sex, and athletic opportunities for members of that sex have previously been limited, members of the excluded sex must be allowed to try-out for the team offered unless the sport involved is a contact sport." HEW's characterization of contact sport was rather nebulous, defining contact sport as "boxing, wrestling, rugby, ice hockey, football, basketball and other sports the purpose or major activity of which involved bodily contact."[17]

Although schools were given until July 1978 to comply with the Title IX regulations, athletic departments immediately challenged the language of

Title IX and its regulations. First, they questioned whether or not an individual could file a lawsuit under Title IX. In other words, nothing in the language of the statute or the regulations specifically said that an individual, Jane Doe, had the right to sue a state university for not allowing her to play a sport, but rather the regulations simply suggested that she could complain to the Office of Civil Rights who in turn would investigate the school. Several Title IX claims were rejected by the courts on these grounds until the United States Supreme Court ruled in 1979 in *Cannon v. University of Chicago* that Title IX had an implied right of action which allowed individuals to sue their schools.[18]

Title IX and its enforcement regulations also failed to define exactly who had to receive federal financial assistance in order for its provisions to apply. One group argued that if any department of an educational institution got federal money, the entire school had to comply with Title IX, and thus if any students received federal aid in the form of student loans and grants, the athletic department had to comply with Title IX. The other side argued that this interpretation was too broad. If the financial aid office received federal money then, yes, Title IX applied to that particular office, but it did not apply to the athletic department unless the athletic department itself received federal money. As very few athletic departments acquired direct governmental aid, this argument would have effectively cut athletics out of Title IX's domain. The Supreme Court agreed with this narrow program-specific interpretation, and in 1984 most athletic departments were exempted from Title IX.[19] In 1988, however, Congress passed the Civil Rights Restoration Act of 1987 (1988 Amendments) over President Ronald Reagan's veto which announced Congress's intention for a broad application of Title IX. If any office of a school received federal money, then the whole institution needed to comply with the law.[20] Only in 1988 did Title IX clearly and without question apply to athletic departments.

Although Title IX had no direct legal impact on sports in the 1970s, it did have an immediate social impact, evident in a dramatic surge of female athletes. During the 1970–1971 academic year, prior to Title IX's enactment, high school girls comprised 7 percent of the pool of athletes; only 268,591 girls played on their schools' teams compared to 3,473,883 boys. Immediately after the enactment of Title IX, in the academic year of 1972–73, those numbers changed dramatically. Some 743,958 girls (17 percent of the athletes) played on high school teams compared to 3,553,084 boys.[21] This huge increase in female athletes came after Title IX was signed into law, but long before the courts and Congress had determined that Title IX applied to athletic departments, well before its regulations went into effect, and even before these regulations had been drafted. Because of the increased number of females in high school and collegiate athletics and because of increased spending on behalf of those female athletes, in July of 1974, *Sports Illustrated* proclaimed, "This year has been the Year of the Woman in Sports." The authors cited the impending threat of Title IX for increasing both the number of female athletes and their budgets.[22] Sports scholars examining the legislation agreed, crediting Title IX with increasing opportunities for female athletes. Peggy Burke, President of the Association of Intercollegiate Athletics for Women (AIAW), suggested, "since Title IX, women and girls in the United States have moved out of the Dark Ages of Athletics."[23] Historian Joan S. Hult called Title IX "the single most significant piece of legislation to affect the direction and philosophical tenets of women in sport. Much of the growth of girls' high school athletics . . . resulted from the act's implementation."[24]

Despite the hoopla in the mainstream white press about the law, when Title IX was enacted, the black press did not devote a great deal of column space to the new legislation. Several weeks after President Nixon signed the bill into law, Bayard Rustin, a long-time activist for human rights and a leader in the black Civil Rights Movement, wrote in a Sunday column for the *Atlanta Inquirer* that black women suffered from both gender and racial discrimination and that they, in fact, actually suffered more than white women. He argued, however, that black women were more concerned about basic life necessities like housing, jobs, and health care than in social (and white) consciousness raising. He added that as a result of their focus on fundamentals, "black women . . . have largely ignored the women's liberation movement."[25] Although he made no direct reference to Title IX or its implications, seemingly assuming that it was something that would benefit white females more than black women, the timing of his column suggested that he was aware of the law's enactment. Seven years later after the Department of Health, Education, and Welfare released the policy interpretations for the athletic component of Title IX, the *Atlanta Inquirer* made no mention of it. The *Pittsburgh Courier* simply reported on December 15, 1979, that the interpretations had been released but made no comment about or reference to its possible impact on African American females.[26] The limited coverage would foreshadow the tension between race and gender in athletics that would grow throughout the decades.

Effect on Black Female Athletes

More than thirty years after the enactment of Title IX, its effect on black females remains a little explored and uncertain subject.[27] Female athletes in general have greatly benefited from Title IX and its perceived impact on athletics. In 1971, fewer than 300,000 girls competed on high school sports teams; at the end of 2001, that number was close to 2.8 million. In 1971, fewer than 30,000 women competed in intercollegiate sports and in 2001 that number was over 150,000.[28] The largest college sports organization in the United States, the National Collegiate Athletic Association (NCAA), did not sponsor any sports for women in 1971, but in 2000–01, 43 percent of their athletes were female.[29]

The number of black women athletes increased as well. In 1971 just 7 percent of female athletes were of color (the vast majority black) and in 2000–01, 15 percent of female athletes were of color. However, black women today are still likely underrepresented compared to their white counterparts since black women and other racial minority groups compose almost a quarter of the United States undergraduate population. This is not to say that black women have not received their share of athletic scholarships: in Division I of the NCAA (the division which awards the most athletic scholarships), only 12 percent of the female undergraduate population was black in 2000–01, while 14 percent of the female athletes on scholarship were black.[30] The cause of the overall gap in participation rates between white and black females, however, is worth consideration. The answer seems linked in part to youth sports, and in what sports black girls compete.

Youth sports, those for children below college age, have had a greater increase in white girls' participation rates than in black girls' participation. In 1999, the Center for the Study of Sport in Society at Northeastern University reported that 85–90 percent of girls in the suburbs (predominantly white communities) engaged in youth sports that year, but only 15 percent of girls in the inner cities (predominantly black communities) competed.[31] Richard Lapchick, a noted scholar of race and sport, reported in 2001 that an African American urban girl had only one-sixth the chance of playing youth sports as a suburban white girl.[32]

The low numbers of urban black girls competing in youth sports seems linked to economic opportunities. Urban schools and youth centers are vastly underfunded compared to their suburban counterparts, and youth teams which must rely on fundraising for travel and equipment are often more successful in more affluent communities. Also, when urban girls do compete in sports, they tend to participate in basketball or track and field, perhaps because their schools have these facilities and because the sports have strong historical roots in the black community. Most urban schools already have basketball courts (young black males are overly represented in this so-called revenue producing sport) and African Americans have historically dominated track and field in the United States. Suburban girls, on the other hand, often have a choice between golf, soccer, volleyball, tennis, swimming, field hockey, gymnastics, equestrian, lacrosse, and other sports.[33]

In the St. Louis, Missouri, metropolitan area for example, two different high schools serve as case studies. Roosevelt High is an urban high school in the St. Louis City School District. The city schools are 81 percent black with almost the same percentage of the student body qualifying as low-income. Roosevelt High in 2002–2003 had 58 percent of its students on the free or reduced-cost lunch program. The school spent $11,840 per student that year and offers seven varsity sports for girls (volleyball, softball, cross-country, track, tennis, soccer, and basketball).[34] Clayton High School is a suburban high school in a wealthy residential neighborhood with a thriving business and government district. The Clayton School District is 22 percent black with just under 14 percent of its students qualifying as low-income. Clayton High School in 2000–2001 spent $14,309 per student that year and offers ten varsity sports for girls (the same seven as Roosevelt plus swimming, field hockey, and golf).[35] While neither school published its athletic budget, the increased opportunities for suburban girls was likely linked to the increased funding in general. The issue among youth and high school athletes of color is opportunity and encouragement.

Many of the popular (white) female sports like tennis and golf require expensive private instruction, and other sports like soccer and softball are geared around a private-club system where the participants pay for equipment and travel. Since the best players are in the club system, college coaches offering athletic scholarships recruit there as well and sometimes instead of the high school leagues. One researcher at the Center for the Study of Sport in America said "the real shame is Black girls could be playing tennis or golf and getting sports scholarships for college but this is not happening because they are either not playing sports or are just interested in basketball."[36] Ironically the few black women and girls who do participate in "white" sports often find it difficult socially being a single minority on the team; sometimes they quit the team because of their sense of isolation.[37]

The emphasis on basketball and track among black girls carries over to college where women of color comprise 40 percent of Division I basketball and track and field athletes but just 11 percent of athletes in other sports.[38] Because fewer black girls compete in sports (other than track and field and basketball) at the youth level, fewer of them are able to compete at the collegiate level given the finite number of collegiate track and field and basketball teams. Because the Office of Civil Rights and the American courts have chosen to use proportionality (meaning that the number of female athletes must be proportional to the number of female undergraduates), as the benchmark for determining whether or not a school is in compliance with Title IX, colleges have been adding additional female sports to their rosters. The NCAA has designated so-called country club and suburban sports such as lacrosse, soccer, crew, and equestrian as emerging sports, and these sports have far more white youth participants who then go on to compete in college. The fastest growing women's collegiate sports since 1987 have been soccer, rowing, golf, and lacrosse with the number of teams at least doubling and, in the case of soccer, tripling. Additionally, with the increase in youth sports (even if it is predominantly for white youths), fewer collegiate sports welcome walk-on novices to their teams. These coaches are paid to win, and to do that they recruit the best-trained athletes and do not necessarily promote diversity on their teams.[39] As a result, despite the doubly protected status that black women should enjoy through their race and gender, Title IX has not opened as many athletic doors for them as it has for white women and girls.

African American Women in Collegiate Coaching and Administration

The one area in which African American and white women are equal in the effects of Title IX is in the failure of the legislation to help women into coaching and sport administration careers. As additional girls played sports and more schools increased funding for female teams, the coaches and administrators of female teams suddenly had money and power unprecedented in women's athletics. In 1972, prior to the enactment of Title IX, an estimated 95–100 percent of women's intercollegiate athletic programs were administrated and coached by women.[40] With the advent of Title IX, however, more college women would play on more teams coached by men in athletic departments headed by men.

In 2000–2001, the numbers of women in collegiate coaching and administration dropped dramatically from almost thirty years earlier, but white women still held more positions than their black counterparts. Although a few white women coached men's teams (white women constituted 2.5 percent of the head coaches on men's teams in Division I and slightly more in Divisions II and III), very few black women were head coaches of men's teams (0.4 percent in Division I and even fewer in Divisions II and III). Compared to their opportunities to coach men's teams, white women coached more women's teams (38 percent in Division I and about the same in Divisions II and III combined), but this means that more males than females coached women's teams. Black women, however, were the head coaches of a paltry 3.2% of Division I women's teams and even fewer Division II and III teams, meaning that almost as many white women coached men's teams as African American women coached women's teams.

College sport administration in 2000–2001 was an even worse career path for black women. Although women constituted 6 percent of Division I Athletic Directors (the most powerful positions in collegiate sport), none of them were African American. Even though more women were athletic directors at Division II and III schools, very few African American women held these positions. At the associate and assistant athletic administrator position, women generally held 27.6 percent of the positions at the Division I level (and even more in Divisions II and III), but African American women only held 1.5 percent of the Divisions I positions and about the same percentage of the Divisions II and III positions. Women in general were much more likely to be Senior Women Administrators (whose job it is to supervise women's sport at the institution under the guidance of the athletic director), holding 90 percent of these positions at the Division I level. More African American women were Senior Women Administrators than any other athletic administrative position, but the numbers were still low: 6.3 percent of Division I positions and even fewer at the other divisions.[41]

Just as athletes of color on predominantly white teams expressed a sense of loneliness, so too did one of the most successful African American female coaches and administrators. *The Voice* ran an article in 1998 about Marian Washington, the women's basketball coach at the

University of Kansas. She began coaching the team in 1973 with a budget of practically nothing, and while building the basketball program, she was named women's athletic director at Kansas. She explained that she often felt "extremely isolated. . . . From coaching to recruiting, the way people responded to me, I did not know if it was because I was a woman or a Black woman."[42] Not only did she reiterate the remoteness of working in a predominantly male and often white arena, she also reiterated the separation she feels as part of a double minority: she is not simply black; she is not simply a woman; she is a black woman who does not know to which aspect of her physical being others react.

Leaders in the African American sporting community have acknowledged the problems for black women in administration. Floyd Keith, the executive director of the Black Coaches Association in 2003, recognized that "Title IX really has not had a significant effect on African-Americans or other minority women. . . . Ethnic minority women face a different struggle in the sports they are most visible—basketball—because they have the most competition. Not only do they have to battle the issue of being hired, but they have to deal with the gender issue." Tina Sloane Green, president and founder of the Black Women in Sport Foundation, argued that "within Title IX there needs to be some sort of initiative that provides an incentive for organizing bodies or colleges to include African-American women or recruit them in sports or to take on administrative roles."[43] While their concerns and frustrations are valid, neither acknowledged the damage that Title IX had done to all women in coaching and administration.

Historically Black Colleges and Universities

Ironically, given the support that historically black colleges and universities (HBCUs) showed women's athletics in the middle part of the twentieth century, these institutions found themselves in trouble with Title IX. In 1997, four HBCUs were cited in a Title IX complaint that named twenty-five schools in total.[44] The Mid-Eastern (MEAC) and Southwestern Athletic Conferences (SWAC), the only historically black college conferences in the NCAA Division I ranks, failed until 2001 to provide proportional spending or proportional opportunities for women. The problem was worse for these HBCUs than for their white counterparts. For example, in 2001 the Southern Conference, a predominantly white conference in the same geographic region as the MEAC, had approximately a 13 per-cent difference between female undergraduates and female athletes. The MEAC had a 20 percent gap. Charles S. Harris, commissioner of the MEAC, blamed the lack of black female athletes at the high school level and added that if non-white children continued to ignore emerging sports to focus on basketball and track and field, the league would continue to have difficulties.[45]

HBCUs had problems with Title IX compliance for several reasons. First, HBCUs, compared to predominantly white schools, were slow to add sports for women. For example, in 1996 Howard University was the only historically black college to offer women's soccer although many white schools had added the sport.[46] Second, the high percentage of females at many of these schools made complying with the proportionality test difficult without drastic increases in female sports or serious cuts in the men's programs. At predominantly black colleges in 1995, 62 percent of the undergraduates were females; the most extreme was Coppin State College where 72 percent of the undergraduate population was female. Causing additional difficulties was the fact that many of the women at Coppin State were returning students, older than the usual eighteen- to twenty-two-year-old undergraduates populating most campuses. Many of these older students did not want to participate in sports because they were focused on academics and had other commitments.[47]

After the complaints about the Title IX violations, the vast majority of HBCUs added a large number of female sports, including some which were also popular in predominantly white schools. In the fall of 2003, these schools' websites reported the following sports would be offered for women: South Carolina State University offered basketball, bowling, cross country, golf, softball, soccer, tennis, track and field, and volleyball for women. Bethune Cookman College supported basketball, bowling, cross country, golf, tennis, softball, track and field, and volleyball. Hampton University sponsored basketball, bowling, cross country, sailing, softball, tennis, track and field, and volleyball. Howard University offered basketball, bowling, lacrosse, soccer, softball, swimming, tennis, track and field, and volleyball. Coppin State University had basketball, bowling, cross country, softball, tennis, track, and volleyball. Many of these sports are so-called "white" sports; golf, tennis, and sailing are definitely country-club sports. An article in 1996 in *Black Issues in Higher Education* describing the growth of women's sports at HBCUs noted that some coaches believed black athletes were out there: they just needed to be recruited. Other coaches believed the HBCUs needed to support youth opportunities in their sports in order to teach their sport to minority girls who could then play at the collegiate level.[48]

Although many of the sports HBCUs have added are prevalent at predominantly white schools, bowling, a popular addition, is more unusual. The HBCUs have added bowling as a varsity sport for women largely because it is seemingly cheap to support and requires no new facilities. Schools discovered, however, that because there are so few varsity programs, the travel budgets for teams were more than they initially expected, but the schools have not yet cut the sport. Bowling has been named an emerging sport for the NCAA, and black colleges in 2001 comprised twenty of the twenty-five Division I varsity women's bowling teams (about fifty other schools offered the sport at the club level). The NCAA sponsored the first bowling national championships in 2003–2004.[49]

The ironic part of adding bowling because of its apparent cost-effectiveness was that it did nothing to increase the number of black female athletes at HBCUs; it just increased the number of female athletes. Many of the bowlers at the historically black colleges are white. Sharon Brummel, the coach at Maryland-Eastern Shore University, noted that "there aren't that many black children who get that involved with bowling." For example, in 2001, Maryland-Eastern Shore, a historically black institution, had only two black bowlers on its seven woman roster.[50]

Title IX and Black Male Athletes

The problems that the HBCUs had initially in complying with Title IX stemmed in part from the numbers and cost of male sports programs, including football. Like many Title IX opponents, some at the HBCUs and other black leaders in sport expressed concern that Title IX was hurting men, specifically that Title IX hurt black men while helping only white women. Eric St. John, a columnist with *Black Issues in Higher Education*, argued that because men's basketball and football are revenue producing sports, black men have financed the athletic opportunities for white women in collegiate sport.[51] These advocates (which often included football coaches) argued that the proportionality requirement of Title IX has reduced the opportunities for black men who are predominantly participants in basketball, football, and track and field. They feared that in a reaction to Title IX or because of budget decreases, colleges would cut the number of scholarships available, especially for football, which would limit the opportunities for black men.

Alex Woods, the head football coach at James Madison University and vice-president of the Black Coaches Association in the late 1990s, was quoted repeatedly, warning that black men would suffer from Title IX, saying that "playing football is the only way that a lot of Black players get to go to college at all."[52] In fact, black male athletes at Blinn College and San Francisco State University did suffer from budget cuts. Blinn cut men's track (75 percent black) and SFSU cut men's football (34 percent black) in order to save money to add women's sports like softball, volleyball, and tennis. The athletic directors at each school said the racial composition of the teams was not a consideration when the cuts and additions were made. Betsy Alden the SFSU athletic director said, "We recruit athletes," but she added that without football the university had the money to focus on recruiting more racially diverse athletes in the new sports.[53]

Craig T. Greenlee, a writer for *Black Issues in Higher Education* consistently found Title IX at fault for what he perceived as dwindling opportunities for black male athletes. In 2002, he blamed Title IX for Howard University's choice to drop baseball as a varsity sport despite the school's statement that it was because of a lack of facilities and not Title IX. He claimed that South Carolina State University dropped baseball in 1993 in order to add softball. He argued that "because of budget limitations and the need to adhere to Title IX, [baseball] could face possible extinction at many schools."[54]

Interestingly, this concern about protecting black male athletes has been based on the argument that Title IX is about quotas. African American male coaches worried about protecting their athletes much like predominantly white organizations such as the College Sports Council (representing men's wrestling, gymnastics, swimming and diving, track and field, and golf) which unsuccessfully sued the U.S. Department of Education to overturn the compliance policy guidelines.[55] The connection of gender at times in sports seems stronger than the bond of race, pitting black men against black women and aligning men of all colors. Alex Woods states that "The race versus gender issue is very real."[56]

Support for Title IX

Support for Title IX, despite its shortcomings, has been strong in the African American press, especially among female writers. Veronica Hendrix, a columnist with the *Los Angeles Sentinel*, wrote an article in celebration of the thirtieth anniversary of Title IX, arguing that Title IX "literally transformed the lives" of young girls and concluding "happy anniversary Title IX. May the next thirty years result in a true and unquestioned level playing field for all women and girls."[57] A Detroit, Michigan, volleyball coach told the *Michigan Chronicle* that "there are only two golden sports, men's basketball and football" and "until the old traditional male values change, the majority of young ladies in the Detroit school system will not reap the advantages Title IX was designed to improve."[58] Carol Ann Webster a columnist in Los Angeles credited Title IX with improving the lot of female athletes noting "no longer are women relegated to being passive observers, or cheerleaders on the sidelines. They are in the game. They are part of the action."[59] A column in the *Pittsburgh Courier* entitled "We Should Encourage Girls to Play Sports," credited Title IX with the increased opportunities to compete and emphasized how sports make girls' lives better.[60] In a story about a woman returning to college and athletics at the age of thirty-seven, one article noted that Title IX increased opportunities and "enriched thousands of women's lives."[61]

Stories about the significance of Title IX, however, transcended the gender of the author. The *Sacramento Observer* published an article saying that Ruthie Bolton (a professional basketball player) and Carolyn Jenkins (a collegiate basketball coach) were just two "of countless African-American women who owe their athletic careers in large part to Title IX."[62] A report on Girls Day in Sports at a New York school described Title IX as being "instrumental in building gender equity."[63]

Even articles in the black press that were less enthusiastic about Title IX did not necessarily call for the abolition of the legislation; instead, these articles called for increasing opportunities for minority girls. *Black Issues in Higher Education* reported in 2003 that minority women's groups wanted the Department of Education and the NCAA to increase minority women's participation in sport rather than modifying Title IX in such a way that might decrease women's opportunities in general.[64] Craig T. Greenlee (a columnist frequently concerned about losing openings for black male athletes) in a 1997 article emphasized that black athletes needed to broaden their sporting base beyond basketball and track and field in order to take advantage of the increased scholarship prospects in the emerging sports for women.[65] The Northern California *Sun-Reporter* noted that "Title IX was designed to meet the needs of girls, but it appears white girls have cashed in." The rest of the article argued that more urban youth centers needed financial support so that more black girls could earn scholarships.[66]

Increasing Participation Rates

The numbers clearly establish that Title IX has not benefited black women as much as it has white women; now the question must be addressed of how to increase their opportunities. Some leaders suggest increasing youth opportunities for black girls. Tina Sloane Green, the director of the Black Women in Sport Foundation and a professor at Temple University, has stated that "Title IX was for white women. I'm not going to say black women haven't benefited, but they have been left out."[67] She argued that urban black girls need to have greater opportunities in sports other than basketball and track and field and her own organization has sponsored golf and tennis clinics in various urban centers.[68] She would also like to see an initiative to recruit African American coaches into coaching and administrative roles, encouraging them to promote their sports in the black community and has added, optimistically, "we can turn what appears to be a negative for African-Americans into a positive."[69] Other suggestions include encouraging coaches to recruit black and minority athletes in sports in which they are underrepresented and requiring colleges to ensure that summer sports camps are available to minority or economically disadvantaged youths.[70]

Still others suggest that change must come from within the community as well as from more institutional support. Funding alone may not be enough to change a long history of black female athletes choosing basketball and track and field over other sports. Opportunities for black girls must be matched by community and family encouragement to try new and different sports. Patricia V. Viverito, then-chair of the NCAA's Committee on Women's Athletics, argued in 1998 that the issue was in part about fathers: "mad dads are the ones making the difference in the white community. They are encouraging, even pushing their daughters into sports. We need more mad black dads."[71]

The tension between race and gender is reflected even in the question of how to promote youth sports in urban America. Donna A. Lopiano, director of the Women's Sports Foundation, has acknowledged that the issue of racial equity is just as important as the question of gender equity and should not be forgotten.[72] But she has also cautioned against simply having unlimited football squads to protect black male athletes. She wants to "remove the obstacles that have created segregation in sport,"[73] but removing those hurdles are incredibly challenging. An anonymous black coach was quoted in the *Sun-Reporter* saying "the problem stems from institutional racism and the increased privatization of sports in America," and the coach added that only black coaches commented on the problems and "they are seen as trouble makers. But if white girls were being shortchanged this would be Topic A."[74]

Conclusion

Title IX has been a law of almost mythic proportions in the American imagination. Long before the law applied to athletic programs, women and girls used the law as a lever to crowbar their way into sports, and the law has greatly benefited female athletes of all races. It has not, however, benefited females of color, and particularly black women and girls, as much as it has benefited white women and girls.

Although historically black female athletes received more support from black communities and had many more opportunities to compete in the first two-thirds of the twentieth century, when Title IX was enacted and white schools began opening athletics to girls, sport became more about economics and, perhaps, tradition. Communities, schools, and families that had enough money to offer a wide range of sports to girls did so. Unfortunately, with most of the wealth in the United States being concentrated in the hands of white families, schools, and communities, poorer youth have not had the same sporting opportunities. Even those black girls with more access to money and opportunities, however, often focus on basketball and track and field, perhaps in part because of the long and storied history of their mothers and grandmothers in those sports.[75]

The battle over dollars for sports in particular, however, has contributed to a tension between race and gender. Black men align themselves ideologically with their white brothers and fear that Title IX will reduce their opportunities. White women recognize that Title IX has not benefited their sisters of color as much but fear that any criticism of Title IX will result in its destruction. Female columnists in the black press have also seemed to follow this policy: they have praised the law but have criticized the social and economic structure of this country that keeps the urban youth from involvement in sports such as lacrosse and equestrian. Even the historically black colleges and universities have been forced to focus on gender more than race, by adding more sports for women but recruiting mostly white athletes to play.

The result is that all too often the experiences of black female athletes are swept into other categories and ignored. Black sport history does not often include the history of black female athletes. The history of women in sport mentions the most outstanding athletes like Althea Gibson and Wilma Rudolph but does not focus on them, and only rarely describes the vast majority of more average black competitors. Even the law focuses on gender alone; Title IX and its surrounding rules and policy say nothing about race, referring only to gender. As a result of the shifting categorizations, women of color have suffered untold levels of discrimination in sport.

In 1998, a children's column in the African American press's *New York Amsterdam News* interviewed John Phillips, a sport sociologist, and asked him to explain why Title IX was important. He explained that gender discrimination in sport was like racial discrimination in the classroom but that "it's just that we don't think that way."[76] We in the United States do need to think that way: we need to examine and respond to discrimination in sport not just for women as an all-encompassing category but also for black women and girls in order to give every female the opportunity to participate in sports.

Notes

1. Education Amendments of 1972, Publ. L. No. 92-318, § § 901-09, 86 Stat. 235 (codified at 20 U.S.C. § § 1681–1688 [1990]) [hereinafter Title IX].

2. For a discussion of the legal limitations of Title IX see Sarah K. Fields, *Female Gladiators: Gender, Law, and Contact Sport in America* (Champaign: University of Illinois Press, 2005).

3. Rita Liberti, "'We Were Ladies; We Just Played Basketball Like Boys': African American Womanhood and Competitive College Basketball at Bennett College, 1928–1942," *Journal of Sport History* 26 (1999): 568.

4. Cindy Himes Gissendanner, "African-American Women and Competitive Sport, 1920–1960," in Susan Birrell and Cheryl L. Cole, eds., *Women, Sport, and Culture*, ed. (Champaign, IL: Human Kinetics, 1994).

5. See A. S. Young, *Negro Firsts in Sports* (Chicago: Johnson Publishing, 1963) as one of the early histories of black sport. Young focuses primarily on male success but devotes several pages to the women's track teams.

6. Susan K. Cahn, *Coming on Strong: Gender and Sexuality in Twentieth-Century Women's Sport* (New York: Free Press, 1994).

7. Gissendanner, "African-American Women," 88.

8. Cahn, *Coming on Strong*, 39.

9. Liberti, "'We Were Ladies,'" 568.

10. David Wiggins, *Glory Bound: Black Athletes in a White America* (New York: Syracuse University Press, 1997), 4–5 and 216–17.

11. Gary A. Sailes, ed., *African-Americans in Sport* (New Brunswick, NJ: Transaction, 1998), xii.

12. Jennifer Lansbury, "The Tuskegee Flash and the Slender Harlem Stroker: Black Women Athletes on the Margin," *Journal of Sport History* 28 (2001): 234.

13. Amy Bass, *Not the Triumph but the Struggle: The 1968 Olympics and the Making of the Black Athlete* (Minneapolis: University of Minnesota Press, 2002), 190.

14. 117 Congressional Record 30, 407 (1971).

15. Javits Amendment to Title IX, quoted in Diane Heckman, "Scoreboard: A Concise Chronological Twenty-five-Year History of Title IX Involving Interscholastic and Intercollegiate Athletics," *Seton Hall Journal of Sport Law* 7 (1997): 395.

16. Margo L. Anderson, "A Legal History and Analysis of Sex Discrimination in Athletics: Mixed Gender Competition, 1970–1987," (PhD diss.: University of Minnesota, 1989), 221–23.

17. 34 C.F.R. § 106.41 (b) (1991).

18. *Cannon v. University of Chicago*, 441 U.S. 677 (1979).

19. *Grove City College v. Bell*, 465 U.S. 555 (1984).

20. 20 U.S.C. § 1687, 102 Stat. 28, Pub. L. 100–259 (1988).

21. Peggy Burke, "The Effect of Current Sports Legislation on Women in Canada and the U.S.A.—Title IX," in Reet Howell, ed., *Her Story in Sport: A Historical Anthology of Women in Sport* (West Point, NY: Leisure Press, 1982), 338.

22. Bil Gilbert and Nancy Williamson, "Women in Sports: A Progress Report," *Sports Illustrated* 34 (July 29, 1974): 28–31.

23. Burke, "The Effect of Current Sports Legislation," 340.

24. Joan S. Hult, "The Story of Women's Athletics: Manipulation of a Dream, 1890–1985," in D. Margaret Costa and Sharon R. Guthrie, eds., *Women and Sport: Interdisciplinary Perspectives* (Champaign, IL: Human Kinetics, 1994), 95.

25. *Atlanta Inquirer*, July 8, 1972.

26. *Pittsburgh Courier*, December 15, 1979.

27. One problem with discussing race in the United States is a matter of definition and classification. The sources for the numbers in this section do not explain how they determined what race an individual was: was it self-identification and if so, what choices was the person given? Was it surname identification or third party observation based on skin color? Since my newspaper and other sources do not offer definitions, neither can I, and this limitation should not be ignored or understated.

28. *Los Angeles Sentinel*, September 4, 2002.

29. Richard E. Lapchick, "2003 Racial and Gender Report Card," Institute for Diversity and Ethics in Sport, 17.

30. "Sidelines," *Chronicle of Higher Education* (July 11, 2003): A31.

31. [Northern California] *Sun Reporter*, January 4, 2001.

32. Richard E. Lapchick, *Smashing Barriers: Race and Sport in the New Millennium* (Lanham, MD: Madison Books, 2001).

33. "Title IX: Black Girls Not Served," 1.

34. Information about Roosevelt High School was found at www.slps.org (accessed on August 17, 2004) and *St. Louis Post-Dispatch*, May 15, 2003.

35. Information about Clayton High School was found at www.clayton.k12.mo.us (accessed on August 17, 2004) and *St. Louis Post-Dispatch*, May 15, 2003.

36. "Title IX: Black Girls Not Served," 1.

37. Welch Suggs, "Title IX Has Done Little for Minority Female Athletes—Because of Socioeconomic and Cultural Factors, and Indifference," *Chronicle of Higher Education* (November 30, 2001): 14.

38. "Title IX: Black Girls Not Served," 1.

39. Suggs, "Title IX Has Done Little," 14.

40. Acosta and Carpenter, "The Status of Women in Intercollegiate Athletics," in *Women, Sport, and Culture*, 114–15.

41. Lapchick, "2003 Racial and Gender Report Card." None of these numbers of coaches and administrators include historically black colleges and universities.

42. Kevin Blackistone, "The Voice Interview: Marian Washington, Champion of Change," [London, UK], *The Voice*, June 1, 1998, 44.

43. Ben Hammer, "Reconsidering the Status of Title IX," *Black Issues in Higher Education* (April 10, 2003): 20.

44. Craig T. Greenlee, "Slow Motion Penalty," *Black Issues in Higher Education* (September 4, 1997): 12.

45. Suggs, "Title IX Has Done Little," A35.

46. Craig T. Greenlee, "Sporting a New Look: Women's Soccer, Sailing, Golf Become Additions to Athletic Menus," *Black Issues in Higher Education* (December 26, 1996): 24.

47. Jim Naughton, "Title IX Poses a Particular Challenge at Predominantly Black Institutions," *Chronicle of Higher Education* (February 20, 1998): A55–56.

48. Greenlee, "Sporting a New Look," 24.

49. Suggs, "Title IX Has Done Little," A35.

50. Craig T. Greenlee, "Bowled Over by Women," *Black Issues in Higher Education* (June 7, 2001): 90.

51. Eric St. John, "Collegiate Athletics Highlights," *Black Issues in Higher Education* (August 19, 1999): 80.

52. Craig T. Greenlee, "Title IX: Does Help for Women Come at the Expense of African-Americans?" *Black Issues in Higher Education* (April 17, 1997): 24–26.

53. Debra E. Blum, "Competing Equities?" *Chronicle of Higher Education* (May 26, 1995): A37.

54. Craig T. Greenlee, "Black College Baseball's Uncertain Future," *Black Issues in Higher Education* (August 1, 2002): 18.

55. Hammer, "Reconsidering," 20.

56. St. John, "Collegiate Athletics Highlights," 80.

57. Hendrix, "Happy 30th Anniversary Title IX," A7.

58. *Michigan Chronicle*, July 4, 2000.

59. *Los Angeles Sentinel*, October 14, 1999.

60. *Pittsburgh Courier*, July 25, 2001.

61. Cheryl D. Fields, "Title IX: The Realization of a Dream Deferred Twenty Years," *Black Issues in Higher Education* (April 17, 1997): 28.

62. *Sacramento Observer*, October 23, 2002.

63. *New York Voice*, July 3, 2002.

64. Hammer, "Reconsidering," 20.

65. Greenlee, "Title IX," 24–26.

66. "Title IX: Black Girls Not Served," 1.

67. Suggs, "Title IX Has Done Little," 14.

68. Blum, "Competing Equities?," A37.

69. Hammer, "Reconsidering," 20.

70. Blum, "Competing Equities?," A37.

71. Naughton, "Title IX Poses a Particular Challenge," A55.

72. Suggs, "Title IX Has Done Little," 14.

73. Blum, "Competing Equities?," A 37.

74. "Title IX: Black Girls Not Served," 1.

75. My thanks to Dean Susan Rollins of Washington University in St. Louis for reminding me of this point. Email correspondence with author on November 25, 2003.

76. *New York Amsterdam News*, March 18, 1998.

7

Mexican Baseball Teams in the Midwest, 1916–1965

The Politics of Cultural Survival and Civil Rights

—Richard Santillan

Sports have been a major presence in Mexican Americans' lives since the early twentieth century. This has been true of Mexican Americans in the Midwest, where sports such as baseball took on a special significance.[1] More than merely games for boys and girls, the teams and contests involved nearly the entire community, and often had political and cultural objectives. Like the fiestas celebrating Cinco de Mayo and September 16, sports are a thread that unites the community.

Sometimes, a thousand people, representing dozens of small Mexican communities, would gather to watch baseball games in the years prior to World War II. People socialized and discussed community issues at the games and strengthened their sense of racial and ethnic solidarity. In the postwar period, sports continued to play a major part in the overall cultural and political agenda of the Mexican American population.

In addition to community unity, two other key benefits of athletics have been the leadership skills and survival tactics that young people developed by participating in team sports skills that have been useful in the political arena and in the fight for social justice. Many parents, in fact, encouraged their children to join teams to develop such skills. Thus, besides the sheer fun of playing and competing, sports have served as a means of establishing community solidarity, developing leaders, and imparting a sense of fair play. Marselino Fernandez of Kansas City noted that sports were: "a means to take out our aggressiveness in a positive way rather than a bad way in fighting or drinking in the streets. Sports definitely helped me become more outgoing, competitive, responsible, articulate, and to take charge. These types of critical skills for success in the real world were not taught to Mexican children in schools or other public places."[2]

Background

In the early part of the twentieth century, a handful of Midwestern Anglo charitable organizations and churches offered recreational activities for Mexican youth. In addition, a few of the YMCA clubs permitted Mexicans to join and use their facilities as members. Nevertheless, Mexican American communities chose to build their own sports networks according to several individuals who came of age in the 1920s, '30s and '40s.[3] They noted that the Mexican community established an elaborate web of athletic associations during the 1920s and 1930s. These included the Aztec Social Club, Los Gallos Athletic Association, El Club Azteca, and El Club Deportivo Internacional. The sports clubs of East Chicago and Gary, Indiana, El Club Deportivo Internacional and the Gary Athletic Club, sponsored a host of sporting events including tournaments in soccer, basketball, and baseball.[4]

In Kansas City, the Mexican Athletic Club was established in 1922 and organized numerous boxing events, bowling tournaments, and track-and-field competitions. In the larger urban Mexican communities, parents pooled their meager finances and purchased buildings and converted the structures into recreational centers. The smaller Mexican communities generally rented buildings for sports activities. These centers and the land around them were the locations of weight rooms, boxing rings, basketball courts, and baseball diamonds.

A handful of Mexican athletic clubs even had swimming pools according to Undo Velandez of Des Moines, Iowa.[5] Lando's father was active with sports activities and tried unsuccessfully to build a gym for the Mexican community in Des Moines. The Anglo power structure prevented the Mexican community from developing a sports center in the early 1920s. His father, nevertheless, did establish the Mexican Athletic Club in Des Moines in 1925. Lando continued his father's work, and in 1962, almost forty years after his father's efforts, spearheaded the creation of the Mexican American Recreation Club.

World War II disrupted the sports movement in the Midwest as young men and women defended the nation both on the battlefield and in defense plants. Nevertheless, the postwar period witnessed a movement to recapture the athletic spirit and superb talent of the community. Both the second generation of Mexican Americans and recent arrivals from Texas and Mexico enjoyed sports immensely in the Midwest. In retrospect, the prewar sports activities among Mexicans were only a prelude to far more significant sports participation between 1945 and 1965.

There was an incredible growth in organized sports in the Midwest Mexican community after 1945. Before the war, major sports were limited primarily to baseball, boxing, and basketball. Afterwards, however, more Mexican Americans began taking part in bowling, tennis, golf, soccer, football, and wrestling. Women's sports came of age during this period as well. Whereas women were mainly involved with softball before the war, they later became active in baseball and basketball leagues, and bowling tournaments. Women's teams in all sports sprung up all over the Midwest.

The Mexican American community followed its rich sports tradition by resurrecting several sports clubs and recreational centers after World War II. These clubs included the El Club Deportivo Azteca, the Mexican American Youth Association, El Club de Deportivos de Joliet, the Azteca Club, the Wichita Mexican American Athletic Club, the Pan American Club, the Mexican American Athletic Club of North Platte, the Argentine Center, El Club Colonia Mexicana, and La Sociedad Deportivo.[6] The Quad-Cities area of Iowa and Illinois formed several sports clubs, including the Quad-Cities Martial Arts Center, Penis Boys Club, and the Silvis Youth Organization. In addition to developing their own clubs, Mexican Americans became active in various city sports and leagues, said Elmer Vega of Newton, Kansas:

> Prior to the war, the Mexican community established its own sports network of clubs, centers, teams, and tournaments. The second and third generations have continued this rich tradition into the 1980s. There is, however, a significant difference. Unlike before, the second and third generations have become directly involved with Little League, Pop Warner, summer sports programs, high school sports, and other mainstream sports activities. We felt that, as taxpayers and citizens, our community and children were entitled to these recreational benefits.[7]

Thus, intergenerational cooperation was a powerful social adhesive that brought together people of all age groups playing sports. Alex Cruz of Parsons, Kansas, noted that: "I was the manager of the Parson's baseball team from 1952 to 1954. Our team was sponsored by several companies, including "Big Heated Red" and Coca-Cola. We played Chanute, Kansas City, Topeka, Coffyville, and Fredonia. . . . My father played baseball for the MKT railroad company during the 1930s. It was not uncommon to have three generations of ballplayers from the same family in the Midwest."[8]

Baseball

Baseball has been the most popular sport among Mexicans in the U.S. The rise of baseball as a spectator sport in the Mexican community simply reflected the rise of mass spectator sports in the nation. Nearly every Midwest Mexican community, small or large, had baseball teams to represent it. The sport became one of the major forms of recreation, and was played before overflowing crowds. Most of the teams selected names from their rich historical past, such as the Aztecas, Mayans, Cuauhtemocs, and Aguilas. The political choice of these names was a way of respecting and reaffirming the Mexican culture.

There were Mexican teams in the Topeka area as early as 1916, and by 1919 several Mexican baseball teams in the Kansas City and East Chicago areas were already playing. Additional clubs were organized and various leagues formed during the 1920s. Some of the early Mexican teams included Los Obreros De San Jose of East Chicago; the Osage Indians of Kansas City; the Mexican All-Stars of Silvis; the Moline Estrellas; the East Chicago Zacatecas Indians; La Libertad and La Victoria of Horton, Kansas; Los Mayans of Lorain, Ohio; Las Aguilas Mexicanas and Los Cometas of Topeka; Los Lobos of Hutchinson, Kansas; Los Aztecas de Kansas City; and Los Nacionales of Wichita, Kansas.

In fact, there were several popular types of baseball leagues in the Mexican Middle West: industrial, Catholic, community, migrant, and women's leagues. It was not unusual for a remarkable player to participate in two or more of these different leagues. Moreover, being an outstanding player was oftentimes a ticket to employment for Mexicans, because businesses wanted to have winning baseball teams. Companies went out of their way to find outstanding Mexican players. Furthermore, many Catholic schools had baseball teams composed largely of Mexican players and called themselves the Guadalupanos. Likewise, most Mexican communities had their own teams that represented them in statewide competitions.

Migrants had their own baseball teams during the summer months. These migrant teams and leagues were found in Western Nebraska, for example, in Scottsbluff, Bayard, Bridgeport, Morrell, Lyman, and Minatare. Other migrant teams could be found in Kansas, Minnesota, South and North Dakota, and Colorado. There were women's teams that played before and after World War II as well. There was also an informal network of Mexicans who played pickup games between regular games and tournaments.

Unfortunately, for those trying to organize baseball games, it was often true that Mexican teams were not allowed to play on city diamonds or in parks owned by local businesses or cities. Elmer Vega of Newton, Kansas, considered one of the finest athletes to come out of the Newton area in both baseball and basketball, remembered: "Most public parks in the Midwest did not permit Mexicans to play organized sports. When we were allowed in the parks, we were given the worst diamonds and undesirable times to play. After World War II, the parks opened for us and we had few problems scheduling games and other recreational activities."[9]

Because they were barred from some public parks before the war, Mexicans made their own ball fields, frequently in vacant lots or in pastures near the railroad tracks, roundhouses, or steel factories. Players, coaches, and supporters constructed their own baseball diamonds. A location would be found, cleared of rocks and debris, and leveled. The women made the bases by sewing anew worn-out pillows. In North Platte, Nebraska, the games were played in a pasture during the 1930s. Dried cow chips were used as bases.[10]

The Mexican communities constructed baseball fields with colorful names such as La Yardita, El Huache, and Devil's Field. Another was known as Rabbit Field because players continuously had to chase rabbits off during games. Sometimes, cars were used in the outfield as bleachers, with people sitting on the hoods, trunks, and roofs, said Perfecto Torrez of Topeka.[11] Eva Hernandez of Hutchinson recalled, "Our baseball team . . . played near the National Armory. Both the Morton Salt and the Carey Salt Company had baseball teams with Mexican players. We played in the cow fields, which we affectionately called Las Vegas."[12] Hernandez's husband, Matt, was an outstanding baseball player and she often watched him play before and after World War II.

El Parque Anahuac, for example, had a seating capacity for five hundred people. It was not unusual for large crowds to show up to see the better Mexican teams. When Los Aztecas de Chicago came to play against the East Chicago team during the first week of June of 1927, the game drew a standing room only crowd of over three thousand spectators. Large crowds were common in the Great Lakes area. This beautiful baseball diamond in East Chicago was eventually destroyed during the Depression because the wooden seats were used as firewood during the cold winter months. Also, someone discovered that beneath the surface of the field were deposits of coal. Apparently a coal or railroad company had left it there. The news spread quickly, and soon the leveled, desolate field became a center of activity with men, women, and children digging for the precious fuel with shovels and sticks.

Sunday was baseball day in Mexican communities across the Middle West. Residents first went to church and then breakfast before heading to the game. The players, on the other hand, ran home after church changing quickly into their uniforms and hurried back to warm-up before the fans arrived, said Phillip Martinez of Dodge City, Kansas.[13] The baseball games started around one in the afternoon. The people wore their Sunday best to the games.

Some of the games in Hutchinson drew better than a thousand people from in town and the surrounding communities, said Bacho Rodriguez.[14] Rodriguez was an outstanding pitcher for the Hutchinson team during the 1930s. He remembers games that usually drew 1,000 to 1,500 spectators. He noted that he and a few other players were scouted by the New York Yankees.

Frequently, admission was charged. Different teams had various methods of raising funds. The money was sometimes used to purchase bats, balls, uniforms, and gas for road games. Most teams charged one dollar for men, fifty cents for women, and five cents for children at the gate. Other teams passed a hat around and collected contributions.[15]

Any money left over after the essentials were paid for was divided among the players. The winners usually received 60 percent of the gate; the losers took home 40 percent. The chance to collect a little money could increase players' energy levels. Ramon Padroza of Newton, Kansas, said that the zeal to win was fierce. He recalled that the Newton Mexican team played highly competitive games against teams from Wichita, Florence, Topeka, Emporia, Hutchinson, and Wellington: "The games were very intense. I was a pitcher and made it a habit to deliberately hit their first batter with a fastball in order to scare the rest of the lineup. Of course, the opposite pitcher did the same thing to our first batter, which sometimes led to brawls. After the game, however, we shook hands and drank beers together."[16]

Kansas City native Marcelino Fernandez said: "Community teams in the Midwest were quite sophisticated when it came to business operations. The Kansas City teams had business agents who negotiated and arranged games with other community teams. We also took a percentage of the gate receipts, and sometimes asked for gas money, meals, and a place to stay from some of the other teams. The good teams generally agreed to our conditions because they also made good money at the gate."[17]

Some Midwest Mexican teams participated in numerous whirlwind tours, playing far away from home according to Abe Morales of East Chicago, and Ernesto Plaza of Omaha.[18] On Saturday, the visiting team and its supporters gathered in the early morning, forming a huge caravan of cars moving along on country roads. It must have been an incredible sight to see dozens of cars packed with Mexican supporters following their teams down the road to the next game. As the line of cars of fans and their team approached, the cars honked their horns, signaling their arrival, said Louis Sanchez of Dodge City.[19] These types of sports activities clearly demonstrated community pride in baseball teams and helped establish important political links between Mexican communities.[20] Frank Lujano of Newton, Kansas, recalled: "Sunday was always a big day for us back then. After working through the week, we always looked forward to the games, and the fans who followed us enjoyed them, too. This was a time for everyone to forget about work and problems and just have a good time. We had several hundred fans who came to the games each week, and when we made an error they let us know about it, but it was all in fun and we had a good time."[21]

Before the Sunday games, players from the two opposing teams would generally get together on Saturday night to party, according to Salvador Gutierrez of Kansas City, Missouri, and Lupe Molina of Kansas City, Kansas.[22] They noted that some teams would attempt to induce the best players on the opposing team to get drunk, so they would be ineffective the next day. Sometimes this ploy backfired because a few players actually seemed to play better with hangovers. Some teams imposed a 10 P.M. curfew before important games to prevent such shenanigans. Mexican men were often utilized as umpires in the Mexican leagues. Ann Antilano of Sterling, Illinois, recalled her father talking about his Midwest umpiring experiences in Gary, Indiana.[23]

Mexican teams from Texas and Mexico barnstormed the region and played exhibition games against local Mexican teams prior to the 1940s. Providing competition for Mexican Midwest teams were Los Cometas from

Morelos; Carta Blanca from Monterey; Los Aztecas, Los Cuauhtemocs, and La junta from Mexico City; and La Fuerza from Guanajuato.[24] The best teams from Texas were the Navarro Club and the Aztecas from San Antonio.

Nearly all of the Mexican ballplayers were big fans of major league teams and players. Many Mexican players took the bus or hitchhiked to major league ballparks to see their favorite teams and idols at Wrigley Field and Comiskey Park in Chicago, Baker's Field in Philadelphia, and Sportsmen's Park in St. Louis. Art Morales of East Chicago said that he and other young men found creative ways to get to the big league games: "I used to hitchhike to old Comiskey Park in Chicago. I tried to make the games when the New York Yankees were in town. My favorite player was Joe DiMaggio, the greatest player to wear a baseball uniform in my opinion. Many of my fondest memories as a boy [are of] the ballpark."[25]

Ramon Padroza of Newton, Kansas, fondly remembered: "We all had our favorite ballplayers during that time. My favorite ballplayers were Lefty Gomez and Babe Ruth. I remember watching a game at Wrigley Field between the Cubs and Pirates. It was one of the biggest thrills in my life. Some of us on the industrial teams were scouted by some of the major league teams and received official invitations to attend spring training. But our families needed us as breadwinners at home."[26]

Leo Barajas of Omaha, who was an outstanding ballplayer, remembers attending a World Series game: "I attended the 1942 World Series between the St. Louis Cardinals and the New York Yankees. We waited nearly two days in line for tickets. The Cardinals' 'Gashouse Gang' was the most popular team among us because it was one of the few teams in the Midwest. Attending the World Series is one of the highlights of my life."[27]

Ralph Rios of Sterling, Illinois, echoed these sentiments. Rios was born in Kansas City in 1927, and as a boy watched the Mexican baseball teams from Kansas and Missouri. Said Rios: "Many of us loved listening to major league baseball during the 1930s and 1940s. My favorite team and player were the St. Louis Cardinals and Stan Musial. I read the box scores every morning to see how the Cardinals and Musial had done the day before."[28]

Victoria Quintana of Parsons, Kansas, recollected that her brothers attended many games in Philadelphia and New York, and were especially fond of Connie Mack's "A's": "Many of us in Kansas had friends and relatives living in Pennsylvania. During the summers, we would visit them and go shopping in New York. Our brothers, however, preferred going to the ballparks to watch the Dodgers, Giants, Yankees, and the Athletics. My brothers were always excited to go to the East Coast because of all the baseball teams, whereas there were no major league teams in Kansas."[29]

Matt Hernandez noted that several communities formed all-star teams showcasing the best Mexican players.[30] He said the all-star games were often reported in the sports sections of the local newspapers with complete box scores. Hernandez played for the Hutchinson Mexican team from 1934 to 1936. His team played Mexican teams from Lyons, Dodge City, Newton, and Wichita. A consequence of these all-star teams was that many players became local sports legends and some even had the thrill of being scouted by teams like the Chicago Cubs, St. Louis Cardinals, New York Yankees, and Cleveland Indians, according to Abraham Vela of Omaha.[31] Sabastian Alvarez of Fort Madison, Iowa, talked about his own experience with the big league scouts: "We had an outstanding baseball team in Fort Madison. We played very good Mexican teams from the Quad-Cities area and several teams from Kansas and Missouri. In the stands were scouts from the various major league teams. I received two letters from the Chicago Cubs asking me to come to a tryout camp. My parents were opposed to it because I needed to work to help the family."[32]

Art Morales of East Chicago had a similar experience: "The Chicago Cub scouts saw me play and gave me a ticket to Chicago to try out for the team. But my parents wouldn't let me go because they believed that Chicago was a wild town and it would corrupt my morals."[33]

Women's Teams

In the years leading up to World War II, there were several Mexican women's teams in the Midwest. These teams were managed and coached by all-male staffs, and games were often played in small, nearby fields while the male teams were playing on the major diamond. The women's teams often traveled with the men's teams. In addition to concurrent games, there were sometimes doubleheaders, with the women playing in the morning and the men playing afterwards.[34] Carol Garcia Martinez, an outstanding pitcher, was born in Mexico in 1923, and later played first base for Las Gallinas of East Chicago. She remembers the green satin uniforms they purchased after taking a collection: "Some young women were active in all types of sports in school. We formed community teams because we enjoyed sports. Most of our parents were supportive as long as our older brothers and male friends were watching over us. We played nine innings and basically played by the same rules as the men. Our games were extremely competitive."[35]

Before the war, the best-known women's teams were Las Gallinas of East Chicago; Las Cuauhtemocs of Newton, Kansas; Las Aztecas of Kansas City; and Las Amapolas of South Chicago. There were also Mexican women's teams in Chicago; Emporia, Kansas; and in Gary and Whitney, Indiana.[36] The state of Nebraska had women's teams in Bayard, Grand Island, Omaha, and Lincoln.[37] *Mexican American Harbor Lights*, an East Chicago publication, noted that the women's baseball teams "performed with devotion, speed, and great skill. The audience loved every great play they made, especially a stolen base. The parents made sure the girls were on time for all games and practice. Hundreds of fans came to see them play."[38]

According to several eyewitnesses, the women's teams were excellent, and exciting to watch. A few of the women might have been better players than some of their male counterparts, according to Frederick R. Maravilla of East Chicago: "The Kansas City and East Chicago teams had several excellent players. Some of the women were gifted athletes, while others learned to play outstanding ball from their brothers. The coaches used to say that we wanted some of the women on our men's team, which nearly always brought laughter from the guys because they thought we were joking. We weren't kidding."[39]

A handful of women became folk heroines because of their exploits on the diamond. As was the case with the men's teams, some of the women's teams had junior or "B" teams. Las Gallinas from East Chicago, for example, had a junior team called Las Gallinas Chicks. Some Mexican girls also played baseball with the Catholic Youth Organization (CYO) and in various city leagues and tournaments prior to World War II.[40]

Postwar Baseball

Baseball had an amazing revitalization throughout the Midwest after 1945, and its popularity was directly linked to the political and civil rights activities of the Mexican American community. Alberto Muniz said: "Sports have been and continue to be an important part of our history. Before the war, the fiestas, politics, and sports were integrated and not viewed as separated activities. Our parents' generation clearly understood the social importance of combining culture, civil rights, and recreation as one enterprise. The second generation continued that strong tradition after the war."[41]

Al Lopez, manager of the Chicago White Sox during the late 1950s and early 1960s, for example, was a member of the Chicago chapter of the American G.I. Forum. In 1962, Lopez received his membership card in a pregame ceremony at Comiskey Park from G.I. Forum local officials. Also, the G.I. Forum National Convention sponsored a game at Wrigley Field in Chicago in 1963.[42]

There were other significant changes in sports that reflected the gains of the Civil Rights Movement. The hiring of Mexican American umpires and league officials was a major breakthrough. For the first time, the postwar period witnessed the mass participation of Mexican American youth in Little Leagues, Pony and Colt teams, and high school teams. Youth were visible in all aspects of school and community sports whereas few Mexican American children played school sports or city-sanctioned teams prior to the 1940s. Ramon Pedroza of Newton, Kansas, said: "After the war, Mexican American teams played in city tournaments and leagues with white teams, which was different [from] when white teams refused to play Mexican teams in the 1920s and 1930s. We felt this was a step in the right direction. At the same time, we maintained our own community tournaments and leagues. The softball team of Newton, for example, took the city championship in the late 1940s."[43]

Another significant change was the skyrocketing popularity of softball after the war. Although there were some slow- and fast-pitch softball teams before the war, they were relatively few in number. The first softball games in the Mexican community in the Midwest were played in the 1930s. In 1937, there were a few softball teams such as Los Diablos of East Chicago. The *Kansas City Star* reported on a Mexican softball tournament which took place in Central Kansas in 1938. The Mexican teams represented at this tournament included Wichita, Hutchinson, Salina, Newton, Kanapolis, and Lyons. The newspaper article further noted that there were big crowds and that the Bravos had won the championship.

Another key reason for the growing popularity of fast- and slow-pitch softball was that most veterans were raising families and getting older. The slower pace reflected their physical condition.[44] They had to be careful not to get hurt and miss work because they had to pay the bills. Yet, these former players still played hard because they were competitive.[45] Nevertheless, a few Mexican American hardball teams and leagues survived after the war, including the Topeka Aztecas and Aguilas.

Between the late 1940s and the early 1960s several Mexican American, Latin American, and Spanish American baseball leagues, as well as state and regional softball tournaments, were established. Many of these tournaments are still going.[46] Tournament games could be found each weekend in places like Newton, Kansas City, Flint, Des Moines, Pontiac, Port Huron, Omaha, Chicago, Emily City, Detroit, Emporia, Capac, Cudahay, Milwaukee, and Bethlehem. A case in point was the Chanute Softball Tournament that was held from 1963 to 1979. Other Mexican communities in Kansas have sponsored their own tournaments, and Kansas City alone had five baseball teams.[47] Something special that has emerged in some of these tournaments is the "old-timers" game, which precedes the championship game. Some of the players from the 1940s, '50s, '60s, and '70s compete for fun and friendship. These games have been sponsored, for example, in Scottsbluff, Nebraska, and in Newton, Kansas. This recognition is a tribute to these pioneers who faced discrimination and, in turn, fought prejudice so that future generations could play sports in public facilities and join mainstream leagues such as the Little League and Pop Warner football.

In fact, one of the oldest softball tournaments takes place each year in Newton. This tournament can be traced back to 1948, when the Latin American Club (formed in 1946) sponsored the first tournament. Dozens of teams throughout the Midwest, Texas, and other southwestern states have participated in the Newton competition during the last fifty years.[48] One of the dominant teams after the war came from Oklahoma. Other championship teams include the Newton Mexican Catholics (1946), Newton McGee (1948), Wichita Guadalupanos (1950), Topeka La Siesta (1963), and Kansas Los Bravos (1969 and 1970).[49]

The Newton Softball Tournament still plays the cultural role that prewar baseball games promoted among Mexican Americans. The tournament events centered around family, friendship, and community unity. The games are only one part of the weekend's events. There are picnics, dances, games for the children, and an opportunity for renewing old friendships. In Omaha they have played the Mexican Softball Tournament for many years at Hitchcock and Upland Parks. Teams have come from Nebraska, Missouri, Iowa, Colorado, and Kansas. Here too, the tournaments have sponsored old-timers games with many former players, some who played during the 1940s and 1950s, competing against their grandchildren and other old-timers from surrounding communities.

Michigan had teams such as the Pontiac Mayans and Aztecs, the Adrian Pirates, and a team in Ecorse called the Latin American Club.

Lalo Perez of Flint said proudly: "The state of Michigan was a hotbed for Mexican baseball during the 1940s through the 1970s. We had a baseball team here in Ecorse sponsored by the Latin American Club. There were teams in Flint, Detroit, Lansing, Adrian, Emily City, Port Huron, and Pontiac. We also played Mexican teams from the state of Ohio."[50]

Over the years, Michigan has produced some outstanding baseball players. The Villareal brothers from Lansing were two of the best in the state. Flint has had its share, too, including one that pitched for Michigan State University. The Castanon brothers, Joe, Frank, Hank, and Marty, from the city of Alma were known for playing great baseball in the 1960s and 1970s. Steve Benavidez of Detroit played baseball at Eastern Michigan University in the 1980s. Saginaw had the Vasquez brothers, Joe and Tiburcio "Tovito," in the 1960s and 1970s. Mexican American baseball in Saginaw goes back to the 1940s and 1950s when the Gallitos were playing.[51]

In 1958, the Spanish American League was formed in Flint.[52] Other baseball tournaments have also been referred to as "Latin American" or "Hispanic." The main reason for this ethnic designation was because players comprised diverse backgrounds, including Mexicans, Puerto Ricans, and other Central and Latin Americans.[53] Aurora, Illinois, for instance, established the Latin American Baseball League.

Ohio and Pennsylvania likewise saw a dramatic increase of Mexican softball teams after the war. A Mexican American team was formed in Toledo as early as 1947. Eventually, teams were established in Bowling Green and Cleveland. Most of those in Ohio were industrial teams as opposed to community or league teams, and frequently traveled to Michigan, Indiana, and Illinois playing in Mexican American softball tournaments.[54]

As was the case before the war, major league baseball scouts continued to visit the Midwest looking for future big league players. Both the Cleveland Indians and the Chicago White Sox sent team representatives to scout Mike Torrez, who was playing for the Topeka Nationals. Torrez later signed a major league contract and later played for the Boston Red Sox and New York Yankees during the 1970s. His brother, Richard Torrez, played with the Topeka basketball team in the Midwest Mexican American Basketball Association.[55] Another great player was Julio Rodriguez from Saginaw, who played for Central Michigan University and later was drafted by the Kansas City Royals. Julio spent a few years in the minor leagues and eventually returned to Saginaw. He was a power hitter outfielder, one of the fastest players around, and had a major league arm. People in the stands were in awe of his tremendous throwing ability and accuracy from the outfield.[56] One of the best fast-pitch softball players in recent memory was Martin "Marty" Castanon from both Alma and Lansing, Michigan. He played in a traveling league that included some of the world's best pitchers and teams in fast-pitch softball.

The Catholic Leagues continued to be popular after the war. There were Catholic Youth Organization leagues and St. Jude's teams. Mexican Americans often played for both Catholic schools and Little League teams. Catholic softball tournaments flourished in several cities in Kansas. There were also city and independent leagues where Mexicans played baseball, but regardless of the level play, Mexican American teams and players were generally talented and competitive.

Mexican women's softball teams began to flourish in the late 1940s and early 1950s. There was a women's softball team in East Chicago by 1949. Las Aztecas of Kansas City won the city championship about the same time. Newton, Kansas, also had established teams in the 1940s, and there were also outstanding women's teams in Sterling, Illinois, and Lincoln, Nebraska, according to Dolores Rios and Marge Villanueva Lambert.[57] Rios played in the summer baseball leagues in Illinois in 1947 and 1948, and noted that baseball was very popular among Mexican women after the war. Lambert also remembered that Nebraska had several women's teams: "Mexican women played baseball before World War II. Many of them worked during the war but resumed playing after the war ended, along with younger women. The state of Nebraska appears to have had several women's teams starting as early as 1946. There was also a team of women in the city of Lincoln."[58]

Fifi Jasso of Newton, Kansas, who was born in Newton in 1932, recalled: "I played third base for the Mexican American women's team of Newton in 1949 and 1950. . . . We had lots of fun and I have many wonderful memories of those days. Sadly, some of my former teammates have passed away."[59]

The employment of women after the war resulted in their playing for industrial teams and leagues as well. Said Juanita Vasquez: "Most of the industrial teams before the war were for men. However, the growing number of women in the workplace after the war resulted in the formation of women's sports in baseball, basketball, and bowling. At the time, we did not realize that our entering factories represented the benefits of industrial sports."[60]

In the 1980s and 1990s the growth of baseball throughout the Midwest continued. Some Mexican communities have both fast-pitch and slow-pitch teams. Saginaw for example, was the host of the Annual Latino State Fast Pitch Tournament during the 1980s. There was also a Mexican American Slow Pitch Softball league in Saginaw that used to take over Hoyt Park and Wickes Park with sixteen teams playing every Sunday. Pontiac and Detroit had some great teams during this period, when Pontiac hosted the Annual State Latino Tournament.[61]

Oklahoma City has recently established a ten-team Liga de Beisbol Mexicana, while Chicago has formed the Aztec and Mayan Leagues. Southeast Kansas, the Quad-Cities, and the Fox Valley of Illinois is experiencing a rise in the number of new baseball teams, leagues, and tournaments. Saginaw, Lansing, and Pontiac had excellent women's softball teams in the 1970s and 1980s. The Saginaw team, coached by Chan Flores and sponsored by Casa del Rey, was dominant and won the Michigan Hispanic Women's State Tournament for years.[62]

Conclusion

Midwestern Mexican American communities, for the better part of seventy years, have produced many talented athletes, as well as numerous teams, leagues, and tournaments. This occurred because of the numerous individuals who put so much effort into developing youth sports programs and other organized sports activities. These sports—especially baseball, but also boxing, basketball, and other contests—played multiple roles in the life of the community. Involvement in sports taught young people the rules of fair play, helped develop their physical and organizational skills, and helped them channel their competitiveness in a positive way. These activities brought Midwestern Mexican people together across miles and circumstances, and brought joy to competitors and spectators alike.

With sports, Midwestern Mexicans had heroes to congratulate, teams to rally around, positive activities for their children, and shared experiences with which they could build a stronger sense of cultural unity and common purpose. To these people, sports were not just games. They were important elements of community identity and political empowerment.

Notes

This article is an excerpt from an unpublished manuscript entitled, *Cuentos y Encuentros: An Oral History of Mexicans in the Midwestern United States, 1900–1979.* The majority of interviews were conducted during my sabbatical leave between 1987 and 1988. Many of the people interviewed resided in Kansas, a state that had the dubious reputation of being considered the most racist state in the U.S. with respect to Mexicans. This helps to explain, in large part, the long history of Mexican organizational resistance there. Many of the individuals cited are now deceased. This chapter is dedicated to them.

1. There are a growing number of books, articles, and videos on the history of Latino baseball in the United States. A sample of these works include James D. Cockcroft, *Latinos en e! beisbol de los Estados Unidos* (Mexico, D.F.: Siglo Veintiuno Editores., 1999); Michael M. Oleksak, *Beisbol, Latin Americans, and the Grand Old Game*, (Hollywood, CA: High Top Sports Production, 1992); USA Home Entertainment, *MLB Latin Superstar*, (New York: MLB Home Video, 2000); Schlessinger Video Productions, *The Hispanic and Latin American Heritage Video Collection*, (Bala Cynwyd, PA, 1995); Carlos Garcia, *Baseball Forever*, (Mexico, 1979); Jonah Winter, *Beisbol! Latino Baseball Pioneers and Legends*, (New York: Let and Low Books, 2001); and Gilbert Garcia's "*Beisboleros*: Latin Americans and Baseball in the Northwest Region," Unpublished paper, Eastern Washington University, no date.

2. Interview with Marselino Fernandez, Kansas City, Missouri, February 26, 1987. Fernandez was an outstanding athlete in the Kansas City area and excelled in several sports. He is also a prominent sports historian regarding the Mexican American communities in Kansas and Missouri. Fernandez was inducted into the Kansas City Mexican American Sports Hall of Fame in the early 1980s.

3. Interviews with Bias Esquivel, Kansas City, Missouri, March 1, 1987; Josephina Jaramillo Martinez Los Angeles, California, April 17, 1995; and Joseph D. Gonzalez, October 16, 1987, author's files. Esquivel was born in Mexico in 1910 and came to the U.S. in 1926 and has an excellent knowledge of sports in the Kansas City area. Martinez was born in Mexico in 1901 and remembers Justine Cordero and Louis Garcia, who were active with youth sports in South Chicago during the 1920s. Gonzalez played baseball for Los Gallos baseball team in East Chicago between 1938 and 1941.

4. Ciro H. Sepulveda, "Social Life and Nativism in La Colonia del Harbor," in James B. Lane and Edward J. Escobar, eds., *Forging a Community: The Latino Experience in Northwest Indiana, 1919–1975* (Chicago: Cattails Press, 1987), 87.

5. Interview with Lando Velandez, Des Moines, Iowa, June 17, 1986.

6. Written correspondence with Ricardo Medina, Blyth, California, March 2, 1995, and Ricardo Parra, Indianapolis, Indiana, author's files.

7. Interview with Elmer Vega, Newton, Kansas, June 10, 1987.

8. Interview with Alex Cruz, Parsons, Kansas, June 9, 1987.

9. Interview with Elmer Vega, Newton, Kansas, June 18, 1987.

10. Written correspondence with Porfy Nila, North Platte, Nebraska, January 11, 1999.

11. Interview with Perfecto Torrez, Topeka, Kansas, February 10, 1987. Torrez was an outstanding player in the Topeka area, especially between the years 1931 and 1937. He pitched for the Piratas, Nacionales, Cometas, and the Bakers. Torrez pitched a perfect game against the Mexican team from Emporia during the 1930–31 season.

12. Interview with Eva Hernandez, Hutchinson, Kansas, March 21, 1988. Some Mexican Midwest baseball teams were allowed to play in public parks, including Block Park, Washington Park, Blackhawk Park, Beaver Park, Credit Inland Park, Burke's Park, Southeast Recreation Center, Sunday Park, Athletic Park, Union Pacific Park, Sinnissippi Park, John Deere Diamond, Douglas Park, Barstow City Park, and Levings Park.

13. Interview with Phillip Martinez, Dodge City, Kansas, June 24, 1988. Martinez played baseball for the Dodge City Aztecas during the 1930s. He played third base and noted that this decade witnessed some of the best Mexican ballplayers and teams throughout Kansas. These Kansas teams included Chanute (Los Toreros and the Eagles), Independence, Coffeyville, Pittsburgh, Garden City (Latin Americans), Dodge City (Mexican Eagles and the Aztecas),

Deerfield, Florence, Emporia (Los Morelos), Parsons, Atchison, Peabody, Iola, Fredonia, Argentine (Eagles), Hutchinson (Lobos), Newton (Cuauhtemocs), Wichita (Aztecas), Horton, Lyons, Wellington (Mayans), Syracuse (Merchants), Topeka (Aguilas and Nationals) Nixon, and Herington.

14. Interview with Bacho Rodriguez, Hutchinson, Kansas, January 28, 1987. Also interview with Francisco Vargas, Topeka, Kansas, February 10, 1987.

15. Interview with Frank Lujano, Newton, Kansas, June 18, 1987. Lujano was born in 1913 and later played baseball for the Newton Cuauhtemocs. He noted that the 1920s and 1930s saw outstanding teams in Topeka, Wichita, and Wellington, Kansas. His wife still has his cotton uniform from the 1930s. Almost everyone agrees in Newton that Lujano was one of the best ballplayers of all time.

16. Interview with Ramon Pedroza, Newton, Kansas, June 18, 1987. Like so many young men of his generation, Padroza served during World War II and saw action in Africa and Italy. Pedroza was born in Newton in 1913. He was an outstanding baseball player in the community of Newton and played pitcher and first base in 1931 for the Cuauhtemocs. I also interviewed Jose G. Calvillo from Hutchinson, Kansas; in author's files.

17. Interview with Marselino Fernandez, Kansas City, Missouri, February 26, 1987.

18. Interviews with Abe Morales, East Chicago, Indiana, May 19, 1987, and with Ernesto Plaza, Omaha, Nebraska, May 30, 1987. Morales was active with sports in the Gary, Indiana, area. He noted that Gary had an outstanding baseball and basketball teams prior to World War II. Morales added that most of the sports activities were sponsored either by companies or the Catholic Church. Plaza played baseball in the western part of Nebraska prior to the 1940s. He added that there were several outstanding Mexican teams in this region including teams in Scottsbluff, Mitchell, Morrill, Lyman, Alliance, and Bayard.

19. Interview with Louis Sanchez, Dodge City, Kansas, January 21, 1987. As a young boy during the 1920s, Sanchez was the batboy for the Mexican teams. Later, Sanchez played for the Santa Fe Railroad baseball team during the 1930s and 1940s. They played several local Mexican teams including the Aztecas from Dodge City and the Garden City Latin Americans.

20. Interview with Marselino Fernandez, Kansas City, February 26, 1987. Fernandez was born in Arizona in 1913. He noted that there were Mexican baseball teams in the Kansas City area as early as 1923. Fernandez eventually joined the Kansas City Aztecas as a star pitcher and first baseman during the 1933–1936 seasons. Some of the players on the 1936 Aztecas included Manuel Zuniga, Lupe Molina, Felipe Camacho, Charlie Mendez, Juan Rodriguez, Meno Hernandez, Caderino Montoya, Milo Hernandez, Carlos Montez, Lalo Nieto, Chico Barbosa, Fidencio Paz, and Fred and Paul Sauceda.

21. Interview with Frank Lujano of Newton, Kansas, June 18, 1987.

22. Interview with Salvador Gutierrez, Kansas City, Missouri, February 25, 1987. Also see *Latin Baseball 50 Years Ago*, author's files. Interview with Lope Molina, Kansas City, Kansas, June 5, 1987. Gutierrez was a promoter of baseball games in the Kansas City area during the 1930s, and also helped establish Mexican baseball leagues. Molina was born in Mexico in 1902 and has a rich history of playing baseball both in the Southwest and Midwest. In 1924, he organized the Azaca baseball team in Kansas City.

23. Telephone interview with Ann Antilano, Sterling, Illinois, March 20, 1998.

24. Interviews with Federico Hernandez, Parsons, Kansas, July 9, 1988, and Robert Segovia, East Chicago, Indiana, May 19, 1987. Segovia was an outstanding player in East Chicago. Also interviewed was Salvador Gutierrez from Kansas City, Missouri, February 26, 1987. Gutierrez was born in Mexico in 1911 and came to Kansas City in 1920 working for a packinghouse. He later served in Europe during World War II. He noted that Mexican players were very dominant in the Catholic leagues. These players were known affectionately as the "Guadalupanas." Also see Jan Wahl, *Mexican and Mexican American Fiestas and Celebrations in*

Scotubluff Nebraska, (The Nebraska Committee for the Humanities, 1988), 15. Wahl found that the earlier Mexican teams formed the Mission League, since most of the teams were sponsored by the Catholic Churches.

25. Interview with Art Morales, East Chicago, Indiana, May 1, 1987. Also interview with Joseph P Gonzalez, Gary Indiana, October 16, 1987. Gonzalez played for Los Gallos baseball team from 1938 through 1941, before serving in the aviation corps during World War II. The Midwest had several outstanding teams and players besides those in Kansas. These popular teams included Las Aguilus of Sterling, Illinois; Los Tigres of Rockford, Illinois; the Aztecas of Joliet, Illinois; La Flor de Mayo of St. Joseph, Missouri; Los Diablos and Los Gallos of East Chicago, Indiana; the Aztecs of Gary, Indiana; El Club Mexicano, and Los Aztecas from Milwaukee, Wisconsin; the South Chicago Excelsiors; Los Estrellas de Toledo; and Los Mexicanos of Des Moines, Iowa.

26. Interview with Ramon Pedroza, Newton, Kansas, June 18, 1987. Telephone interview with George Robles, Milwaukee, Wisconsin, June 24, 1994. Robles has been very involved with Mexican American sports in Wisconsin, and was an outstanding athlete in several sports.

27. Interview with Leo Barajas, Omaha, Nebraska, June 3, 1987.

28. Interview with Ralph Rios, Sterling, Illinois, May 26, 1987.

29. Interview with Victoria (Vicki) Quintana, Parsons, Kansas, July 9, 1988. Interview with Anthony (Tony) Navarro, Davenport, Iowa, June 25, 1986. In the 1980s, several Midwest communities paid tribute to the old-time baseball players. The 1923 Mexican All-Stars team was saluted, for example, by the Quad-Cities Mexican American communities in 1981. The eight surviving members included Cruz Sierra, 78; Socorro Nache, 77; Isaac Rangel, 77; Augie Martel, 77; Joseph Ybarra, 73; Lewis Sierra, 72; and Eleuterio Martel and Jess Castillas, both 70. The community of Horton, Kansas, recognized several players from the 1930s, including Nate Vallejo, Gilbert Martinez, Julio Vallejo, Lolo Vallejo, Nick De La Cruz, Benito De La Cruz, Lupe Espinosa, Phillip Picon, and Fidel Cortez.

30. Interview with Matt Hernandez, Hutchinson, Kansas, January 23, 1987.

31. Interview with Bacho Rodriguez, Hutchinson, January 28, 1987. Also interview with Abraham Vela from Omaha, Nebraska, June 1, 1987. He was born in Horton, Kansas, in 1917. His father arrived in 1904 to work on the railroad. Vela played baseball in Nebraska during the 1930s.

32. Interview with Sebastian Alvarez, Fort Madison, Iowa, June 19, 1986. Alvarez was one of the best all-around athletes in Fort Madison during the 1920s and 1930s. He played baseball, basketball, and football in high school. Alvarez played on several Mexican baseball teams and he was later scouted by the Chicago Cubs. Also interview with Antonio (Tony) Rojas from Garden City, Kansas, January 10, 1987. Rojas noted that Margarito "Maggie" Gomez of Newton, Kansas, received a letter from the New York Yankees for a tryout as a right-fielder. After World War II, Gomez received a letter from the St. Louis Cardinals about a tryout.

33. Interview with Art Morales, East Chicago, Indiana, May 1, 1987. Morales noted that nearly 98 percent of Mexican American players in East Chicago either volunteered or were drafted when the war broke out. Morales played for the service team along with some professional players of the Chicago White Sox. He said it was a great thrill to play with some of the players that he had watched at Comiskey Park. Morales also stated that some of the armed forces baseball teams had Mexican American players.

34. Interview with Juanita Vasquez, East Chicago, Indiana, May 18, 1987.

35. Interview with Carol Garcia Martinez, East Chicago, Indiana, May 18, 1987. Garcia's sister was a professional singer and performed at Chicago hotels. Her father had a band in East Chicago during the 1930s. Mariano Guereca and Nieves Lombrano, for example, organized the 1942 Las Aztecas of Kansas City. Some of the players included Mary and Sarah Fernandez, Vicki

Franco, Chona Martinez, Epifinia Carpeo, Nacha Barbosa, Santos Olivia, Lola Oliva, Margarite Rodriquez, Grace Briones, Irene and "Choppy" Ibarra, and Annie Molina.

36. Interview with Lola Aguilar, Emporia, Kansas, July 2, 1988. Also interview with Lali Garcia, Kansas City, Kansas, June 5, 1987. She has an excellent history of the women's baseball team in Kansas City.

37. Interview with Mary Sousa, Omaha, Nebraska, September 17, 1987. Sousa was born in 1918 and later played baseball with the Our Lady of Guadalupe Church girl's team between 1938 and 1940.

38. *Mexican American Harbor Lights* (East Chicago, Indiana, 1992), 80. This book was published by a group of Mexican American women known as Senoras of Yesteryear (SOY). The East Chicago Mexican women's team played against South Chicago, Whiting, Gary, Hessville, and other local teams.

39. Interviews with Frederick R. Maravilla, East Chicago, October 16, 1987. Maravilla was the team manager of Las Gallinas starting in 1937 and also played on the men's baseball team.

40. These teams were primarily concentrated in the states of Kansas and Nebraska.

41. Interview with Alberto Muniz, Lincoln Park, Michigan, May 16, 1987.

42. Both the G.I. Forum and LULAC chapters had several baseball teams, which entered tournament play in the Midwest. One of the better teams was the Topeka G.I. Forum. In addition, there were other sponsors of Mexican softball teams including the Elks, Lions, Kiwanis, and other Lodge sponsorship.

43. Interview with Ramon Pedroza, Newton, Kansas, June 18, 1987.

44. Interview with Pete M. Guardian, Chanute, Kansas, June 10, 1987.

45. Interview with Harley Ponce, Chanute, Kansas, June 10, 1987. Ponce was born in Chanute in 1939.

46. Interview with Lalo Perez, Flint, Michigan, May 6, 1987. Perez was born in San Antonio, Texas, in 1920 and came to Flint in 1937. Several of his brothers served in the military. To cut costs, teams generally stayed with members of the opposition. The Wichita Aztecs often stayed in the homes of opposing team members because it was one way of saving money.

47. Interviews with Harley Ponce and Raul Quirarte, Chanute, Kansas, June 10, 1987, and Linda de Leon Cabrera, Bethlehem, Pennsylvania, July 10, 1988. Over the years, Midwest softball teams have included the Emporia Brown Eagles, Cudahay Dukes, Flint Pirates, Bethlehem Mexicans, Wichita Aztecs, Argentine Eagles, Emporia Los Chicanos and Bandaleros, Silvis Aztecas, Kansas City Bravos, Milwaukee Los Amigos, Chicago All-Stars, Blue Island Latinos, Wichita North End and Builders, and the Waukegan Aguilas.

48. *Fiesta Program's Tribute to Softball Tournaments, 1948–1988*, author's files.

49. Other champions have included the Wichita Padres (1972), Hutchinson Los Lobos (1976), Oklahoma Casa Dulce (1978), Omaha Mestizos (1980), Kansas City Aztecas (1981), Houston Nine (1982), Pueblo Colorado Angels (1983), and Austin Jokers (1987).

50. Interview with Lalo Perez, Flint, Michigan, May 6, 1987.

51. Written correspondence with Ricardo Medina, Blythe, California, March 2, 1995.

52. Interview with Lalo Perez, Flint, Michigan, May 16, 1987.

53. Interview with Irene Campos Carr, Aurora, Illinois, author's files.

54. Written correspondence with Ricardo Medina, Blythe, California, March 2, 1995.

55. Interview with Robert Gomez, Topeka, Kansas, author's files.

56. Written correspondence with Ricardo Medina, Blythe, California, March 2, 1995.

57. Interview with Ray Olias, Newton, Kansas, March 25, 1987.

58. Interview with Marge Villanueva Lambert, Lincoln, Nebraska, June 3, 1987, and Dolores Rios, Sterling, Illinois, May 2, 1987.

59. Interview with Fifi Jasso, Newton, Kansas, March 25, 1987. Her grandparents and parents came from Mexico to Newton in 1907. Interview with Ila Placencia, Los Angeles, California, December 30, 1994. Placenia shared an incredible amount of history regarding the Mexican community in Des Moines, Iowa. As a young woman, she was active with sports.

60. Interview with Juanita Vasquez, East Chicago, Indiana, May 18, 1987.

61. Written correspondence with Ricardo Medina, Blythe, California, March 2, 1995.

62. Written correspondence with Ricardo Medina, Blythe, California, March 2, 1995.

8

Roberto Clemente

Images, Identity, and Legacy

—Samuel O. Regalado

Roberto Clemente did not come to the United States mainland with the purpose of pioneering change. He came to pursue his dream of success in the major leagues. Driven by his competitive spirit, when he left Puerto Rico in 1953, he carried with him the credentials for baseball greatness: a keen batting eye, sprinter's speed, defensive quickness, and a powerful throwing arm. Moreover, his athletic skills were augmented by his tremendous self-confidence. Through the course of his career, his achievements on the field led to well-earned notoriety as being one of the most talented players both of his generation and within the history of the game itself. "There isn't anything he can't do," crowed the *Sporting News* in a 1968 article about Clemente. "He can hit, hit with power at times, run, throw and there just isn't a better fielder."[1]

But Clemente proved to have other credentials, too: a generous heart, compassion, and outrage at injustice. As evidenced in a 1971 interview, Clemente, by then, assumed a self-proclaimed duty beyond the field of play. "Lots of kids will try to imitate me, and maybe I will have the chance to do some good for people," he told the *New York Times*.[2] Combined with his talents as a player, Clemente understood the difference between mere athletic skills and his role as a leader. His apprenticeship to greatness, however, came in an age when other Latinos and blacks in baseball experienced the difficult world of racial discrimination and prejudice. Moreover, he discovered, images of Latinos were, too often, uncomplimentary. Yet Clemente's emergence into stardom also illuminated the internal conflict Puerto Ricans, in their transition from island to mainland, encountered regarding race and identity. On three fronts, as a player, a symbol, and a legend, Roberto Clemente's presence challenged the perceptions that mainstream Americans held of Latinos. However, for Puerto Ricans, his role and heroic legacy also brought into focus the delicate balance between race and status.

Contrary to the notion that all Latino players emerged from impoverished backgrounds, Clemente, born in 1934 near San Juan, Puerto Rico, came from a middle-class family. His father, Melchor, was a foreman at a local sugar mill. Like other youths in his upbringing, baseball stole Clemente's heart and he played in the San Juan sandlots armed with a bat "fashioned from the branch of a guava tree, a glove [that] was improvised from a coffee bean sack, and [a] ball [that] was a tight knot of rags."[3] The young Puerto Rican also experienced his first lessons in race relations. Since the early years of the twentieth century, San Juan, like other Caribbean cities, was a major hub for barnstorming teams and players from the United States looking to make extra money during the winter months. From that bunch, Clemente most admired Monte Irvin, an outfielder for the New York Giants who was among the first blacks in the major leagues and went on to the Hall of Fame. Clemente, himself a black man, considered race irrelevant in determining the quality of an individual. "I don't believe in color, I believe in people," he later stated as a big leaguer.[4]

Even in Puerto Rico, Clemente's idealism proved to be an anomaly. His brethren, indeed, did believe in color as a factor in status. On the surface, of course, race was seemingly not a problem in Puerto Rico. Since its days as a colonial entity under Spain, blacks in Puerto Rico, by virtue of slave protection laws, the practice of compadrazgo (god parenting), and varied socioeconomic opportunities based on merit, had some degree of latitude and acceptance not found in the North American continent. Thus, in Puerto Rico, that local or regional laws barred no blacks from public accommodations was not uncommon, nor was there any history of lynch mobs in the commonwealth or continual violence against blacks there.

Clemente's vision of Puerto Rico, thus, was not entirely unwarranted and, in fact, advanced in the world he knew best—baseball. Puerto Rican players of color frequented many sports and competed with whites. Notable black ballplayers from the states, when on tour in Puerto Rico, stayed at the lavish LaFrance Hotel in San Juan, and some, like Negro

Leaguer Dick Seay, even settled on the island.[5] Black stars like Willard
Brown and Monte Irvin, through their achievements and public freedom,
painted a picture of such racial tolerance that Clemente and his Latino
contemporaries understandably could hardly conceive of the kind of circumstance they later found north of their homeland.

Yet, though Puerto Rico did not have an extended period of black
slavery and did not maintain overt racially segregated laws and customs,
race was a factor in the determination of status. Largely because of Spanish
rule in the years prior to 1898, Caucasians held a higher status than blacks
on the island. People of prominence were either white or made convincing arguments to that effect. By the 1960s, as a new middle class emerged,
evidence of a stratified society also appeared. Joseph P. Fitzpatrick argued:
"Admission to certain societies and clubs, social acceptance by some
groups of middle and upper class people, and particularly marriage, are
[a serious hindrance] for a person who is identified as colored."[6] Even
Pedro Zorilla, who sat at the top of the island's baseball echelon during
Clemente's upbringing, was white. The reality of race and society on the
island did not escape the attention of those affected. "If I was back in
San Juan, I wouldn't have any office job," recalled a black Puerto Rican
migrant in New York City during the 1950s. "You don't see girls of my
color in an office—unless they're cleaning up or something."[7] Indeed, the
ever-observant Vic Power confirmed that "You can go anywhere that you
want. . . . But the funny thing about it is if you go to a lot of places like a
bank or hotel, the white Puerto Ricans—they get the jobs."[8] As racial barriers were quietly apparent in the commonwealth, on the mainland they
were, of course, far more overt.

Puerto Rican blacks, like Clemente, were not ignorant of racism in
the states. Stories of racial discrimination were in abundance from those
that had spent considerable time in the states and had returned to the
island. However, the degree of resistance to integration raised, by the
1950s, a new level of intensity in the struggle to bring about civil rights.
Prior to World War II, proponents of segregation were comforted by the
fact that no one in the three branches of government seemed to have an
appetite to change the status quo. However, cracks in that veneer were
apparent in the immediate years that followed the end of the war. Almost
in succession, the executive and judicial branches adopted policies and
rendered decisions that shot holes into Jim Crow. Those actions helped
to stimulate what was once a grass roots desire for civil rights into a full-
fledged movement.

Events in baseball, of course, also played a role in the dynamics of that era. The integration of the major leagues, for example, occurred seven years before the landmark U.S. Supreme Court's decision, *Brown v. School Board of Topeka, Kansas* (1954). Jackie Robinson's entry and subsequent success rightfully won praise from proponents of integration who concluded those gigantic strides in race relations had been accomplished. These successes, however, did not come without a price. On the ball diamond, Robinson hardly got a free ride. Throughout the 1947 season, disgruntled segregationists dogged the Brooklyn rookie with racial epithets regularly. And in the days following the 1954 decision, backlash in the streets and in the schools were also common as segregation aficionados determined to prevent legal integration from attaining success.

Old stereotypes also heightened in this period of racial stress. Among the most popular was the alleged lack of intelligence of people of color. Watermelon-eating, slow-witted images of blacks were not an uncommon image in many circles within the mainstream, but Latinos, too, bore the brunt of unflattering portraits. Tales of ignorant people from Latin America, through the years, was reinforced via the media in the 1950s. The halting English spoken by Desi Arnaz's "Ricky Ricardo" character on the *I Love Lucy* show, seen as charming by many viewers, also did little to advance any notion of Latino virtues.

Roberto Clemente began his major league career in this difficult time. Not entirely naive about the racial characteristics found in the United States, Clemente, in advance of going to the mainland, often muttered his displeasure about the injustice towards blacks within an earshot of those around him. Any thoughts of launching racial change, however, were usually quelled by elders such as his mentor, Robert Marin. "They've been like that for two hundred years. You're going there to play ball. That's all."

Despite early warnings regarding the racial environment in the states, Clemente's experience with players who were prone to use racial epithets in their lexicon proved to be difficult. The derogatory images of Latinos, as exhibited in the mainstream media and sports pages in the newspapers, added to his displeasure and fueled a temperament that journalists often described as rage. Described by *The Sporting News* as a person with "the hot blood of defiance," the proud Puerto Rican did not accept his lot quietly.[9] "Lots of times I have the feeling people want to take advantage of me, especially the writers," he argued. "They talk to me but maybe they don't like me so they write about me the way they want to write."[10] Encounters with the press staff were common. Often he concluded that his being "black and Puerto Rican" tainted the media's perceptions of him.[11] Clemente's most ardent defenders were, of course, fellow Puerto Ricans. His hometown paper, *The San Juan Star*, declared: "Clemente is a black Puerto Rican. That makes him doubly dubious. His native tongue is foreign to button-down America, and so is his color. He has felt as much. He has frequently complained that other Puerto Ricans and blacks—as well as himself—have been skirted for endorsements of products and media commercials."[12]

The *Star's* defense of a "black Puerto Rican," however, belied the fact that once on the mainland, race, to Puerto Ricans, was not a subtle matter. On the mainland, argued Oscar Handlin, Puerto Ricans "found themselves in a dilemma, for color, which was of slight importance back home, was crucial [in the states]."[13] He went on to observe that "The colored Puerto Rican wished above all to avoid the stigma of identification with the [American] Negro."[14] "The colored Puerto Rican," observed Joseph P. Fitzpatrick, "is identified primarily as Puerto Rican, not as a Negro."[15] Racially apathetic on social matters, Puerto Ricans who had migrated to the mainland also came to practice its racial principles of segregation. So determined were some Puerto Ricans in displaying themselves as being white, that they often avoided any participation in the growing civil rights movement of the 1950s and 1960s. Fear of being categorized as "blacks" stigmatized many of the darkest Puerto Ricans who were "often the most reluctant to learn English."[16] Their reluctance to racially categorize themselves was such that, even though the 1950 United States Census included a section of nonwhite and white Puerto Ricans, a decade later, no such designation was listed.[17]

Balancing the concerns of race, as defined by mainland standards, and their Puerto Rican identity, however, was not easy. During the 1950s, in an effort to offset migrant anxieties in advance of moving northward, the Puerto Rican Department of Education, in a series of pamphlets entitled *Emigracion*, prepared islanders as best they could for their forthcoming "cultural shock."[18] Among their guidelines came a warning not to contaminate ourselves with the prejudices of some Americans.[19] *Emigracion* went on to firmly state that: "There is nothing more terrible to see than a Puerto Rican in the United States who is contaminated by the prejudice there. He begins by attacking the American blacks, and winds up attacking his own Puerto Rican brothers."[20]

Cubans, by comparison, faced similar travails. Having migrated from a country where miscegenation was historically common, their recognition of the racial dynamics in the United States was not unlike that of intuitive Puerto Ricans. Two factors distinguished them from the Puerto Ricans, however. First, few of those who were poor and distinctively black before and after 1959 migrated to the United States. Second those who did, unlike the Puerto Ricans, dwelled in segregated communities. Yet Cubans were selective in their prejudice. Orestes "Minnie" Minoso, a black Cuban, held a place of distinction among Cubans long before his 1949 major league appearance and subsequent stardom. Apart from the norteamericano perceptions of Minoso as the "happy-go-lucky" player, to Cubans, his notoriety was as "a serious-minded, generous, and honest man who gave everything he had."[21] Yet Minoso's popularity was already in place before his arrival to the United States to, first, play in the black leagues and subsequently reach the major leagues. Clemente, on the other hand, developed his career in a land bedeviled by race and stereotypes of the Latino people.

Clemente clearly recognized that perceptions of Puerto Ricans in the United States were not good, but these drawbacks gave him greater incentive to succeed. In doing so, the Pittsburgh outfielder emerged as a symbol for not only Latino recognition, but also Puerto Rican achievement. However, Clemente's earlier "color blind" declarations were as much a pronouncement of his commonwealth heritage as it was about race. A Puerto Rican identity far exceeded any concerns about ethnicity. Language, culture, and tradition were the ingredients that fed into Clemente's consciousness. And so, too, did Puerto Ricans in the mainland respond to him not as a black islander, but as a Puerto Rican citizen. Thus, Clemente's growing notoriety in the 1950s and 1960s not only greatly tempered the negative profile of his brethren, but also bridged the uncomfortable gap between white and nonwhite Puerto Ricans in their American enclaves. Most of all, he never wavered from his commonwealth's most important rule: "Everyone is first a Puerto Rican and only second a member of a particular racial group."[22]

Though he contemplated retirement after the 1971 championship season, Clemente decided to play the following year in part to continue his quest to defuse the negative images of Latinos in professional baseball. At that point, given the many successes that he and his brethren had accumulated since the 1950s, the great outfielder increased his campaign on behalf of the Spanish-speaking quarter of the big leagues. Clemente stated in a 1972 interview: "the writers, at first, they thought Latinos were inferior to the American people. Now they know they can't be sarcastic about Latinos. Which is something I have fought all of my life."[23]

Clemente, however, did not live to see the fruits of his labors. On December 31, 1972, while personally escorting humanitarian aid to earthquake victims in Nicaragua, the plane with Clemente and four others crashed off the coast of Puerto Rico killing all onboard. The eulogies were immediate. Clemente "had the touch of royalty," stated baseball commissioner Bowie Kuhn.[24] "We have lost not only a great baseball player but a very wonderful human being," added Pirates' general manager Joe Brown.[25] From the Puerto Rican community in New York City, one shocked admirer said, "It is a terrible thing. He was trying to help people in Nicaragua when it happened."[26] "Roberto Clemente lived nobly, gloriously, and with generosity. He fulfilled a high destiny for his family and for his people," said a grief-stricken Puerto Rican in San Juan.[27]

In April 1973, the Baseball Writers of America voted to induct Clemente into the United States Baseball Hall of Fame. The induction came five years before the traditional period of entry and, in keeping with Clemente's career, did not occur without controversy. Some believed that early induction was not necessary alleging that "special privilege" could only hurt his legacy.[28] However, Larry Catlin of the *Boston Herald* maintained that with Clemente, "there could be no better candidate to be the pioneer" in the representation of Latinos in the Hall of Fame.[29]

Following Clemente's passing and induction, the Pirates struggled to regain their emotional equilibrium. "He's gone," said pitcher Dave Giusti, "and there's not a thing we can do about it. And it may not be wise to talk too much about it."[30] Willie Stargell added, "we'll miss the man more than the ballplayer. There are a lot of men going around saying they're great, but there aren't many good men left."[31] "Clemente is still on the ball club. His spirit [belongs] here. You know how great he was in the outfield. And he gives his life for somebody he don't know," Manny Sanguillen pondered.[32] The Pirates completed the decade as one of the most competitive clubs in the National League. Only once after Clemente's death did they fall below second place in the Eastern Division standings, captured three division titles, and, in 1979, climbed back into the World Series and won the title. By then, Clemente's legacy had gained considerable life.

Immediately after his death, a relief-aid organization for the Nicaraguan earthquake victims called the Roberto Clemente Memorial Fund came into existence.[33] President Richard Nixon, an avid baseball fan, was among those who set the tone for the contributions. In fact, after having donated $1,000 from his personal checking account, the president then brought executives from the Pirates to Washington and together they initiated the fund.[34] Within a short time thereafter, donations grew to $350,000.[35]

Other eulogies followed. On April 4, 1973, Cardinal Luis Aponte Martinez of San Juan celebrated a special mass in Brooklyn to honor Clemente. The service drew 2,500 patrons.[36] Five days later, the Pittsburgh Youth Symphony Orchestra performed "Roberto's Youth City Benefit Concert." Nelson Briles, a teammate of Clemente's was the vocal soloist.[37] In the next few years, hundreds of other testimonials to the fallen star took place. Among the most prominent occurred in 1973 when Major League Baseball renamed its Commissioner's Award, an honor extended to the ballplayer whose humanitarian efforts were notable, the "Roberto Clemente Award." Years later, Sammy Sosa, a Dominican who admired Clemente and adopted his number "21," won the award in 1998 and 1999. The Pittsburgh Pirates, too, created a "Roberto Clemente Award" of their own, for reasons similar to that of the major league baseball version. Outside of baseball, the United States Postal Service in 1982 issued a Roberto Clemente commemoration stamp. In Puerto Rico, its largest indoor sports arena adopted the name Roberto Clemente Coliseum. Moreover, several schools took on the name of the great ballplayer and, not surprisingly, city officials in San Juan, christened the street of his home as Calle Roberto Clemente.[38]

Through the years Clemente's legacy continued to grow. Several books about his life emerged in one manner or another. In 1999, Bob Cranmer, Chairman of the Allegheny County Commissioners, announced that Pittsburgh's Sixth Street Bridge, one that spanned the Allegheny River and connected it to the new Pirates' PNC Park, would be named Roberto Clemente Bridge. In 2002, Major League Baseball Commissioner, Allan "Bud" Selig, proclaimed September 18 to be "Roberto Clemente Day."[39]

During his lifetime, however, the Pirates' star had made clear his desire to create a "sports city" for disadvantaged youth. As early as 1967, Clemente shared his blueprint for this project with reporters. "The biggest thing I want to do is for the youths . . . for the kids. When I am ready to quit baseball, I will have my sports center. It will be only a little thing to some but to me it will be the most important thing in the world."[40] This project was so important to the great outfielder that shortly before attaining his 3,000th hit, he confided to his manager, Danny Murtaugh, the most important moment of his life was not the hit, but the creation of his sports center. "I have a project going in Puerto Rico for the underprivileged and

I have made so much progress with the political men in our country that I'm beginning to think my dream will come true."[41]

Despite the early euphoria in the wake of Clemente's death, his "Ciudad Deportiva Roberto Clemente" (Roberto Clemente Sports City) struggled for stability. The project trudged along for the remainder of the 1970s and into the next decade. The Puerto Rican government initially allocated three hundred acres for its development, but attempting to survive largely on personal donations, by 1985, little had been accomplished. Clemente would be "terribly angry," reporter Dick Young reflected after he toured the grounds.[42]

In the late 1980s, however, Vera Clemente, the outfielder's widow, attained corporate help. "Finally we are on the right course, again," she commented.[43] Luis Mayoral, a longtime Spanish-language sportscaster and close friend of Clemente's added, "With the support of private business we will work miracles here in the next three years."[44]

For many, Clemente's legacy already had contributed mightily to the miracles of those who followed him. By the end of the 1990s, three major leaguers—Carlos Baerga, Ruben Sierra, and Ivan Rodriguez—were alumni of Clemente's center. Many other Puerto Ricans in professional ball trained there. Indeed, almost thirty years into its existence, Clemente's dream appeared achieved. Moreover, thanks to an annual government donation of $784,000, the institution grew to offer a variety of recreational facilities, which went well beyond baseball. "My goal is to carry out my father's mission at the Sports City," said Luis Roberto, now executive director of the facility.

Clemente's legacy, perhaps most importantly, found expression in a newer generation of Latinos in the major leagues. Those who came into the big leagues in the years following Clemente's death expanded baseball's cultural horizons still further. Moreover, mainstream audiences and the press responded to the achievements of Latinos in a manner unseen during Clemente's early years. Luis Tiant, Fernando Valenzuela, Pedro Martinez, and Sammy Sosa, to name a few, were arguably heroes nationally to many people beyond the Latino community. Indeed, Sammy Sosa's 1998 momentous home run race with Mark McGwire catapulted the Dominican's prestige to an unprecedented level for Latinos. As well, their achievements were earned. Since Clemente's death, Latino pitchers captured five Cy Young awards; four Rookie of the Year trophies; eight Most Valuable Player awards, and captured ten batting championships. Finally, five Latinos followed Clemente into the United States Baseball Hall of Fame.

The new element of recognition also came as a result of an increase in the Spanish-language media in the United States. "Only a generation ago, the national Hispanic media landscape was a sparse one, populated by a handful of old-line community newspapers, low-wattage AM radio stations and one struggling television network," a recent article stated in the *Washington Post*. However, by 2000, it went on, "Spanish-language television stations are top-rated in major cities."[45] The increased visibility also included Spanish-language broadcasts of major league games. Saddled with a lack of recognition by the English-speaking press, Clemente, in his era, had little recourse but to struggle in his relationships with the mainstream press corp. But in the years following his passing, no longer did Latino players face limited options in advancing their own notoriety. Indeed, with the increase of the Latino media also came an increase in Spanish-language advertisers who routinely selected major league stars to sell their products.

Through it all, Clemente was not forgotten. "For me he is the Jackie Robinson of Latin baseball," said Ozzie Guillen, a Venezuelan who came up to the big leagues in 1985, and is currently the manager of the Chicago White Sox, who won the 2005 World Series.[46] Puerto Rican, Ivan "Pudge" Rodriguez, born in 1972 explained, "I saw Roberto in videos and [my father] told me about his life and personality. Roberto is a hero in Puerto Rico." Rodriquez went on to say, "To every Latin American Roberto is a hero; in Venezuela, Panama, Santo Domingo, everybody knows Roberto."[47]

Roberto Clemente left San Juan, Puerto Rico in 1953 to succeed as a baseball player. His stamp on the game he loved was unquestionable, and his constant hustle inspired his teammates throughout his career. Clemente's goals evolved into a larger mission, however. As his prominence grew, so did his sense of obligation to his brethren. "By insisting over and over that the Spanish-speaking son of a sugar cane worker is as good a man as the native son, Clemente helped reshape our concept of the Latin American player," writer Robert Heurer explained.[48]

Clemente's prominence also helped to bring the Puerto Rican identity, particularly for those who had migrated onto the mainland, into greater focus. That a black man became the island's favorite son resonated with other islanders who were abroad. Clemente was an outspoken ambassador for Puerto Ricans and an outspoken defender of blacks on and off the island. In this respect, he bridged several uncomfortable gaps Puerto Ricans faced in their quest to both assimilate and maintain their heritage amidst an English-speaking mainstream. His success in that endeavor resonated in the years following his untimely death, and his spirit pro-vided motivation to those Puerto Rican players whose time came well after the plane crash that took his life.

His legacy was also built upon his celebrated challenges to undermine the aged poor perception of Latinos, particularly during an era in which the American mainstream struggled with the issue of race. And, as he real-ized, his outspoken approach, combined with his skills as a ballplayer, was needed to alter those unfounded images. This was his formula and one which inevitably accumulated dividends. As the scales of perception tipped in Clemente's direction, he comfortably summed up in the last years of his career: "My greatest satisfaction comes from helping to erase the old opinion about Latin American and black ballplayers."[49]

Notes

1. Les Beiderman, "Clemente—The Player Who Can Do It All," *Sporting News* 144 (April 20, 1968).

2. *New York Times*, September 24, 1971.

3. Samuel O. Regalado, *Viva Baseball!: Latin Major Leaguers and Their Special Hunger* (Urbana: University of Illinois Press, 1998), 118.

4. Ibid., 70.

5. Donn Rogosin, *Invisible Men: Life in Baseball's Negro Leagues* (New York: Atheneum, 1985), 164.

6. Joseph P. Fitzpatrick, *Puerto Rican Americans: The Meaning of Migration to the Mainland* (Englewood Cliffs, NJ: Prentice-Hall, 1971), 105.

7. Dan Wakefield, *Island in the City: Puerto Ricans in New York* (New York: Corinth Book, 1959), 39.

8. Regalado, *Viva Baseball!*, 71.

9. *Sporting News*, 137 (October 11, 1961).

10. Lou Prato, "Why the Pirates Love the New Roberto Clemente," *Sport* (August 1967): 36.

11. *Sporting News*, 145 (April 19, 1969).

12. *San Juan Star*, November 4, 1971.

13. Oscar Handlin, *The Newcomers: Negroes and Puerto Ricans in a Changing Metropolis* (Garden City, NY: Anchor Books, 1962), 60.

14. Ibid.

15. Fitzpatrick, *Puerto Rican Americans*, 109.

16. Wakefield, *Island in the City*, 41.

17. Fitzpatrick, *Puerto Rican Americans*, 101.

18. Kal Wagenheim, *The Puerto Ricans: A Documentary History* (Garden City, NY: Anchor Books, 1973), 290.

19. Ibid.

20. Ibid.

21. Roberto Gonzalez Echevarria, *The Pride of Havana: A History of Cuban Baseball* (New York: Oxford University Press, 1999), 289–90.

22. C. Wright Mills, et. al., *The Puerto Rican Journey: New York's Newest Migrants* (New York: Russell & Russell, 1967), 7.

23. C. R. Ways, "'Nobody Does Anything Better Than Me in Baseball' Says Roberto Clemente," *New York Times Magazine* (April 9, 1972).

24. *Newsday* (New York), January 2, 1973.

25. Ibid.

26. *New York Times*, January 3, 1973.

27. *San Juan Star*, January 2, 1973.

28. Regalado, *Viva Baseball!*, 153.

29. Ibid.

30. Roberto Clemente file. Baseball Hall of Fame, Cooperstown, New York.

31. Ibid.

32. Ibid.

33. (Newark) *Star Ledger*, January 26, 1973.

34. *Sporting News*, 149 (January 20, 1973).

35. *Star Ledger*, January 26, 1973.

36. (New York) *Daily News*, April 4, 1973.

37. Ibid., April 9, 1973.

38. *New York Times*, February 22, 1976.

39. See, for example, Phil Musick, *Who Was Roberto? A Biography of Roberto Clemente* (Garden City, NY: Doubleday, 1974); Bruce Markusen, *Roberto Clemente: The Great One* (Champaign, IL: Sports Publishing, 1998); Kal Wagenheim, *Clemente!* (New York: Praeger, 1973). This book was re-released in 2001. Jonah Winter and Raul Colon, *Roberto Clemente: Pride of the Pittsburgh Pirates* (New York: Simon & Schuster, 2005).

40. Prato, "The New Clemente," 82.

41. *New York Times*, February 22, 1973.

42. *New York Post*, November 25, 1985.

43. Ibid.

44. Ibid.

45. *Washington Post*, August 11, 2003.

46. *Orlando* (Florida) *Sentinel*, March 31, 2002.

47. Interview with Ivan Rodriquez, June 23, 1994, Anaheim, California.

48. *New York Times*, January 2, 1983.

49. *Syracuse Herald-American*, April 25, 1971.

9

The Pigskin *Pulpito*

A Brief Overview of the Experiences of Mexican
American High School Football Coaches in Texas

—*Jorge Iber*

On the evening of October 18, 1991, the Duval County town of
Benavides provided one of its former head football coaches with
the highest honor that can be granted to a Texas field general,
naming the community's gridiron stadium in his honor. The tribute was
well deserved for between the years 1940 and 1955, Coach Everardo Carlos
(E. C.) Lerma guided the hometown Eagles to an impressive—even by
Texas standards—run of success. The 1942, 1947, 1950, and 1952 squads
won district championships. The 1948, 1949, and 1951 clubs earned bi-
district titles and the 1943 and 1949 contingents finished with undefeated
seasons and claimed regional crowns. In addition to his remarkable
success on the gridiron, Lerma, like many of his colleagues during that
era, directed all the school's other team sports and produced district titles
in track, baseball, and another regional championship in basketball.[1] The
accomplishments of Lerma's charges generated a sense of pride among
Benavides' residents and, as another student of Texas high school football
history has noted, impacted the community because success on the
gridiron affected "how outsiders viewed [such] places."[2] In addition to on-
field success, Lerma, reflecting the experiences and convictions of most of
his coaching contemporaries, believed it was his responsibility to instill in
his athletes the values of "self-reliance, sacrifice, discipline, accountability
and survival—in a word that coaches so often used, manliness, in its most
positive sense."[3]

Over the past seven decades, numerous individuals have chronicled the role of high school football coaches in Texas. Writers such as Harold Ratcliff, Bill McMurray, and Carlton Stowers have generated works with heroic titles such as *Autumn's Mightiest Legions, Texas Schoolboy Football,* and *Friday Night Heroes: A Look at Texas High School Football.* These tomes had two principal purposes: first, to "record and preserve the sport's high-water marks," and second, to regale "readers with riveting vignettes of greatness on the high school gridiron."[4] While such works are important in capturing the lore and statistics of on-the-field action, they are limited in their analysis of the historical impact of football and coaches on community life in the Lone Star State.

A more scholarly perspective of this subject matter is provided in Ty Cashion's 1997 work, *Pigskin Pulpit: A Social History of Texas High School Football Coaches.* Here, using oral history interviews with coaches active primarily between the late 1940s and late 1960s, the author examines the "ways and outlooks" and societal impact of these men. Unanimously, Cashion's interviewees, whether white, African American, or Hispanic, embraced a belief in the value of football as a way to improve one's economic and social standing as well as a similar philosophy regarding the game. These coaches believed that football presented their players with some of the same obstacles that these young men would confront in later life. It was a coach's task, then, to use sport to instill the "keystones of character" to the next generation of Texan males. One individual Cashion quotes, Panhandle High School's Stocky Lamberson, succinctly noted the significance of this phenomenon: "I teach history in the morning. In history you try to show how our forefathers reacted under pressure. In athletics you can experience it for yourself. The most satisfying moment is seeing a young person achieve something he didn't think he could. He had a doubt in his mind, and all along the way you tried to convince him he could do it."[5]

It is doubtful that E. C. Lerma would have disagreed with Lamberson's assessment of the goals of coaching. Still, an analysis of Lerma's career, and other Mexican American coaches, reveal some important differences in their experiences from their white and African American colleagues. As many scholars of the Mexican American experience in Texas have noted, while Spanish-speaking people did not face segregation that was as strict as the segregation that African Americans experienced, they were also not treated as the "equal" of the state's white majority population.[6] How did this trend manifest itself in the hopes, philosophy, goals, and experiences of Mexican American coaches?

Clearly, *Pigskin Pulpit* provides a more sophisticated analysis of the Texas high school football coaching profession than do previous works, but the study does have certain limitations. Cashion does a thorough job of highlighting the significance of African American coaches to their communities and schools, but the impact and role of Mexican American coaches, for example, is not as well delineated. Of the eighty-two interviews Cashion conducted, only two, Lerma and Ralph Martinez, were coaches of Spanish-speaking descent. Given the substantial presence of Mexican Americans in the population of Texas, especially in locales such as the lower Rio Grande Valley, Laredo, and El Paso, this leaves a significant lacuna in our understanding of the experiences and influence of high school football coaches. The preliminary goal of this research, then, is to build upon Cashion's work and provide a brief overview of the experiences of two Spanish-surnamed coaches of the generation discussed in *Pigskin Pulpit*. Also, this chapter will examine some of the "ways and outlooks" of younger (men born in the 1950s and later), current Mexican American football coaches. What obstacles did these men face in their career paths? Finally, through an analysis of *Dave Campbell's Texas Football* and the *Texas Sports Guide of High School and Colleges* the essay documents a disturbing trend which finds that, even at the dawn of the twenty-first century, there are still few Hispanics outside the Valley, Laredo, and El Paso heading high school football programs in Texas.

In his research, Cashion notes that most of the "old-time" coaches who entered the profession during the years after World War II shared similar, humble backgrounds and a sense that sport could provide them with "the upward mobility necessary to escape the vestiges of the rural, nineteenth-century environment that had trapped their undereducated and underemployed parents."[7] As the game of football increased in popularity throughout Texas in the early part of the 1900s, young men of modest means realized "athletics provided one of the few paths to college." Also, football, "to young men for whom even a high school diploma was outside of their family's experience, opened the door to a new life, the likes of which they had never conceived."[8] Such youngsters grabbed onto the "teachings" of Texas's early football coaches and many managed to get an education far beyond anything they had ever hoped. Not surprisingly, some of these former players felt the inclination to pass on that which had worked so well for them to the next generation. Additionally, especially during the 1940s and 1950s, the coaching profession allowed men of humble upbringing to achieve great status in communities throughout the state. One interviewee, Moon Mullins, who spent most of his career in West Texas recalled that during this era: "The coach was the cornerstone of the community along with the preacher and the mayor. He had access to the kids and he guided their lives. In return, coaches got their respect and were even beloved. And the parents trusted you with teaching moral lessons."[9]

Before moving on to the specifics of this research, however, it is important to contextualize two topics relevant to the investigation: an overview of the significance of sport to ethnic minorities in the United States (as well as to note the general neglect by the historical profession of the sporting experiences of Mexican Americans) and a succinct synopsis of white Texans' perceptions of both the physical and intellectual capabilities of Mexican Americans.

During the 1980s and 1990s, scholars of various minority groups began a systematic examination of the impact of sport on the lives and communities of Native Americans, African Americans, Jews, Italian Americans, and Asian Americans. During these years, authors such as Robert Ruck, Jeffrey T. Sammons, Elliot J. Gorn, Gerald R. Gems, Roberta J. Park, Susan G. Zieff, Peter Levine, Steven A. Riess, Gary Ross Mormino, and Anthony A. Yoseloff chronicled how athletic competition impacted these groups' communities or schools and how many minority athletes used sport as a way to break down vicious stereotypes about their people as well as gaining a measure of opportunity for themselves.[10]

Although the participation of Mexican Americans (and other Latinos) has not garnered the attention that it deserves, one noted writer, Samuel O. Regalado, has almost single-handedly carried the torch in regard to bringing this story to a scholarly audience. His research includes works on the social significance of baseball *ligas* (leagues) to *barrio* (neighborhood) life in southern California, the social impact of Spanish-language broadcasts by the Los Angeles Dodgers, and an examination of the majority population's perception of Hispanic big leaguers such as the late Pittsburgh Pirate great, Roberto Clemente.[11]

Recently, and fortunately, other historians specializing in the study of Mexican Americans have incorporated some of Regalado's trailblazing spade work into their own research and have started providing more than a passing mention of the role of sport in the lives of Spanish-speaking *comunidades* (communities) in the United States. For example, both Gilbert Gonzalez and Matt Garcia provide examinations of the role of baseball in the lives of citrus workers in southern California during the early decades of the 1900s.[12] Douglas Monroy's work encapsulates various aspects of *barrio* life, including what he terms the "Passions of Mexico de afuera" (Mexico outside of Mexico). Among these were food, religion, music, politics, and sports.[13] In regard to athletic competition, Monroy argues that it fulfilled three vital roles for the Mexicans living in Southern California. First, it provided an opportunity for competition and success for men and boys who faced severe limitations in both the workplace and school. Second, it permitted Spanish-speakers to pit themselves against other "races" and compete for community pride. Finally, it was believed by many in the *barrio*, sport presented Mexicanos with an opportunity to dispel some of the negative perceptions of their people by the majority population. Every triumph by local teams was important because "The task these boys are undertaking on the sports field, which is the most appreciated among the American people (was) to elevate the good name of our *raza* (race) (and this) should not be overlooked."[14] These works' use of sport are evident in the career and experiences of E. C. Lerma during his tenure at Benavides, as well as in the lives of the other football coaches that participated in the oral history phase of this research. Before moving on to the results, however, it is necessary to present a short discussion of the perceived "limitations" of Mexican Americans outlined by Texas educators and academicians during the first half of the twentieth century.

Arnoldo De Leon's classic study, *They Called Them Greasers: Anglo Attitudes towards Mexicans in Texas, 1836–1900*, offers an exhaustive examination of how whites in the Lone Star State "constructed" both the intellectual and physical abilities (Or would it be more appropriate to say inadequacies?) of their Spanish-speaking neighbors.[15] Not surprisingly, many Texans fully embraced the notion that men, women, and children of Mexican descent were intellectually inferior and inherently lazy. Such perceptions found their way into the literature of numerous educators. While it is possible to cite many theses, dissertations, and scholarly publications for examples of such thinking, two particularly glaring illustrations will suffice to make this point here.[16] First, in a 1927 thesis, James Kilbourne Harris (principal of a San Antonio elementary school), noted that his Mexican American charges lacked capacity and ambition and that "their brains do not seem to work as rapidly as do the brains of English speaking pupils." In regards to athletics, the arguments were mixed; some authors postulated that Spanish-surnamed *estudiantes* were not interested in sports, while others made the blanket statements that Spanish-speakers "excel in these, but they mar [games] . . . by being poor losers."[17] Either way, during the early 1900s, the Mexican Americans of Texas were perceived as not having the "tools" or "drive" necessary to succeed in a demanding sport such as football. It was against such negative assumptions that E. C. Lerma battled and, as this research reveals, it appears that many current Hispanic football coaches continue to struggle against some of the same misperceptions.

Everardo Carlos Lerma was born in Bishop in 1915, the son of migrant workers from Mier, Tamaulipas, Mexico. When E. C. turned eight, both parents had died and he was left in the care of his siblings. His older brothers and sisters decided that they would all work to support the family and to provide E. C. with the opportunity to attend school.[18] Although he grew up poor and attended segregated institutions in Kingsville, the young Lerma dreamed of becoming a member of the varsity football squad at the local high school. E. C. faced a great deal of initial difficulty in convincing his "teammates" to accept him as part of their group. One response by Anglo players to this affront was to toss Lerma into a swimming pool. "I couldn't even swim," he recalled many years later.[19]

Through his diligence and ability, however, E. C. eventually won over his classmates and topped off his career in 1933 by being named all-district in his senior year. His prowess on the gridiron drew the attention of coaches at Texas Christian University who offered the young Spanish-surnamed man a scholarship. Lerma, however, did not wish to leave his hometown and decided to attend the local college, Texas A & I. Again, he faced circumstances similar to those of his high school years. Most of the white upperclassmen worked diligently to drive Lerma off the squad. One member of the 1934 freshman team, Dr. L. E. Ramey, recalled that varsity players were especially rough with Lerma during intrasquad scrimmages: "By this time the freshmen had developed a respect and admiration for E. C. We knew he was a hard-nosed football player that would not be intimidated. Consequently, when we scrimmaged the varsity, we did all we could to see that E. C. got a fair shake. It took only two or three scrimmages for the varsity to realize that Lerma was here to stay, and they also developed respect." Eventually, E. C. played for the A & I Javelinas until 1937, and many of the players that had wanted to eliminate him from the team became defenders of their Mexican American teammate when he endured physical attacks and racial slurs during games throughout his career.[20]

Lerma graduated in 1938 and took a position as an assistant at Benavides High School. When the head coaching post came open in 1940, E. C. applied and the "reaction in town was as expected. Did a 'Mexican' have the intellectual capacity to guide one of the town's flagship institutions?"[21] The school's administration was well rewarded for making

Lerma one of the first Mexican American head football coaches in Texas. He remained in Benavides until moving on to Rio Grande City in 1955 and resurrecting their moribund program. Lerma retired in 1965 with an overall record of 154 wins, 98 losses and 13 championships in various sports. In addition to coaching, he served as teacher, mentor, and administrator to students. Although he was always proud of his success on the field, his main goal was that his boys practiced "Good conduct [and] good living."[22] Clearly, this son of migrant workers used football as a way to improve both his life and that of other Mexican Americans.

The life and career of Modesto Garcia mirrored Lerma's. Coach Garcia was born in 1928 in San Diego, Texas. His father had a third grade education and worked as a sharecropper in the Rio Grande Valley his entire life while Modesto's mother dedicated herself to raising the family's seven children. The family's financial situation, like that of most Mexican Americans in this part of Texas during the early part of the twentieth century, was bleak. Garcia's mother stressed education and he recalls that "She fought my dad about this (going to school) all the time." Modesto benefited from his mother's encouragement and graduated from San Diego High School in 1946. He then joined the military to take advantage of the educational benefits of the GI Bill. After a two-year enlistment, he entered Laredo Junior College and played one year of football while working on an education degree and then transferred to Southwest Texas State in 1949. Garcia graduated in 1953 and became coach at San Diego Junior High School in 1954.

Modesto's ties to San Diego were one reason for his being hired as coach, but Garcia also benefited from the success of E. C. Lerma in nearby Benavides. Lerma had demonstrated that it was possible to win on a consistent basis (in various sports) at a school that was, as Garcia described SDHS in the early 1950s, "almost 100 percent Mexican American (both teachers and students)." In 1957, Modesto became athletic director at his alma mater. Unfortunately, his stint was not as successful as Lerma's. He remembers that he "had very little help, no facilities, and no tradition (of winning)." Often assistant coaches for the various teams were not even trained coaches, just volunteers from the faculty. Garcia finally left San Diego in 1965 and, ironically, followed Lerma as head football coach at Rio Grande City.[23] Both E. C. Lerma and Modesto Garcia were Mexican American pioneers in the coaching profession and Garcia, while not as successful as his senior colleague, also served as a role model for the Spanish-surnamed youth of his South Texas community.

Although by the early 1950s, path breakers such as E. C. Lerma and Modesto Garcia had proven themselves as winners on the field and capable administrators, the number of Mexican American high school football coaches in Texas remained quite limited. An examination of *Texas Sports Guide of High Schools and Colleges* for the years 1955–1965, reveals that, even with Lerma and Garcia's educational, civic, and on-field efforts, there were very few Mexican Americans given the opportunity to serve as head football coaches during this era. Also, and this trend continues to the present, these men were hired overwhelmingly in the poorest areas of Texas; locales usually characterized by high percentages of Mexican American students. Table 1 reveals the names and places where some of the earliest Spanish-surnamed head football coaches in Texas plied their trade.[24]

The oral history research for this paper produced twenty-three interviews with coaches of Mexican American heritage and Lerma and Garcia were the only individuals whose tenures began before the early 1970s. Although by this era the Mexican American population of Texas had not achieved academic parity with their white counterparts, the Chicano Movement in the state had provided some stimulus for increased opportunities for Spanish-surnamed students to attend college and eventually move into professional careers such as teaching and academic administration. In turn, with more Mexican American teachers and bureaucrats (particularly in places like the Rio Grande Valley, Laredo, and El Paso), opportunities for coaches increased.[25] The responses of the field generals interviewed reflect these societal changes. While most did not enjoy affluent childhoods, many had parents who held semi-skilled, skilled, if not white-collar, occupations and stressed the importance of educational attainment. Among the jobs of the fathers of the interviewees were sales representative, lumberyard foreman, field caseworker for an ISD, maquiladora superintendent, businessman, bakery owner, police officer, and civil servant.

The present-day coaches continue the philosophical tradition of their professional forefathers and contend that their primary job is to mold young people into productive, responsible citizens. To a man, the coaches argued that it was necessary to be positive role models so students would have before them examples of steadfast, dedicated *hombres*. Ronald Hernandez, former head coach (and now athletic director) at Fabens High School (near El Paso) believes that his primary responsibility is to "battle apathy . . . [because parents] expect the school to do it all for them, and they pass that attitude on to the kids."[26] Similarly, coach Robert Gomez

Table 1. Head football coaches, by year and location

Coaches' names	Schools	Year
A. Ortiz	San Diego	1955
J. H. Roquemore	Edcouch-Elsa	
J. F. Martinez	San Felipe	
E. C. Lerma	Rio Grande City	
A. Ortiz	San Diego	1956
J. H. Roquemore	Edcouch-Elsa	
J. F. Martinez	San Felipe	
E. C. Lerma	Rio Grande City	
Jose Sanchez	Southside (SA)	
A. Ortiz	San Diego	1957
J. H. Roquemore	Edcouch-Elsa	
J. F. Martinez	San Felipe	
E. C. Lerma	Rio Grande City	
Jose Sanchez	Southside (SA)	
A. Ortiz	San Diego	1958
Nick Garza	Sydney Lanier (SA)	
Gus Mireles	San Felipe	
Frank Villareal	Valentine	
E. C. Lerma	Rio Grande City	
A. Ortiz	San Diego	1959
Joe Valencia	EP Jefferson	
Armando Gutierrez	EP Tech	
Lucio Diaz	San Felipe	
Nick Garza	Sydney Lanier (SA)	
Isaac Gonzalez	Benavides	
Rene Hinojosa	Sharyland (Mission)	
E. C. Lerma	Rio Grande City	
Joe Valencia	EP Jefferson	1962
Armando Gutierrez	EP Tech	
Isaac Gonzalez	Benavides	
Rene Hinojosa	Sharyland (Mission)	
E. C. Lerma	Rio Grande City	
Ramiro Jaime	Asherton	
Gus Zavaletta	St. Joseph (Brownsville)	
Gus Mireles	San Felipe	
Joe Valencia	EP Jefferson	1963
Armando Gutierrez	EP Tech	
Isaac Gonzalez	Benavides	
Rene Hinojosa	Sharyland (Mission)	

Coaches' names	Schools	Year
E. C. Lerma	Rio Grande City	
Ramiro Jaime	Asherton	
Rogerio Garcia	La Joya	
Vicente Vicinaiz	San Isidro	
Joe Valencia	EP Jefferson	1964
Armando Gutierrrez	EP Tech	
Armando Balderrama	JFK (SA)	
R. Garcia	San Diego	
T. W. Celaya	Uvalde	
Isaac Gonzalez	Benavides	
Manny Aguilar	EP Cathedral	
E. C. Lerma	Rio Grande City	
Robert Chavaria	San Felipe	
Oscar Saenz	Ben Bolt-Palito Blanco	
Santos Canales	Mirando City	

Source: *2002–2003 Texas Sports Guide of High Schools and Colleges* (El Paso, TX: Craftsman Publications and the North American High School Football Coaches Association, 2002).

of El Paso Bowie High School urges his charges to "strive for success in everything they do." He also argues that, while most of these kids do not go on to play football at the collegiate level, the sport provides structure and discipline that makes it possible for most to complete high school and pursue higher education.[27] Chris Soza of Mathis High School (county, near El Paso) maintains that, in addition to building upon the concept of personal responsibility, his job is to increase the sense of community and teamwork among his athletes. He offers that most of his *jugadores* (players) have little individual talent, but that by working together (on the field and in their communities), "the team concept can overcome the [individual] liabilities."[28]

Clearly, the coaches share the belief system of their *Pigskin Pulpit* era colleagues, but many are ambivalent about the claim that sport is a great equalizer in American (or in this case, Texas) society. While about one half of the interviewees argued that conditions have improved, approximately one-third alleged that hard work and success on the field were still not enough to break down barriers keeping Hispanics out of head coaching positions in areas outside the Valley, Laredo, and El Paso.[29]

Typical of the positive comments from the coaches are those by "Bucky" Rodriguez of Weslaco High School, Henry Yzaguirre of Premont

High School, Pat Alvarado of Houston Northbrook High School, Bobby Ortiz of Seguin High School, and Felix Martinez of Lorenzo High School. In Rodriguez's estimation, ethnicity is irrelevant because "a good coach with a good record can be hired anywhere."[30] Yzaguirre notes that he has never been denied a job because of his background. When he attends coaching clinics throughout the state, he believes that "most coaches respect me and see me as just another coach, not a Hispanic coach." Alvarado declares that most "jobs come through hard work, no matter what color you are."[31] Coach Ortiz declared that the perception of Mexican American coaches is quite positive and "it is an ever-growing status" and that one can "use their ethnic background as a plus, [because] people are looking for Hispanic coaches."[32] Finally, and in probably the most positive assessment of all the men interviewed, Felix Martinez stated that: "As long as the door is open, stick your foot in it in any way you can. Hispanic coaches have to not look at it (the dearth of Mexican American head coaches) as a racial thing; people will notice what you do . . . those who really care will see what you do. Just keep doing the best you can and they'll notice you and hire you."[33]

Other head coaches who provided positive comments regarding the current employment situation tempered statements with an acknowledgment that circumstances are not the same throughout the state. Chris Soza of Mathis High School stressed that Mexican American head coaches are accepted, but "Down here (in South Texas), it is probably easier."[34] Oscar Villasenor of Eagle Pass High School acknowledged that the chances for hiring a Mexican American head coach "probably depends on where the job is available: the areas north of San Antonio may not be so great [of an opportunity]."[35] Elvis Hernandez of Santa Rosa High School reaffirmed Sosa and Villasenor by arguing that demographics and geographic location are just as important as record in getting jobs.[36]

Circumstances for Spanish-surnamed coaches at the start of the twenty-first century appear to be better than those encountered by trailblazers like E. C. Lerma, but problems remain and many of the coaches interviewed were candid about their concerns. Roque Hernandez who directed the football fortunes of Calhoun County High School in the late 1990s (and is now an administrator), believes there is an "unspoken situation regarding Mexican American head coaches" which tends to limit the hiring of such men primarily to the Valley. "Outside the Rio Grande Valley there is resistance to hire a Hispanic coach . . . (because other regions) looks down on the Valley schools."[37] Joe Carillo of San Elizario

High School believes there are places in Texas where "no Hispanic coach would be hired."[38] A final example of some of the problems faced by some of these coaches is seen in the interview with David Guerra of Fort Worth Paschal High School. After graduating with a degree in education in 1993 from Angelo State University, Guerra began his career as an assistant at Fredricksburg High School. After coaching for two years at the junior high level, he was promoted to linebacker's coach at the high school. Everything was fine, according to Coach Guerra, until he married a local Anglo woman. "I began to receive hate mail and the superintendent received a letter from an anonymous source asking for my firing." Given the situation, Guerra and his wife moved to the Metroplex where he became the defensive coordinator at Paschal and head coach in 1998.[39]

While the anecdotal evidence provided is important, it is imperative to impart some statistical evidence to appraise the value of the coaches' observations. In order to do this, it is necessary to turn to the twin "bibles" of the gridiron in the Lone Star State: *Dave Campbell's Texas Football* (published since 1961) and *Texas Sports Guide of High Schools and Colleges* (published since 1954). The first publication provides aficionados of the high school gridiron with a preseason overview of the numerous classifications (ranging from 1A to 5A and six-man),[40] districts (the state is divided into thirty-two districts for each classification) and individual teams throughout the state.[41] One point to keep in mind about the classifications is the higher the classification, the larger the school. Therefore, 5A (1900+ students) institutions are considered the most prestigious jobs since most of these schools are located in the state's larger metropolitan areas. In turn, these schools receive more media attention and success at this level provides greater opportunity for coaches to move on to the collegiate, or possibly even the professional ranks.

The *Texas Sports Guide of High Schools and Colleges* does not provide prognostications, but rather offers a listing of individual coaches and assistants for all teams. Information gleaned from these publications was used to tabulate the number of Spanish-surnamed football head coaches and assistant coaches in Texas. In addition, these materials provided a breakdown of coaches by region and district as well.

Table 2 is an overview of the six classifications over the last two seasons and presents a numerical count of Spanish surnamed head-coaches. The figures in parentheses represent the percentage of Hispanic coaches in that particular classification and the numbers in the total row represent the percentage of Spanish-surnamed coaches out of all head coaches in Texas.

Table 2. Head football coaches with Spanish surnames by classification

Classification	2001	2002
5A	33 (15)	25 (11)
4A	18 (8)	25 (11)
3A	16 (8)	15 (7)
2A	6 (3)	7 (3)
1A	9 (6)	5 (4)
Six man	3 (3)	4 (4)
Total	85 (8)	81 (7)

Source: *2002–2003 Texas Sports Guide of High Schools and Colleges* (El Paso, TX: Craftsman Publications and the North American High School Football Coaches Association, 2002).

Tables 3 and 4 reveal the location of Spanish surnamed coaches during the 2001 and 2002 seasons. These tables demonstrate a troubling pattern: Mexican American coaches (regardless of classification) tended to

Table 3. Head football coaches with Spanish surnames (by district, 2001)

District #	5A	4A	3A	2A	1A
1	2 (7)	1 (6)	0	0	1 (11)
2	2 (7)	2 (11)	0	1 (17)	1 (11)
3	0	0	2 (13)	0	0
5	2 (7)	0	0	0	1 (11)
7	1 (3)	0	0	0	1 (11)
11	2 (7)	0	0	0	0
12	0	1 (6)	0	1 (17)	0
13	0	1 (6)	0	0	0
19	0	0	0	1 (17)	0
21	1 (3)	0	1 (6)	0	0
25	1 (3)	0	0	0	0
26	1 (3)	0	0	0	0
27	2 (7)	0	1 (6)	0	0
28	1 (3)	4 (22)	1 (6)	0	0
29	2 (7)	1 (6)	0	0	2 (22)
30	4 (12)	0	1 (6)	1 (17)	0
31	4 (12)	(6)	4 (25)	1 (17)	0
32	8 (24)	7 (39)	6 (38)	1 (17)	3 (33)
Totals:	33	18	16	6	9

Source: *Dave Campbell's Texas Football* (Dallas, TX: Host Communications, 2001), 52; *Dave Campbell's Texas Football* (Dallas, TX: Host Communications, 2002), 53.

Table 4. Head football coaches with Spanish surnames (by district, 2002)

District #	5A	4A	3A	2A	1A
1	3 (12)	3 (12)	0	1 (14)	1 (17)
2	0	2 (8)	1 (7)	0	0
4	1 (4)	0	0	0	0
5	1 (4)	0	1 (7)	0	1 (17)
9	0	1 (4)	0	0	0
10	1 (4)	0	0	0	0
14	0	0	0	1 (14)	0
20	0	0	1 (7)	0	0
21	1 (4)	0	0	0	0
22	0	0	1 (7)	0	0
23	1 (4)	0	0	0	0
26	0	1 (4)	0	0	0
27	2 (8)	1 (4)	0	0	0
28	2 (8)	4 (16)	0	0	0
29	1 (4)	1 (4)	1 (7)	0	1 (17)
30	4 (16)	0	1 (7)	1 (14)	0
31	6 (24)	6 (24)	4 (27)	1 (14)	0
32	3 (12)	6 (24)	5 (33)	3 (43)	2 (33)
Totals:	25	25	15	7	6

Source: *Dave Campbell's Texas Football* (Dallas, TX: Host Communications, 2001), 52; *Dave Campbell's Texas Football* (Dallas, TX: Host Communications, 2002), 53.

concentrate in the three most distinctly "Mexican" areas of the state, Districts 1, 2, 27, 28 and 30–32. Not surprisingly, Districts 1 and 2 encompass El Paso and surrounding areas, Districts 27 and 28 cover San Antonio, District 30 takes in the Laredo area, and 31 and 32 comprise the lower Rio Grande Valley (which include the counties of Willacy, Cameron, Starr, and Hidalgo). The figures presented in these tables tend to support the contention of the more pessimistic coaches: it appears quite difficult for a Spanish-surnamed individual to get a football head coaching position outside the areas of highest Mexican American concentration.[42]

A final analysis of the raw numbers of Hispanic participation in the high school football coaching profession in Texas can be observed by determining the number of Spanish-surnamed assistant coaches and the locations where they are coaching throughout the state. The information in the Table 5 comes from the 2002–2003 edition of the *Texas Sports Guide of High Schools and Colleges*.[43]

As with the information on head coaches, the results presented in this table are striking. While Spanish-surnamed assistant coaches work

Table 5. Spanish-surnamed assistant football coaches by districts (not subdivided by classification)

District #	# of Spanish-surnamed coaches
1	54 (9)
2	31 (5)
3–26	167 (28)
27	11 (2)
28	50 (8)
29	40 (7)
30	55 (9)
31	91 (15)
32	93 (16)
Total	592

Source: *Dave Campbell's Texas Football* (Dallas, TX: Host Communications, 2001), 52; *Dave Campbell's Texas Football* (Dallas, TX: Host Communications, 2002), 53.

at all levels and all districts throughout Texas, the overwhelming majority of these individuals toil in Districts 1, 2 (the El Paso area), 27, 28 (San Antonio), 29 (the Corpus Christi, southern Texas area), 30 (Laredo) and 31 and 32 (the Valley). These eight districts account for approximately 72 percent of all Hispanic assistant football coaches in the state of Texas. The remaining districts account for only 28 percent of the total, even though they encompass major metropolitan areas such as the Dallas-Arlington-Fort Worth Metroplex and Houston. In summary, it appears the more "pessimistic" coaches provided a more realistic perspective of the opportunities of Hispanic football coaches in the Lone Star State. Job openings, especially for Spanish-surnamed head coaches, are severely limited outside the areas of greatest Mexican American concentration.

The men who prowl the high school gridiron have a special place in the social and sporting history of Texas. For almost a hundred years, football field generals have guided and instilled values into future generations of Texas youths. While some social scientists and reporters have ridiculed and criticized the impact of football on Texans, the overwhelming majority of the state's citizens embrace the institution, its rituals, and philosophy.[44] The Hispanic coaches interviewed for this research continue many of these traditions. They see themselves as role models of how *hombres verdaderos* (real men) should behave. In this regard, it is positive that most of Spanish-surnamed coaches work in areas of high Mexican

American concentration. Still, it is curious why there are so few outside areas like the Valley, El Paso, and Laredo. Further research is necessary to determine why opportunities for such coaches are so geographically limited. It is time for historians of Texas sport and society to insert a missing piece, the Mexican American coach and athlete, into the study of this important aspect of the state's history.

Notes

1. For an examination of the career of Coach Lerma, please see: Jorge Iber, "Mexican Americans of South Texas Football: The Athletic and Coaching Careers of E. C. Lerma and Bobby Cavazos, 1932–1965," *Southwestern Historical Quarterly* 55 (April 2002): 617–33.

2. Ty Cashion, *The Pigskin Pulpit: A Social History of Texas High School Football Coaches* (Austin: Texas State Historical Association, 1998), 2.

3. Cashion, *The Pigskin Pulpit*, 14.

4. Harold Ratliff, *Autumn's Mightiest Legions: History of Texas Schoolboy Football* (Waco: Texian, 1963); Bill McMurray, *Texas High School Football* (South Bend: Icarus, 1985); Carlton Stowers, *Friday Night Heroes: A Look at Texas High School Football* (Austin:, 1983).

5. Cashion, *The Pigskin Pulpit*, 14.

6. While a number of books and articles could be cited here, the works which provide the most complete examination of this theme are by David Montejano, *Anglos and Mexicans in the Making of Texas, 1836–1986* (Austin: University of Texas Press, 1987) and Arnoldo De Leon, *They Called Them Greasers: Anglo Attitudes toward Mexicans in Texas, 1836–1900* (Austin: University of Texas Press, 1983).

7. Ibid., 16.

8. Ibid.

9. Ibid., 32.

10. The following is a brief listing of some of the articles and books touching upon such topics during the past decade: Rob Ruck, *Sandlot Seasons: Sport in Black Pittsburgh* (Urbana: University of Illinois Press, 1993); Jeffrey T. Sammons, "'Race' and Sport: A Critical, Historical Examination," *Journal of Sport History* 21 (Fall 1994), 203–78; Elliott J. Gorn, ed., *Muhammad Ali: The People's Champ* (Urbana: University of Illinois Press, 1995); Gerald R. Gems, *For Pride, Profit and Patriarchy: Football and the Incorporation of American Cultural Values* (Lanham: Scarecrow, 2000); Roberta J. Park, "Sport and Recreation Among Chinese Americans of the Pacific Coast from the Time of Arrival to the 'Quiet Decade' of the 1950s," *Journal of Sport History* 27 (Fall 2000): 445–80; Susan G. Zieff, "From Badminton to Bolero: Sport and Recreation in San Francisco's Chinatown, 1895–1950," *Journal of Sport History* 27 (Spring 2000): 1–29; Peter Levine, *Ellis Island to Ebbets Field: Sport and the American Jewish Experience* (New York: Oxford University Press, 1992); Steven A. Riess, *Sport and the American Jew* (Syracuse: Syracuse University Press, 1998); Gary Ross Mormino, "The Playing Fields of St. Louis: Italian Immigrants and Sports, 1925–1941," *Journal of Sport History* 9 (Summer 1982): 5–19; Anthony Yoseloff, "From Ethnic Hero to National Icon: The Americanization of Joe Dimaggio," *International Journal for the History of Sport* 16 (September 1999): 1–20.

11. Samuel O. Regalado, *Viva Baseball: Latin Major Leaguers and Their Special Hunger* (Urbana: University of Illinois Press, 1998); idem., "Baseball in the Barrios: The Scene in East Los Angeles Since World War II," *Baseball History* 23 (Summer 1996): 47–59; idem., "Dodgers Beisbol Is on the Air: The Development and Impact of the Dodgers' Spanish-Language Broadcasts,

1958–1984," *California History* 74 (Fall 1995): 282–89; idem., "'Image Is Everything': Latin Baseball Players and the US Press," *Studies in Latin American Popular Culture* 13 (1994): 101–14. See chapter eight regarding Roberto Clemente.

12. Gilbert G. Gonzalez, *Labor and Community: Mexican Citrus Worker Villages in a Southern California County, 1900–1950* (Urbana: University of Illinois Press, 1994), especially 65–74; Matt Garcia, *A World of Its Own: Race, Labor, and Citrus in the Making of Greater Los Angeles, 1900–1970* (Chapel Hill: University of North Carolina Press, 2001); especially 87–120.

13. Douglas Monroy, *Rebirth: Mexican Los Angeles from the Great Migration to the Great Depression* (Berkeley: University of California Press, 1999).

14. Ibid., *Rebirth*, 48.

15. De Leon, *They Called Them Greasers.*

16. Iber, "Mexican Americans of South Texas Football," 620–23.

17. Ibid., 621–22.

18. Oral history interview with John Lerma (E. C. Lerma's son), July, 2001. Copy of tape in author's possession.

19. *McAllen Monitor*, September 26, 1997, Sunday Special section, 1C.

20. Iber, "Mexican Americans of South Texas Football," 625–27.

21. Ibid., 627.

22. Cashion, *The Pigskin Pulpit*, 37.

23. Oral history interview with Modesto Garcia, January 2001. Copy of tape in author's possession.

24. Information from the 2000 Census confirms this economic and demographic pattern: El Paso County, where the Hispanic population comprises 78.2 percent of the population, has a median household income of $31,051 versus $39,927 for the remainder of Texas. The figures for other counties with high Mexican American concentrations are as follows: Webb County (Laredo metropolitan area) is 94.3 percent Hispanic and has a median household income of $28,100; Nueces County (Corpus Christi metropolitan area) is 55.8 percent Hispanic and has a median household income of $35,959; Bexar County (San Antonio metropolitan area) is 54.3 percent Hispanic and has a median household income of $38,328; Cameron County (Brownsville-Harlingen, San Benito metropolitan area) is 84.3 percent Hispanic and has a median household income of $26,155; Hidalgo County (McAllen, Edinburg, Mission metropolitan area) is 88.3 percent Hispanic and has a median household income of $24,863; Starr County is 97.5 percent Hispanic and has a median household income of $16,504; and finally, Willacy County is 85.7 percent Hispanic and has a median household income of $22,114. These final four counties comprise the Rio Grande Valley, or in the parlance of Texans, simply "the Valley." All of this information comes from: http://quickfacts.census.gov/qfd/states.

25. For more specific information on the history of Mexican Americans in the educational system of Texas, see: Guadalupe San Miguel, *"Let Them All Take Heed": Mexican Americans and the Campaign for Educational Equality in Texas, 1910–1981* (Austin: University of Texas Press, 1987); idem., *Brown, Not White: School Integration and the Chicano Movement in Houston* (College Station: Texas A & M University Press, 2001). Additionally, more information on the Chicano Movement in Texas can be found in David Montejano, *Anglos and Mexicans in the Making of Texas: 1836–1986* (Austin: University of Texas Press, 1987).

26. Oral history interview with Ronald Hernandez, December 2000. Copy of tape in author's possession.

27. Oral history interview with Robert Gomez, December 2000. Copy of tape in author's possession.

28. Oral history interview with Chris Sosa, January 2001. Copy of tape in author's possession.

29. The remaining coaches were either noncommittal on this question or chose not to address it directly.

30. Oral history interview with Camilo "Bucky" Rodriguez, January 2001. Copy of tape in author's possession.

31. Oral history interview with Pat Alvarado, December 2000. Copy of interview in author's possession.

32. Oral history interview with Bobby Ortiz, January 2001. Copy of interview in author's possession.

33. Oral history interview with Felix Martinez, December 2000. Copy of interview in author's possession.

34. Oral history interview with Chris Sosa, January 2001. Copy of interview in author's possession.

35. Oral history interview with Oscar M. Villasenor, December 2000. Copy of interview in author's possession.

36. Oral history interview with Elvis Hernandez, January 2001. Copy of interview in author's possession.

37. Oral history interview with Roque Hernandez, December 2000. Copy of interview in author's possession.

38. Oral history interview with Joe Carillo, December 2000. Copy of interview in author's possession.

39. Oral history interview with David Guerra, December 2000. Copy of interview in author's possession.

40. *Campbell's* also analyzes the football fortunes of the state's private institutions. These schools, however, were not included in the calculations for these tables.

41. This is an enormous undertaking for at the start of the 2002 season, there were over 1,100 public and private institutions fielding football programs in the state of Texas.

42. The information in these three tables comes from an analysis of *Dave Campbell's Texas Football* 52 (2001) and 53 (2002).

43. *2002–2003 Texas Sports Guide of High Schools and Colleges.*

44. For a negative interpretation of the sport in Texas, please see: H. G. Bissinger, *Friday Night Lights: A Town, A Team, and A Dream* (New York: HarperCollins, 1990), and Douglas E. Foley, "The Great American Football Ritual: Reproducing Race, Class, and Gender Inequality," *Sociology of Sport Journal* 7 (1990), 111–35.

Conclusion
A Contested Terrain

The Sporting Experiences of African American and Latino Athletes in Post–World War II America

—Billy Hawkins

Racial issues in sport appear to be moving at the speed of light. Tremendous cosmetic changes have been made within the past thirty years. For example, there are more people of color occupying leadership positions in sport, on and off the field. The National Basketball Association (NBA) has diversified ownership with Robert L. Johnson becoming the first African American majority owner of a professional basketball franchise. There are more black quarterbacks leading teams at predominantly white National Collegiate Athletic Association (NCAA) Division I institutions and in the National Football League (NFL). This is a monumental transition in the sport of football because blacks are being recruited by major universities and drafted into professional football mainly to play and stay in the quarterback position. Venus and Serena Williams have elevated the game of tennis with their performances and presence in a previously predominantly all-white (American and European) sport, especially as it pertains to top rankings, earnings, and endorsements. Major League Baseball (MLB) has experienced an increase in representation with Latino ballplayers making social and cultural transitions into professional baseball in the U.S. The list of diversification continues for people of color in other sports and at different levels of athletic administration.

Despite these gains, the road to racial equality in sport is yet a long, winding, and often an uphill battle. The seventy-two-year-old Southeastern

Conference (SEC),[1] the last major conference to integrate black players, has its first black head football coach with Sylvester Croom taking over at Mississippi State University. He will be one of four black coaches heading an NCAA Division I football program.[2] Also noteworthy, regarding the SEC, is the University of Georgia (UGA) hiring Damon Evans as the first African American Athletic Director for UGA and the SEC. Although these can be considered signs of progress in the SEC, they are relatively slow and minimal in comparison to the percentage of football and basketball teams that have been predominantly black for the past ten years.

Furthermore, Latino ballplayers are replacing blacks in being racially segregated and stereotyped into certain positions. Although they have made strides on the playing field, blacks and Latinos are still experiencing resistance at the high school, collegiate, and professional level as they desire to move into leadership positions off the field.

In addressing these issues, research on race and sport has also increased significantly in the past twenty-five years.[3] With the addition of new research methodologies and interdisciplinary means of inquiry, there is an increase in the number of scholars and nonscholars engaging the topic of race and sport. This increase in scholarly and nonscholarly inquiry has produced new insights into the interworkings of this phenomenon. Emerging from these insights are new questions and perspectives that broaden our overall conceptualization of race and sport.

This anthology makes a significant contribution to the literature on race and sport by engaging the sporting experiences of African Americans and Latinos in post–World War II America. It provides a variety of new perspectives and addresses new questions. It further highlights how the intersection of race and sport has provided opportunities of triumph and controversy. These essays emphasize how at times, sport supports dominant ideas about race and racial supremacy, and at other times sport is used as a platform to address racial and social injustices, within sport and in the larger society. Besides being original contributions to the research literature on race and sport, these essays incorporate various sources for data collections: oral interviews, newspapers, and archival sources.

Because of their elevated status above their racial peers, African American professional athletes were often overlooked in the public's eye as recipients of major forms of discrimination (e.g., employment, housing, and transportation). Thus they were least expected to be contributors to the cause of civil rights. Professional and collegiate black athletes in particular have often been considered apolitical, neutral sociopolitical activists, or they have been slighted as catalysts and contributors to sociopolitical activity. However, Maureen Smith dispels this notion by showing how twenty-one African American athletes in the American Football League were instrumental not only in bringing national attention to racial injustices in New Orleans, but in having the All-Star game relocated to a different venue. The significance of this article is in showing how some professional black athletes were willing to risk their temporary comforts to speak to racial injustices and discomforts, not only in professional sport, but also in the larger southern community.

The boycott of the East-West All-Star game exemplified Manning Marable's assessment of the young people who conceived, planned, and carried out the desegregation battles of the 1960s. Eight of the twenty-one boycotters attended historically black colleges and universities at a time when all the impatience and idealism which characterizes youth was an organic and integral aspect of this campaign for racial justice. They viewed the legalistic maneuvers of the NAACP with a politely hidden contempt. The Urban League was perceived as the "enemy's camp," and they knew little, if any, of the earlier efforts of civil rights activists like W. E. B. Du Bois and A. Philip Randolph. Even more importantly, as historian Vincent Harding indicated, the desegregation battles of the 1960s was not a rejection of the American Dream. It generated necessary, albeit ambiguous, steps towards its culmination.[4]

Clearly the East-West All-Star boycott reflected the mind and mood of the black youths who participated in the desegregation battles of the 1960s. Black stars in the AFL recognized their advantageous position. By the mid-1960s the AFL was on the brink of stability. In 1964 the league signed a lucrative TV deal with NBC for $42 million over five years. By 1965, the AFL sold $5 million worth of season tickets before the kickoff of its first regular season game. Viewed in this light, AFL owners would have been reluctant to allow All-Pros, like Art Powell and Cookie Gilchrist, to defect to the NFL.

Michael Ezra's investigation of Muhammad Ali provides insights into how sport has served as a platform from which public attention and apolitical sports fans are made aware of blacks' plight to distance themselves from whiteness and regain control of their economic and cultural destinies. At the time, this was a monumental and controversial move, and it spoke volumes to the issue of black empowerment and the need for blacks, and professional black athletes specifically, to be proactive in taking responsibility for and control of their fate. The selection of a predominantly black management team with a pro-black philosophy incited resistance from members of the white power structure (sportswriters, owners of media venues, promoters, and managers).

Ali's attempt to empower blacks illustrates the continuity of early twentieth-century self-help economic initiatives promoted by Booker T. Washington and W. E. B. Du Bois. Ali recognized early in his career that in order to conduct business in America, he would have to negotiate with the white power structure. But, as Ezra points out, Ali's career began with blacks in key positions, and when he was able to make that possible, he often did. To Ali, Black Power meant using his boxing career to employ and enrich other African Americans. His philanthropic efforts throughout his early reign as heavyweight champion further demonstrate his commitment to black economic uplift.

Yet the plight of Main Bout Inc. illustrates how race can override economic considerations and good business sense. The aforementioned white power structure had a vested interest in professional boxing's profitability. Therefore, it was in their best economic interests to maximize the sport's revenues through its most prestigious prize—the heavyweight championship. Main Bout Inc.'s formation met with resistance because of the presence of a predominantly black management team, and Ali's refusal to enter the military draft. What was revealing about this was that the boxing establishment, evidently, were more comfortable with organized crime figures around boxers like Sonny Liston than the Muslims around Ali. More important, virtually ignored by the boxing establishment was the fact that by the 1960s the Nation had built an $80-million business empire.

Another insightful issue dealt with Jim Brown's statement about the purpose of Main Bout Inc.: to use its profits to generate capital for African American businessmen. Brown's assertion represented the rhetoric of activists who referred to Black Power as Black Capitalism. In other words, Black Power meant creating independent, self-sufficient black business enterprises by encouraging black entrepreneurship. Quickly perceiving this, Richard Nixon, who was running for the presidency in 1968, took an aggressive pro-Black Power posture. As Nixon defined the term in a Milwaukee, Wisconsin, speech on March 28, 1968, Black Power was "the power that people should have over their own destinies, the power that comes from participation in the political and economic process of society." Nixon's endorsement of Black Power as Black Capitalism was applauded by major corporations and the financial sector's chief organ, the *Wall Street Journal*. It was also supported by Floyd McKissick of CORE and Roy Innis of the NAACP.[5]

Harry Edwards's attempt to organize a boycott of the 1968 Olympic Games was rooted in the pluralistic tradition. Like other ethnic groups before them, African Americans realized that American society operated through the competitive interaction of its various interest groups. By attempting to form a power bloc within the sporting community, African Americans were not being antiwhite but pro-black. As Michael Lomax explains, African American athletes and students sought a greater degree of empowerment—not the rise of a Black Power autarky. Striving to negotiate a viable existence for themselves through self-directed action, they believed that both student and athletic governance should be kept as close to the students and athletes as possible. Demands for hiring black coaches on the U.S. track and field team and the creation of both the United Black Students Association and a special committee at San Jose State College to evaluate circumstances involving the possible demotion or expulsion of black athletes illustrated this aspiration.

Edwards's ideal of highlighting the plight of African Americans in a "world court," and linking the black athlete revolt to the overall struggle for black liberation, was comparable with the Black Panther Party's (BPP) endorsement of global liberation strategies. Ron Briley points out that the BPP's ideology of internationalism did make for a common cause with the heroic individualism of a Muhammad Ali resisting the Vietnam War and Edwards's OPHR cooperative approach to combating racism in sport on the international level. The BPP, as Yohura Williams indicates, exported black nationalism and "tied Black liberation to an international struggle for freedom and independence and pledge leadership and unity with oppressed peoples of the world." Whereas their primary focus was on police brutality, economic colonialism, and struggles for national liberation, the BPP began focusing more on sport in the Bay Area when they sought to gain political control of Oakland's city government through the ballot box.[6]

Both Harry Edwards and the Black Panther Party epitomized what historian Harvard Sitkoff refers to as the heirs of Malcolm X. Malcolm X's Black Nationalism crystalized the feelings of those whose expectations had been thwarted and those whose lives had received little or no impact from the Civil Rights Movement. Insightful in portraying the cultural and psychological legacies of African American oppression, Malcolm imparted a positive sense of black identity among his followers. His ideas of racial pride and African American control of black community institutions both expressed and shaped the changing consciousness of young black activists.[7]

Kurt Kemper examines the UCLA Bruins all-black cheerleaders' struggle for recognition and equality within the larger context of the Black Power Movement. Although the presence of black women in athletic departments and on college campuses in the late 1960s and early 1970s was often considered insignificant and grossly underrepresented, Kemper shows that they were significant contributors to the tenets of the Black Power Movement. These black women, although in a "peripheral" nonrevenue generating sport—cheerleading—sought equality in a predominantly white sport at a predominantly white institution. Enduring threats of violence and verbal criticism, this group of women persevered in order to achieve equal participation and to control their destinies.

Kemper also highlights the perseverance some student organizations employed to maintain whiteness and white privilege. The valiant efforts of these black women were met with considerable resistance, because they demanded opportunities and privileges once exclusively reserved for whites. The tragedy was that these organizations that resisted equal opportunity and participation were housed in institutions of higher learning and, in many cases, supported by them. In addition, the presence of African American cheerleaders represented a direct challenge to traditional undergraduate femininity as it had been defined by generations of college students on predominantly white campuses. Up to that period white skin, sorority membership, and passive behavior had been the norm. Successful participation in campus activities like beauty contests and cheerleading required complete conformity to the existing ideal of traditional undergraduate femininity. The Black Power Movement required embracing what had traditionally been held in contempt, the physical features of blacks, particularly women.

The willingness of students to wear their hair in the natural or "Afro" fashion, to lead "soul cheers," to dance demonstratively in the black style not only rejected the existing norms, but embraced a new Black Power aesthetic. It was an effort to define and establish their own values while rejecting the cultural norms of their oppressors. On an individual level, Black Power represented a fundamental revolution in self-worth. Head cheerleader Marilyn Joshua explained: "It was a self-esteem issue. We were not ready to accept [second-class status]," a sentiment shared by many during the Black Power era.[8]

Sarah Fields's essay brings to light how race has often trumped gender in regards to equality for black women. This essay provides an excellent example of how black women have not benefited from Title IX as much as their white counterparts, not only as participants but also as coaches and administrators. In the past thirty years, data has shown a marked increase in the amount of opportunities women have as participants in various sport settings. However, Fields provides examples of how the number for women of color lagged behind significantly.

It was often assumed that increased sporting opportunities for women meant an increase for women of all races or socioeconomic background. It is clear that Title IX has increased the sporting opportunities for women, and more specifically white women. However, it has not been able to address the socioeconomic and racial disparities of the larger society, which influences the access women of color have to certain sports. Fields's analysis provides insight into the sociostructural and economic forces that prevent many young black women from taking advantage of traditional "white" sports. It is in these traditional "white" sports that increased opportunities for women are being generated, and white women are the main beneficiaries of these opportunities. Welch Suggs found that only 2.7 percent of women receiving scholarships in sports other than basketball and track and field on predominantly white colleges in Division I are black. However, those are precisely the sports—golf, lacrosse, soccer, and rowing—that colleges have been adding to comply with Title IX.[9]

In the essay on "Mexican Baseball Teams in the Midwest, 1916–1965," Richard Santillan details the presence and functions of sport in Mexican American communities in the Midwest. Not only does sport serve the functions of uniting communities and strengthening racial and ethnic solidarity, but it also provides youth with leadership skills and survival tactics that benefit them later in the struggle for social justice. Santillan shows how several associations and athletic clubs were created to serve as sport networks in these Mexican American communities. In conjunction with the rise of spectator sports throughout the U.S., baseball emerged as the most popular sport among Mexicans in the U.S. Although each Mexican American community had a baseball team to represent it, the teams met with resistance in using public facilities throughout the Midwest. Met with this white resistance, these communities constructed their own fields to compete in their favorite pastime. Santillan also illustrates the support and success Mexican American women had in competing in baseball initially and later in softball. This essay highlights the significant role sport played in these communities in creating racial and ethnic solidarity and political and economic empowerment.

Santillan shows how baseball had a comfortable and important home in Mexican agricultural communities in the Midwest. The sport provided a social setting where people could come together and discuss community issues and strengthen their sense of racial and ethnic solidarity. The local baseball diamond on Sunday was similar to the Jewish kitchen, which author Irving Howe described as a "place where immigrants might recall to themselves that they were not mere creatures of toil and circumstances, but also human beings defined by their sociability."[10]

Samuel O. Regalado gives an overview of the dynamic life of Roberto Clemente. This essay illustrates how Clemente played a pivotal role in what is now a norm on many Major League Baseball teams—the Latino presence. Regalado provides a view of Clemente's greatness as a player, a humanitarian, and a social activist for other Latino baseball players. This essay illustrates how Clemente, faced with racial challenges similar to those of black ballplayers, paved the way for the reception of other Latino players into this favorite American pastime. His life in professional baseball was an example of the experiences many pioneers made to achieve racial equality for the generations that followed. Regalado documents how Clemente's life transcended racial issues and embarked on other social issues to relieve the burdens of less fortunate individuals. His ability to use professional sport as a platform to resist whiteness and pursue justice for socially and racially marginalized people is truly a mark of greatness.

Of importance was Clemente's unwillingness to accept the status quo. He fought against stereotypes that portrayed him and other Latinos as absurd, hypochondriacal, and unintelligent. He also contested social habits and restrictions that he believed belittled not only Puerto Ricans, but all people of color. Moreover, Clemente sought to win what he felt he earned but had been denied—recognition. The 1971 World Series served as his public platform to address this issue. Without question Clemente put on an impressive performance, hitting .414, with two home runs and four runs batted in.

Clemente's greatest satisfaction, however, appeared to come in the locker room when he addressed the press during the post-series celebration. As he paused for questions, one journalist asked if the series was his greatest moment. "The greatest moment in my career is now, this precise instant, when I'm going to answer your questions," he replied. "This is the first time I've ever been able to have all of you together in one room, and I want to tell all of you that you're a bunch of good-for-nothing bums! Now that I got that off my chest, you'll see a different Roberto Clemente. I won't complain anymore." Clemente's post-series press conference represented a radical departure in the way Latinos were supposed to behave—to be seen and not heard. The outstanding credentials he accumulated over the years and his World Series performance afforded him this privilege.[11]

Jorge Iber's essay discusses the experiences of Mexican American football coaches in Texas. He draws from several foundational works on the Mexican American football coaching experience to expand and examine current trends among Mexican American coaches in Texas. Iber highlights the resistance many are facing as they seek opportunities into coaching and administration in areas that are predominantly white. This essay also points to an important trend of Spanish-surnamed coaches being employed mainly in areas where there are a high percentage of Mexican Americans. Although hiring Mexican American football coaches in these school settings gives an illusion of racial progress, it is merely a change in demographics that has increased the number of Mexican American football coaches, not social consciousness. Changes in the demographics and the structure of these coaching staffs does not necessarily equate to ideological changes. It is, however, a start that has the potential to change the mindsets of those proponents of whiteness.

Collectively, these essays provide new perspectives into the African American and Latino sport experiences in post–World War II America. Two themes that emerge throughout each essay are nationalism and the power of whiteness and the resistance to whiteness. The essays dealing with the African American sporting experience illustrate the continued support of the ideas of Black Nationalism—racial solidarity, black empowerment, and an affinity to fight against white racism. African American athletes made attempts to mobilize, close ranks, and move toward a position of group strength both on and off the field. They sought to define and establish their own values while rejecting the cultural norms of their oppressors. Moreover, by moving toward a position of group strength, African American athletes were not being antiwhite, but pro-black. In this way, African American athletes sought a greater degree of empowerment over their destinies—not the creation of a Black Power autarky.

The Latino sporting experience was also an expression of nationalistic sentiments during this era. Whereas Latinos did not encounter outright segregation in sports like African Americans, they did confront several obstacles to athletic participation. Poverty was the central factor that kept Latinos off the playing field. The majority of young Latinos did not enter high school due to the economic limitations of most families. This lack of opportunity made it problematic to even consider athletic participation. Strong young men had no time for sports when they were needed to help the family as they worked in the sugarcane, cotton, or vegetable field.

To Latinos, sport was a vehicle for community celebrations, a way to express pride in ethnic and religious heritages, a diversion from a long week of backbreaking work. Sport served as a means to develop leadership skills and survival tactics that were useful in the political arena and in the fight for social justice. Baseball and football players and coaches took center stage in several communities that sought a larger and more defined presence in the American mainstream. Sport became a means to combat the negative stereotypes Latinos faced, and shaped their own sense of racial and ethnic identity; it was an essential factor in the construction of that identity.

The power of whiteness and the resistance to whiteness constitutes the second theme that links these essays together. Because of the centrality of whiteness within the dominant national identity of being "American," most Americans make few distinctions between their "ethnicity" and their "race," and the two concepts are usually used interchangeably. "Black" and "white" are usually perceived as very fixed, specific categories that define millions of human beings and their behavior. Yet in reality, "ethnicity" refers to the values, traditions, rituals, languages, music, and family patterns created by human beings within all social groups. All people have some kind of ethnic identity that has nothing to do with the color of their skin.[12]

"Race" as it is understood in the United States is completely different. Race should be understood not as a thing that exists in every human society, or as an ethnicity based on certain biological or genetic differences between people. A race is actually an inequitable relationship between social groups, reinforced by the sophisticated patterns of power, ownership, and privilege that may exist inside the social, economic, and political institutions of society.

These essays demonstrate how at times the structure and culture of sport in America has been a contested terrain that produced and reinforced ideals of whiteness. It has also been an institution that has provided privileges in the form of benefits and access to certain members of this society. Even when sport has been classified as the great racial equalizer, it has simultaneously reproduced various forms of racial discrimination and perpetuated racial myths and stereotypes. Thus, sport has been a corporate industry, social institution, and cultural practice that has defined race (i.e. who is White, Black, or Latino).[13]

Important to note also is that regardless of sport's role in informing us about race, perpetuating racial myths, and reproducing racial discrimination, it continues to be a site of racial resistance—a platform to address social inequalities. These essays show how the sporting experiences of black and Latino athletes were similar in nature, forging new territories and existence against racial segregation and institutional forms of racism. Sport has contributed to notions about race by denying access and opportunity or through stereotyping, and it has been a sight of resistance where these notions are challenged. These essays reveal individuals and small groups of people who have used sport as a platform to speak to injustices within the institution of sport and to greater social injustices at the local, regional, national, and international levels. These essays on the sporting experiences of African Americans and Latinos in post–World War II America exposed sport in the U.S. as a contested terrain: reinforcing and resisting the status of "white privilege."

Because of this dual role, sport is much more than mere entertainment. It is not apolitical. It is an influential cultural practice that informs cultural ideology and determines race relations. Its complexity has not only been expressed and visible in the major mediated men's and women's sporting experiences, but also in activities associated with sport, yet often taken for granted, such as cheerleading. It is effective in maintaining whiteness, and its ineffectiveness in consistently resisting whiteness has been in its ability to be masked as merely a source of entertainment—that is, "it's just a game."

As sport in the U.S. becomes more culturally diverse and the world becomes smaller through international sporting practices and an increase migration of foreign athletes into professional and intercollegiate sports, the use of sport will change in its configuration and utility. As stated earlier, structural changes does not necessarily equate to ideological changes. However, exposure can impact dominant ways of thinking about individuals that are different from ones own gender, race, and ethnic origins. Sport has proven to be a means of providing exposure, social interaction, and cultural interchange among a variety of cultures. Its continual impact depends on how valuable it is in maintaining whiteness for a limited few, or how effective it is in capturing the human expression in athletic performance and advancing the human potential in reaching racial harmony.

Notes

1. The Southeastern Conference is one of the wealthiest football conferences in college football. The 2003–04 Bowl season produced around $30–34 million dollars in revenue generated from bowl appearances of eight SEC teams. The twelve teams that make up the SEC are University of Alabama in Tuscaloosa, Alabama (founded in 1831); University of Arkansas in Fayetteville, Arkansas (founded in 1871); Auburn University in Auburn, Alabama (founded in 1856); University of Florida in Gainesville, Florida (founded in 1853); University of Georgia in Athens, Georgia (founded in 1785); University of Kentucky in Lexington, Kentucky (founded in 1865); Louisiana State University in Baton Rouge, Louisiana (founded in 1860); University of Mississippi in Oxford, Mississippi (founded in 1848); Mississippi State University in Starkville, Mississippi (founded in 1878); University of South Carolina in Columbia, South Carolina (founded in 1801); University of Tennessee in Knoxville, Tennessee (founded in 1794); and Vanderbilt University in Nashville, Tennessee (founded in 1873). In 1966, the SEC admitted its first black athlete, Kentucky football player Nat Northington (http://www.secsports.com/local/about.htm).

2. This is out of 117 NCAA Division I-A major college athletic programs. See The Institute for Diversity and Ethics in Sport's 2003 Racial and Gender Report Card (http://www.bus.ucf.edu/sport/public/downloads/media/ides/release_report.pdf).

3. Several volumes of edited and original contributions to research have been published in recent years: Dana Brooks and Ronald Althouse, *Racism in College Athletics: The African American Athlete's Experience* (Morgantown, WV: Fitness Information Technology, 2000); Gary A. Sailes, *African Americans in Sport: Contemporary Themes* (New Brunswick, NJ: Transaction, 1998); Michael E. Lomax, *Black Baseball Entrepreneurs, 1860–1901: Operating by Any Means Necessary* (Syracuse, NY: Syracuse University Press, 2003); Richard E. Lapchick, *Smashing Barriers: Race and Sport in the New Millennium* (Lanham, MD: Madison, 2001); John Hoberman, *Darwin's Athletes: How Sport Has Damaged Black America and Preserved the Myth of Race* (Boston: Houghton Mifflin, 1997); Gerald Early, Eric Solomon, and Loïc Wacquant, *The Charisma of Sport and Race* (Berkeley: University of California, 1996); Billy J. Hawkins, *The New Plantation: The Internal Colonization of Black Student Athletes on Predominantly White NCAA Institutions* (Winterville, GA: Sadiki, 2001); Kenneth L. Shropshire, *In Black and White: Race and Sports in America* (New York: New York University Press, 1996).

4. Manning Marable, *Race, Reform, and Rebellion: The Second Reconstruction in Black America, 1945–1982* (Jackson: University Press of Mississippi, 1984), 70–71; Vincent Harding, *The Other American Revolution* (Los Angeles: Center for Afro-American Studies, 1980), 159.

5. The notion of Black Power as Black Capitalism and the Nixon speech is in Robert L. Allen, *Black Awakening in Capitalist America: An Analytic History* (New York: Doubleday, 1969), 190–95.

6. Yohuru Williams, "American Exported Black Nationalism: The Student Coordinating Committee, the Black Panther Party, and the Worldwide Freedom Struggle, 1967–1972," *Negro History Bulletin* 60 (July–September 1997): 14.

7. Harvard Sitkoff, *The Struggle for Black Equality 1954–1992*, rev. ed. (New York: Hill and Wang, 1993), 196–202.

8. See chapter five.

9. Welch Suggs, "'Left Behind': Title IX and Black Women Athletes," in David K. Wiggins and Patrick Miller, eds. *The Unlevel Playing Field: A Documentary History of the African American Experience in Sport* (Urbana: University of Illinois Press, 2003), 387–93.

10. Irving Howe, *World of Our Fathers: The Journey of the East European Jews to America and the Life They Found and Made* (New York: Simon and Schuster, 1976), 172.

11. Samuel O. Regalado, *Viva Baseball!: Latin Major Leaguers and Their Special Hunger* (Urbana: University of Illinois Press, 1998), 150–52.

12. A significant amount of information on whiteness and white skin privilege has been produced in the past fifteen years since Peggy McIntosh's seminal piece "White Privilege: Unpacking the Invisible Knapsack," *Independent School* 49 (Winter 1990): 5, 31. A few other works that have addressed this topic include Alice McIntyre, *Making Meaning of Whiteness: Exploring Racial Identity with White Teachers*, (Albany: State University New York Press, 1997); Richard Delgado and Jean Stefancic, *Critical White Studies: Looking behind the Mirror* (Philadelphia: Temple University Press, 1997). For an account regarding the construction of race in the U.S., see Manning Marable, *Black Liberation in Conservative America* (Boston: South End, 1997).

13. For secondary accounts on the concept of the contested terrain, see Douglas Hartmann, *Race, Culture, and the Revolt of the Black Athlete* (Chicago: University of Chicago Press, 2003); idem., "Rethinking the Relationships between Sport and Race in American Culture: Golden Ghettos and Contested Terrain," *Sociology of Sport Journal* 17 (2000): 229–53; Susan Birrell, "Racial Relations Theories and Sport: Suggestions for a More Critical Analysis," *Sociology of Sport Journal* 6 (1989): 212–27; Pierre Bourdieu, "Program for a Sociology of Sport," *Sociology of Sport Journal* 5 (1988): 153–61.

Contributors

Ron Briley is assistant headmaster and a history teacher at Sandia Preparatory School in Albuquerque, New Mexico. He is also an adjunct professor of history at the University of New Mexico, Mexico Valencia campus. His work on film and sport history is published in various anthologies, reference works, and academic journals. Briley is the author of *Class at Bat, Gender on Deck, and Race in the Hole: A Line-up of Essays on Twentieth-Century Culture and America's Game.*

Michael Ezra is an associate professor in the Department of American Multicultural Studies at Sonoma State University. He received his PhD in American studies from the University of Kansas. His work has been published in the *Journal of Sport History, American Studies,* the *Journal of African American Men,* and the *Encyclopedia of American Social Movements.* He is completing a book that considers Muhammad Ali's boxing career within the context of the Black Power Movement.

Sarah K. Fields is an assistant professor at The Ohio State University. She holds a JD from Washington University in St. Louis and a PhD in American studies from the University of Iowa. Her book *Female Gladiators: Gender, Law, and Contact Sport in America* examines the intersection of gender, law, and contact sport.

Billy Hawkins is an associate professor of sport sociology at the University of Georgia. His book *The New Plantation: The Internal Colonization of Black Student Athletes at Predominantly White NCAA Division I Institutions* examines the experiences of black student athletes in intercollegiate athletics. He has also written several scholarly articles on black athletes and their intercollegiate athletic experiences, the media representation of black male and black male athletes, religion and sport, and youth and sport.

Jorge Iber is a professor of history and an associate dean at Texas Tech University in Lubbock. His first book, *Hispanics in the Mormon Zion, 1912–1999*, deals with the origin and development of the Hispanic community in the Salt Lake City area. Since arriving at Texas Tech, he has worked on a series of articles and book-length projects dealing with the sporting experience (particularly high school football) of Mexican Americans.

Kurt Edward Kemper is an assistant professor of history at the University of South Dakota. He received his MA in American history from George Mason University and PhD from Louisiana State University and A & M College. His most recent experience is as an assistant professor at River Parishes Community College. Kemper's research interests include history of sports, and history of the Civil Rights Movement and social activism.

Michael E. Lomax is an associate professor of sport history at the University of Iowa. His book *Black Baseball Entrepreneurs 1860–1901: Operating by Any Means Necessary* examines the ways entrepreneurs transformed the black game into a commercialized amusement. He has also written several articles dealing with the African American sporting experience and labor relations in professional sports.

Samuel O. Regalado is a professor of history at California State University, Stanislaus, located in Turlock, California. He is the author of *Viva Baseball!: Latin Major Leaguers and Their Special Hunger*. Regalado, whose area of United States history includes a specialization of U.S. ethnic and immigration and U.S. sport, has written articles that have appeared in such journals as *Pacific Northwest Quarterly*, *Journal of Sport History*, and *Indiana Journal of Global Legal Studies*.

Richard Santillan is a professor emeritus of the Ethnic and Women's Studies Department at California State University at Pomona. Santillan has published and edited extensively on Chicano/political history, voting rights, and Mexican history in the Midwest. He is working on two books: *Encuentros y Cuentos: An Oral History of Mexican Americans in the Midwestern United States, 1900–1950*; and *The Politics of Cultural Nationalism: El Partido de La Raza Unida in Southern California, 1969–1978*.

Maureen Smith is an associate professor in the Department of Kinesiology and Health Science at California State University, Sacramento. She received her BS and MS from Ithaca College and her MA and PhD from The Ohio State University. Her research interests are in race and gender issues in sport, the Olympic Movement and the social construction of race and ethnicity, and the post–World War II African American sporting experience.

Index